# Contents

# Pronunciation

This section is designed to familiarize you with the sounds of Arabic using our simplified phonetic transcription. The pronunciation of the Arabic letters and sounds is explained below, together with their "imitated" equivalents. This system is used throughout the phrase book. When you see a word spelled phonetically, simply read the pronunciation as if it were English, noting any special rules.

## The Arabic language

There are over 20 countries where Arabic is the official language. These are the main areas where you can expect to hear Arabic spoken (but see notes about differences in dialects):

### North Africa

Egypt (**muSr**) has the largest population of any Arab country (63 million), and Arabic is spoken by almost the entire population. The dialect is also widely understood everywhere else through Egyptian films and TV programs.

Other North African countries include Libya (**libyaa**), Tunisia (**toonis**), Algeria (**al-jazaa'ir**), Morocco (**al-maghrib**), and Sudan (**as-soodaan**). The total population of these countries is around 100 million, with Algeria, Morocco, and Sudan accounting for approximately 28 million each. Most of the population speak Arabic but often in a regional dialect. English and French are also widely spoken in the area, as well as other indiginous languages, such as Berber.

### The Levant

Includes Lebanon (**lubnaan**), Syria (**sooriya**), Iraq (**al-AHiraaq**), Jordan (**al-urdunn**), and Palestine (**filasteen**). Of these countries, Iraq and Syria have the largest populations with around 20 million and 15 million respectively. Jordan has around 6 million and Lebanon only just over 3 million. The Palestinian population is scattered throughout the West Bank, Israel, the Gaza strip, and the wider diaspora. The Levant Arabic dialect is reasonably pure, but French is a strong influence in Lebanon.

### The Gulf

Saudi Arabia (**as-sAHoodeeyya**) has the biggest population in the Gulf region (19 million). However, many of these are immigrant workers who may not speak Arabic. Yemen (**al-yaman**) has a population of over 15 million. The other Gulf countries have relatively small populations: Bahrain (**al-baHrayn**) – 570, 000; Kuwait (**al-koowayt**) – 1.7 million; Oman (**AHumaan**) – 2.3 million; Qatar (**qaTar**) – 560, 000; United Arab Emirates (**al-imaaraat al-AHrabeeya al-muttaHida**) – 2.3 million. Dialects vary between countries.

Uniting all these different countries and dialects is what is known as "Modern Standard Arabic" (MSA) – the more formal version of the language used for almost all written material and sometimes for oral communication, particularly if it involves different nationalities. Almost all Arabic speakers will speak their own dialect but also be able to communicate in Modern Standard.

So that you can use this *Berlitz Arabic Phrase Book* in as many countries as possible, we have chosen to use a modified Modern Standard Arabic, which includes elements of colloquial pronunciation and vocabulary.

Below you will find the sounds of the Arabic language explained. (➤ 9 for more details on how the Arabic letters are joined.)

## Consonants

| Letter | Approximate pronunciation | Symbol | Example | Pronunciation |
|--------|---------------------------|--------|---------|---------------|
| ب | *b* as in *b*at | *b* | بنت | *bint* |
| ت | *t* as in *t*in | *t* | تلفون | *tilifoon* |
| ث | *t* as in *t*in (*colloq.*) [or *th* as in *th*in (*MSA*)] | *t* | ثلاثة | *talaata* |
| ج | soft *j* as in French *je* (*g* as in *g*ate in Northern Egypt) | *j* | جميل | *jameel* |
| ح | strong, breathy *h* | H | حلو | *Hilw* |
| خ | *h* from back of throat as in Scottish lo*ch* | kh | خالد | *khaalid* |
| د | *d* as in *d*ad | *d* | دار | *daar* |
| ذ | *d* as in *d*ad or *z* as in *z*ebra (*colloq.*) [hard *th* as in *th*at (*MSA*)] | *d/z* | ذهب هذا | *dahab* *haaza* |
| ر | *r* as in *r*ain | *r* | رجل | *rajul* |
| ز | *z* as in *z*ebra | *z* | زبيب | *zibeeb* |
| س | *s* as in *s*un | *s* | سلام | *salaam* |
| ش | *sh* as in *sh*ut | sh | شمس | *shams* |
| ص | strong, emphatic *s* | S | صباح | *SabaaH* |
| ض | strong, emphatic *d* | D | ضاني | *Daanee* |
| ط | strong, emphatic *t* | T | طالب | *Taalib* |

7

# Consonants (cont.)

| Letter | Approximate pronunciation | Symbol | Example | Pronunciation |
|--------|---------------------------|--------|---------|---------------|
| ظ | strong, emphatic z | Z | ظلام | Zalaam |
| ع | a guttural sound made by tightening the throat | AH | عرب | AHrab |
| غ | like French "r," as in rue | gh | غير | ghayr |
| ف | like f in fan | f | فارس | faaris |
| ق | q pronounced from back of throat (sometimes dropped in spoken Arabic ) | q | قبل | qabl |
| ك | k as in kart | k | كرفس | karafs |
| ل | l as in lip | l | لماذا | limaazaa |
| م | m as in man | m | مارس | maaris |
| ن | n as in never | n | نور | noor |
| ه | h as in hat | h | هنا | huna |
| و | w in win | w | وسط | wasT |
| ي | y as in yet | y | يمين | yameen |
| ء | short pause, like the sound when you drop the ts in butter ("bu'er") | ' | أسد | 'asad |

## Short vowels

There are three short vowels which are written above or below the letter they follow. However, they are not normally shown in most Arabic text as the reader is expected to know them:

| | | | | |
|--------|---------------------------|--------|---------|---------------|
| ﹷ | a as in English bat, but sometimes nearer to an e | a | وَلَد | walad |
| ﹹ | u as in English but | u | كُل | kul |
| ﹻ | i as in English bit | i | بِنت | bint |

## Long vowels/Dipthongs

Long vowels and dipthongs are formed by a combination of the short vowels and the letters alif (ا), waaw (و), and yaa (ي):

| | | | | |
|---|---|---|---|---|
| ـَا | ar as in English far | aa | دَار | daar |
| ـُو | oo as in English boot | oo | نُور | noor |
| ـِي | ee as in English meet | ee | فِيل | feel |
| ـَو | o as in English home | au | يَوم | yaum |
| ـَي | ay as in English say | ay | سِير | sayr |

## Stress

In Arabic the stress in a word tends to fall on syllables with long vowels or be relatively even. So a word like **yameen** would have the stress on the long vowel: **yameen**; but **laban** would be pronounced with equal stress on both syllables.

## Arabic alphabet and script

Arabic is written right to left (except numbers ➤ 216). The letters also change their shape depending on whether they are at the beginning, in the middle, or at the end of a word. Here is the alphabet and script:

| | beg: | mid: | end: | | beg: | mid: | end: | | beg: | mid: | end: |
|---|---|---|---|---|---|---|---|---|---|---|---|
| 'alif | ا | ـا | ـا | raa' | ر | ـر | ـر | ghayn | غـ | ـغـ | ـغ |
| baa' | بـ | ـبـ | ـب | zaa' | ز | ـز | ـز | faa' | فـ | ـفـ | ـف |
| taa' | تـ | ـتـ | ـت | seen | سـ | ـسـ | ـس | qaaf | قـ | ـقـ | ـق |
| thaa' | ثـ | ـثـ | ـث | sheen | شـ | ـشـ | ـش | kaaf | كـ | ـكـ | ـك |
| jeem | جـ | ـجـ | ـج | Saad | صـ | ـصـ | ـص | laam | لـ | ـلـ | ـل |
| Haa' | حـ | ـحـ | ـح | Daad | ضـ | ـضـ | ـض | meem | مـ | ـمـ | ـم |
| khaa' | خـ | ـخـ | ـخ | Taa' | طـ | ـطـ | ـط | noon | نـ | ـنـ | ـن |
| daal | د | ـد | ـد | Zaa' | ظـ | ـظـ | ـظ | waaw | و | ـو | ـو |
| dhaal | ذ | ـذ | ـذ | AHyn | عـ | ـعـ | ـع | yaa' | يـ | ـيـ | ـي |

9

# Basic Expressions

## ESSENTIAL

| Yes./No. | naAHm/laa | نعم./لا. |
| Okay. | Hasanan | حسنا. |
| Please. | min faDlak/lau samaHt | من فضلك/لو سمحت. |
| Thank you. | shukran | شكراً. |
| Thank you very much. | shukran jazeelan | شكراً جزيلاً. |

## Greetings/Apologies الترحيب/الاعتذار

| Hello./Hi! | as-salaam AHlaykum/ahlan السلام عليكم./أهلا! |
| Good morning. | sabaaH al-khayr. صباح الخير. |
| Good afternoon/evening. | masaa al-khayr. مساء الخير. |
| Good night. | tiSbaH[ee] AHla khayr تصبح [تصبحي] على خير. |
| Good-bye. | maAH as-salaama. مع السلامة. |
| Excuse me! (getting attention) | lau samaHt[ee]! لو سمحت [سمحتي]! |
| Excuse me. (May I get past?) | laa mu'aakhaza لا مؤاخذة. |
| Excuse me!/Sorry! | aasif[a]! آسف [آسفة]! |
| Don't mention it. | AHfwan عفواً. |
| Never mind. | walaa yuhimmak [yuhimmik] ولا يهمك. |

# Communication difficulties
## الصعوبة في التفاهم

| | |
|---|---|
| Do you speak English? | *tatkallam[ee] injileezee*<br>تتكلم [تتكلمين] إنجليزي؟ |
| I don't speak much Arabic. | *laa atkallam AHrabee kateer*<br>لا أتكلم عربي كثير. |
| Could you speak more slowly? | *mumkin tatkallam[ee] bibuT'*<br>ممكن تتكلم [تتكلمي] ببطء؟ |
| Excuse me?/What was that? | *AHfwan/maaza qult[ee]؟* عفواً؟/ماذا قلت؟ |
| Please write it down. | *uktubuh [uktubeeh] lau samaHt[ee]*<br>أكتبه [أكتبيه] لو سمحت. |
| Can you translate this for me? | *mumkin tutarjim[ee] lee haaza*<br>ممكن تترجم [تترجمين] لي هذا؟ |
| What does this/that mean? | *maa maAHnaa haaza* ما معنى هذا؟ |
| Please point to the phrase in the book. | *ashir [asheeree] ilaal AHibaara feel kitaab, lau samaHt[ee]*<br>أشر [أشيري] إلى العبارة في الكتاب، لو سمحت. |
| I understand. | *afham* أفهم. |
| I don't understand. | *laa afham* لا أفهم. |
| Do you understand? | *hal tafham[ee]؟* هل تفهم [تفهمين]؟ |

## GRAMMAR

Arabic has a masculine and a feminine form of "you," which means the sentence will change slightly depending on whether you are talking to a male or a female. In the *Basic Expressions* section you will find these changes in brackets [ ] in the Arabic column. In the rest of the book only the masculine is shown (► 169 for more details).

– *mee'a khamsa wa arbAHeen juhayh.*
– *laa afham.*
– *mee'a khamsa wa arbAHeen juhayh.*
– *uktubeeh lee lau samaHtee ... aah,*
  "145 pounds" ... *tafaDDalee.*

## Questions أسئلة

Arabic questions are simple to form. There are two types:

1. Questions to which the answer is "yes" (**naAHm**) or "no" (**laa**). These are formed either by simply raising the intonation at the end of a statement or by adding the question word **hal**:

**ismak sameer.**   Your name is Samir.

**ismak sameer?/hal ismak sameer?**   Is your name Samir?

2. Other questions are formed by using the relevant question word (➤ 12–17):

**maa ismak?**   What's your name?

**matta yiftaH al-matHaf**   When does the museum open?

---

### Where? أين؟

| | |
|---|---|
| Where is it? | أين هو/هي؟ *ayn huwa/hiya* |
| Where are you going? | الى أين تذهب [تذهبين]؟ *ilaa ayn tazhab[ee]* |
| at the meeting place [point] | عند نقطة اللقاء *AHnda nuqTit al-liqaa'* |
| downstairs | تحت *taHt* |
| from the U.S. | من أمريكا *min amreeka* |
| far away from me | بعيد عني *bAHeed AHnee* |
| here (to here) | هنا (إلى هنا) *hunaa (ilaa hunaa)* |
| in the car | في السيارة *fees sayyaara* |
| in Egypt | في مصر *fee muSr* |
| inside | داخل *daakhil* |
| near the bank | قريب من البنك *qareeb min al-bank* |
| next to the apples | بجانب التفاح *bijaanib at-tufaaH* |
| opposite the market | مقابل السوق *muqaabil as-sooq* |
| on the left/right | على اليسار/اليمين *AHlaal yasaar/yameen* |
| there (to there) | هناك (إلى هناك) *hunaak (ilaa hunaak)* |
| to the hotel | إلى الفندق *ilaal funduq* |
| outside the café | خارج المقهى *khaarij al-maqhaa* |
| up to the traffic lights | حتى إشارة المرور *Hatta ishaarit al-muroor* |
| upstairs | فوق *fauq* |

# When? متى؟

| | |
|---|---|
| When does the museum open? | *matta yaftaH al-matHaf* |
| | متى يفتح المتحف؟ |
| When does the train arrive? | *matta yaSil al-qiTaar* |
| | متى يصل القطار؟ |
| 10 minutes ago | *munzu AHshar daqaa'iq* |
| | منذ ١٠ دقائق |
| after lunch | *bAHd al-ghadaa'* بعد الغداء |
| always | *daa'iman* دائما |
| around midnight | *Hawaala muntaSif al-layl* |
| | حوالى منتصف الليل |
| at 7 o'clock | *as-sAHa sabAHa* ٧ الساعة |
| before Friday | *qabl yaum al-jumAHa* قبل يوم الجمعة |
| by tomorrow | *khilaal al-ghad* خلال الغد |
| early | *baakir* باكر |
| every week | *kull usbooAH* كل أسبوع |
| for 2 hours | *limuddit sAHatayn* لمدة ساعتين |
| from 9 a.m. to 6 p.m. | *min tisAHa SabaaHan Hatta* |
| | *sitta masaa'an* من ٩ صباحا حتى ٦ مساء |
| immediately | *fauran* فورا |
| in 20 minutes | *fee AHishreen daqeeqa* في ٢٠ دقيقة |
| never | *abadan* أبدا |
| not yet | *laysa bAHd* ليس بعد |
| now | *al-aan* الآن |
| often | *kateer* كثيرا |
| on March 8 | *fee tamanya maaris* في ٨ مارس |
| at the weekend | *fee nihaayat al-usbooAH* |
| | في نهاية الأسبوع |
| sometimes | *aHyaanan* أحيانا |
| soon | *qareeban* قريبا |
| then | *fee haazal waqt* في هذا الوقت |
| within 2 days | *khilaal yaumayn* خلال يومين |

## What sort of ...? ؟... ما نوع

|  |  |  |
|---|---|---|
| I'd like something ... | ureed shay' ... | ... أريد شيئا |
| It's ... | haaza ... | ... هذا |
| beautiful/ugly | jameel/qabeeH | جميل/قبيح |
| better/worse | afDal/aswa' | أفضل/أسوأ |
| big/small | kabeer/Sagheer | كبير/صغير |
| cheap/expensive | rakheeS/ghaalee | رخيص/غال |
| clean/dirty | naZeef/wisikh | نظيف/وسخ |
| dark/light | ghaamiq/faatiH | غامق/فاتح |
| delicious/revolting | lazeez/muqrif | لذيذ/مقرف |
| easy/difficult | sahl/SAHb | سهل/صعب |
| empty/full | faarigh/malyaan | فارغ/مليان |
| good/bad | jayyid/sayyi' | جيد/سيء |
| heavy/light | taqeel/khafeef | ثقيل/خفيف |
| hot, warm/cold | saakhin, daafi'/baarid | ساخن، دافئ/بارد |
| modern/old-fashioned | Hadees/qadeem | حديث/قديم |
| narrow/wide | Dayyiq/waasiAH | ضيق/واسع |
| old/new | qadeem/jadeed | قديم/جديد |
| open/shut | maftooH/mughlaq | مفتوح/مغلق |
| pleasant/unpleasant | murDee/ghayr murDee | مرض/غير مرض |
| quick/slow | sareeAH/baTee' | سريع/بطيء |
| quiet/noisy | haadi'/muzAHij | هادئ/مزعج |
| right/wrong | SaHeeH/khaaTi' | صحيح/خاطئ |
| tall/short | Taweel/qaSeer | طويل/قصير |
| vacant/occupied | faarigh/mashghool | فارغ/مشغول |
| young/old | Sagheer as-sinn/AHjooz | صغير السن/عجوز |

## Why? لماذا؟

|  |  |  |
|---|---|---|
| Why? | limaaza? | لماذا؟ |
| Why not? | lima laa? | لم لا؟ |
| because of the weather | bi-sabab al-jau | بسبب الجو |
| because I'm in a hurry | li'annee mustAHjil | لأني مستعجل |
| I don't know why. | laa adree limazaa | لا أدري لماذا. |

## GRAMMAR

Arabic grammar has two genders: masculine and feminine.
Most feminine nouns end with the sound **a** or obviously
refer to feminine people (**umm** – mother; **bint** – girl/
daughter, etc.). **al** (also pronounced **il**) means *the* and is used for
both genders. There is no equivalent of the English *a/an* or of the verb
*to be* in the present (*is/am/are*). This means you can have many
sentences and questions with no verb at all:

| | |
|---|---|
| **ana mudarris** | I (am a) teacher. |
| **ayn al-bank?** | Where (is) the bank? |
| **bikam haaza?** | How much (is) this? |

Adjectives come <u>after</u> the noun. Those referring to feminine nouns
also have to be feminine, again usually by adding **a**:

| | |
|---|---|
| **bayt jameel** | (a) beautiful house |
| **buhayra jameela** | (a) beautiful lake |

Arabic plurals are complicated and need to be learned individually
(▶ 215 for more details).

## How much/many? عدد/ثمن كم

| How much is that? | bikam haaza? | بكم هذا؟ |
|---|---|---|
| How many are there? | kam AHdadhum? | كم عددهم؟ |
| 1/2/3 | waHid/itnayn/talaata | ٣/٢/١ |
| 4/5 | arbAHa/khamsa | ٥/٤ |
| none | laa shay | لا شيء |
| about 100 pounds | meet junayh taqreeban | ١٠٠جنيه تقريبا |
| a little | qaleel | قليل |
| a lot of milk | Haleeb kateer | حليب كثير |
| enough | kifaaya | كفاية |
| few/a few of them | bAHD/bAHDuhum | بعض/بعضهم |
| more than that | aktar min zaalik | أكثر من ذلك |
| less than that | aqall min zaalik | أقل من ذلك |
| much more | aktar bi-kateer | أكثر بكثير |
| nothing else | laa shay aakhar | لا شيء آخر |
| too much | kateer jiddan | كثير جدا |

## مَن؟/أي واحد؟ Who?/Which one?

| | | |
|---|---|---|
| Who's there? | *man hunaak?* | من هناك؟ |
| Me! | *ana* | أنا! |
| someone | *aHad maa* | أحد ما |
| no one | *laa aHad* | لا أحد |
| Which one do you want? | *ayy waaHid tureed* | أي واحد تريد؟ |
| this one/that one | *haaza/zaalik* | هذا/ذلك |
| one like that | *waaHid misl zaalik* | واحد مثل ذلك |
| something | *shay maa* | شيء ما |
| nothing/none | *laa shay/walaa waaHid* | لا شيء/ولا واحد |

## لمن؟ Whose?

| | | |
|---|---|---|
| Whose is that? | *liman haaza* | لمن هذا؟ |
| It's ... | *innahu ...* | إنه ... |
| mine/ours/yours | *lee/linaa/lak [lik]* | لي/لنا/لك |
| his/hers/theirs | *lahu/lahaa/lahum* | له/لها/لهم |
| It's ... | *innahu ...* | إنه ... |
| my/our/your turn | *dooree/doornaa/doorak [doorik]* | دوري/دورنا/دورك |
| his/her/their turn | *dooruh/doorhaa/doorhum* | دوره/دورها/دورهم |

---

### GRAMMAR

To express possession (*my/your/our*, etc.) in Arabic, you need to add a particular ending to the noun, e.g.:

**kitaab** book      **kitaab<u>ee</u>** <u>my</u> book

Here is a table of the most important endings:

| | ending | example |
|---|---|---|
| my | **ee** | kitaab<u>ee</u> |
| your (masculine sing.) | **ak** | kitaab<u>ak</u> |
| your (feminine sing.) | **ik** | kitaab<u>ik</u> |
| your (plural) | **kum** | kitaab<u>kum</u> |
| his/its | **uh** | kitaab<u>uh</u> |
| her/its | **haa** | kitaab<u>haa</u> |
| our | **naa** | kitaab<u>naa</u> |
| their | **hum** | kitaab<u>hum</u> |

16

## How? كيف؟

|  |  |
|---|---|
| How would you like to pay? | kayf tureed an tadfAH<br>كيف تريد أن تدفع؟ |
| by credit card | bi-baTaaqat al-i'timaan<br>ببطاقة الائتمان |
| in cash | naqdan نقدا |
| How are you getting here? | kayf sa-taSil ilaa hunaa<br>كيف ستصل إلى هنا؟ |
| by car/by bus/by train | bis-sayyaara/bil-baaS/bil-qiTaar<br>بالسيارة/بالباص/بالقطار |
| on foot | maashiyan ماشيا |
| quickly | bi-surAHa بسرعة |
| slowly | bi-buT' ببطء |
| too fast | sareeAH jiddan سريع جدا |
| very | jiddan جدا |
| with a friend | maAH Sadeeq مع صديق |
| without a passport | bidoon jawaaz safar بدون جواز سفر |

## Is it ...?/Are there ...? هل هو/هل هناك ...؟

|  |  |
|---|---|
| Is it ...? | hal huwa هل هو ...؟ |
| Is it far? | hal huwa bAHeed هل هو بعيد؟ |
| It isn't ready. | laysa jaahiz. ليس جاهزا. |
| Is there ...? | hal hunaak هل هناك ...؟ |
| Are there ...? | hal hunaak هل هناك ...؟ |
| Is there a shower in the room? | hal hunaak dush feel ghurfa<br>هل هناك دش في الغرفة؟ |
| Are there buses into town? | hal hunaak baaSaat ilaal madeena<br>هل هناك باصات الى المدينة؟ |
| There's a good restaurant near here. | hunaak maTAHam jayyid qareeb<br>هناك مطعم جيد قريب. |
| There aren't any towels in my room. | laysa hunaak ayy manaashif fee ghurfatee<br>ليس هناك أي مناشف في غرفتي. |
| Here it is/they are. | haa huwa/haa hum hina<br>ها هو/ها هم هنا. |
| There it is/they are. | haa huwa/haa hum hunaak<br>ها هو/ها هم هناك. |

## Can/May? ممكن؟

| | | |
|---|---|---|
| Can I have …? | mumkin aakhud | ممكن آخذ ...؟ |
| Can we have …? | mumkin nakhud | ممكن نأخذ ...؟ |
| May I speak to …? | mumkin atkallam mAHa | ممكن أتكلم مع ...؟ |
| Can you tell me …? | mumkin taqool lee | ممكن تقول لي ...؟ |
| Can you help me? | mumkin tusaAHidnee | ممكن تساعدني؟ |
| Can you direct me to …? | mumkin tadullnee AHlaa | ممكن تدلني على ...؟ |
| I can't. | laa astaTeeAH | لا أستطيع. |

## What do you want? ماذا تريد؟

| | | |
|---|---|---|
| I'd like … | ureed … | أريد ... |
| Could I have …? | mumkin aakhud … | ممكن آخذ ...؟ |
| We'd like… | nureed … | نريد ... |
| Give me … | AHTeenee … | أعطني ... |
| I'm looking for … | abHas AHn … | أبحث عن ... |
| I need to … | aHtaaj an … | احتاج أن ... |
| go to … | az-hab ilaa … | أذهب إلى ... |
| find … | ajid … | أجد ... |
| see … | ara … | أرى ... |
| speak to … | atkallam mAHa … | اتكلم مع ... |

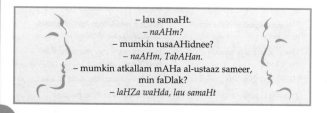

– lau samaHt.
– naAHm?
– mumkin tusaAHidnee?
– naAHm, TabAHan.
– mumkin atkallam mAHa al-ustaaz sameer,
min faDlak?
– laHZa waHda, lau samaHt

# Other useful words كلمات أخرى مفيدة

| | |
|---|---|
| fortunately | li-Husn al-HaZZ لحسن الحظ |
| hopefully | atmanna أتمنى |
| of course | TabAHan طبعا |
| perhaps/possibly | rubbamaa/jaa'iz ربما/جائز |
| probably | min al-muHtamal من المحتمل |
| unfortunately | lil-asaf للأسف |

# Exclamations علامات تعجب

| | |
|---|---|
| At last! | akheeran! أخيرا! |
| Go on. | akmil. أكمل. |
| Damn! | lAHeen! لعين! |
| Good God! | yaa ilaahee! يا إلهي! |
| I don't mind. | laa umaaniAH. لا أمانع. |
| No way! | laa majaal! لا مجال! |
| Really? | bijadd? بجد؟ |
| That's enough. | haaza kifaaya. هذا كفاية. |
| That's true. | haazihil Haqeeqa. هذه الحقيقة. |
| Well I never! | mish mAHqool! مش معقول! |
| How are things? | kayf al-amoor? كيف الأمور؟ |
| Fine, thank you. | bi-khayr, shukran بخير، شكرا. |
| great/terrific | raa'iAH رائع |
| very good | AHZeem عظيم |
| fine | bi-khayr بخير |
| okay | mashee al-Haal ماشي الحال |
| not good | laysa jayyid ليس جيدا |
| terrible | sayyi' jiddan سيء جدا |

# Accommodations

There is a wide range of accommodation to choose from in the Middle East, from luxury Western-style hotels to youth hostels, rented apartments, and camping sites. You should try to reserve in advance, particularly during local holidays. In many parts of the Middle East an unmarried man and woman will not be allowed to share a room. Women traveling alone should be especially careful to reserve appropriate accommodation. Types of accommodation available vary from country to country, but the main ones are listed below:

### فندق *fundooq*
Hotel. These vary from Western-style hotels, comparable to hotels in Europe and the United States and offering Western-style facilities and cuisine (as well as Arabic food), to small local hotels. Tourist information bureaus often have lists with details of price ranges. Reservations can be made through a travel agent or by directly contacting the hotel.

### بنسيون *bensyoon*
Boarding house. Usually family run and often occupying part of an apartment block or the owner's house. Prices are usually reasonable, but facilities are often shared. Rates are often negotiable for longer stays.

### شقة مفروشة *shaqqa mafroosha*
Furnished rented appartment. These can be found in many of the major cities in the Middle East – and can be an economic option for a longer stay. For details, contact the tourist information office for the country concerned before you leave.

### بيت شباب *bayt shabaab*
Youth hostel. These can be found in many Arab countries, including Egypt, Bahrain, Qatar, and Saudi Arabia. You may need a Hostelling International card to get a discount.

# Reservations الحجز

## In advance مسبقاً

Can you recommend
a hotel in …?

*mumkin tanSaHnaa
bi-funduq fee*

ممكن تنصحنا بفندق في ...؟

Is it near the center of town?

*hal huwa qareeb min wasT il-madeena*

هل هو قريب من وسط المدينة؟

How much is it per night?

*kam ujrat il-layla*

كم أجرة الليلة؟

Is there anything cheaper?

*hal hunaak arkhaS*

هل هناك أرخص؟

Could you reserve a
room for me there, please?

*mumkin taHjiz lee ghurfa hunaak,
lau samaHt*

ممكن تحجز لي غرفة هناك، لو سمحت؟

How do I get there?

*kayf aSil hunaak*

كيف أصل هناك؟

## At the hotel في الفندق

Do you have any vacancies?

*hal AHndakum ghurfa faarigha*

هل عندكم غرفة؟

Is there another hotel nearby?

*hal hunaak funduq aakhar qareeb*

هل هناك فندق آخر قريب؟

I'd like a single/double room.

*ureed ghurfa li-shakhS/li-shakhSayn*

أريد غرفة لشخص/لشخصين.

Can I see the room, please?

*mumkin araa al-ghurfa,
lau samaHt*

ممكن أرى الغرفة، لو سمحت؟

I'd like a room with …

*ureed ghurfa bi*

أريد غرفة بـ...

twin beds

*sareerayn*

سريرين

a double bed

*sareer muzdawij*

سرير مزدوج

a bath/shower

*banyo/dush*

بانيو/دش

---

– hal AHnaakum ghurfa faarigha?
ureed ghurfa li-shakhSayn.
– aasif, al-funduq mumtali'.
– wah. hal hunaak funduq aakhar qareeb?
– naAHm, sayyid/sayyida. al meeridiyaan qareeb jiddan.

21

# الاستقبال Reception

| | |
|---|---|
| I have a reservation. | عندي حجز. *AHndee Hajz* |
| My name is … | اسمي … *ismee …* |
| We've reserved a double and a single room. | *Hajaznaa ghurfa li-shakhSayn wa ghurfa li-shakhS* حجزنا غرفة لشخصين وغرفة لشخص. |
| I confirmed my reservation by mail. | *akkadt Hajzee bil-bareed* أكدت حجزي بالبريد. |
| Could we have adjoining rooms? | *mumkin ghurfatayn maftooHayn AHla bAHDhuma* ممكن غرفتين مفتوحين على بعضهما؟ |

## التسهيلات ووسائل الراحة Amenities and facilities

| | |
|---|---|
| Is there (a/an) … in the room? | *hal hunaak … feel ghurfa* هل هناك … في الغرفة؟ |
| air conditioning | تكييف هواء *takyeef hawaa* |
| TV/telephone | *tilifizyoon/tilifoon* تلفزيون/تلفون |
| Does the hotel have (a) …? | *hal feel funduq* هل في الفندق …؟ |
| cable TV | *tilifizyoon kawaabil* تلفزيون كوابل |
| laundry service | *maghsala* مغسلة |
| solarium | *shurfat Hammaam shamsee* شرفة حمام شمسي |
| swimming pool | *masbaH* مسبح |
| Could you put … in the room? | *mumkin taDaAH … fee ghurfatee* ممكن تضع … في غرفتي؟ |
| an extra bed | *sareer iDaafee* سرير إضافي |
| a crib [child's cot] | *sareer lil-Tifl* سرير للطفل |
| Do you have facilities for children/the disabled? | *hal ladaykum tas-heelaat lil-aTfaal/lil-muAHaaqeen* هل لديكم تسهيلات للأطفال/للمعاقين؟ |

# How long ...? كم مدة ...؟

| | |
|---|---|
| We'll be staying for ... | sa-nuqeem li-muddat ...<br>سنقيم لمدة ... |
| one night only | layla waahda faqaT<br>ليلة واحدة فقط |
| a few days | biDAHat ayyam<br>بضعة أيام |
| a week (at least) | usbooAH (AHlaal aqall)<br>أسبوع (على الأقل) |
| I don't know yet. | laa aAHrif bAHd<br>لا أعرف بعد. |
| I'd like to stay an extra night. | awadd al-iqaama layla iDaafeeya<br>أود الإقامة ليلة إضافية. |
| What does this mean? | maa maAHna haaza<br>ما معنى هذا؟ |

---

– as-salaam AHlaykum. ismee joon nyootun.
– wa-AHlaykum as-salaam sayyid nyootun.
– awadd al-iqaama laylatayn.
– Hasanan. hal tasmaH bi-tAHbi'at waseeqat at-tasjeel?

---

| | |
|---|---|
| ممكن أرى جواز سفرك، لو سمحت؟ | May I see your passport, please? |
| املأ الاستمارة، لو سمحت. | Please fill in this form. |
| ما هو رقم لوحة سيارتك؟ | What is your car registration number? |

---

| | |
|---|---|
| غرفة فقط | room only |
| بالفطور | breakfast included |
| وجبات متوفرة | meals available |
| اسم العائلة/الاسم الاول | last name/first name |
| عنوان البيت/الشارع/رقم | home address/street/number |
| الجنسية/المهنة | nationality/profession |
| تاريخ/مكان الولادة | date/place of birth |
| رقم جواز السفر | passport number |
| رقم لوحة السيارة | car registration number |
| المكان/التاريخ | place/date |
| التوقيع | signature |

23

## Price السعر

| | | |
|---|---|---|
| How much is it …? | *kam tamanuh* | كم ثمنه …؟ |
| per night/week | *feel layla/usbooAH* | في الليلة/الأسبوع |
| for bed and breakfast | *lis-sareer wal-ifTaar* | للسرير والإفطار |
| excluding meals | *bidoon al-wajbaat* | بدون الوجبات |
| for full board [American Plan (A. P.)] | *li-iqaama kaamla* | لإقامة كاملة |
| for half board [Modified American Plan (M. A. P.)] | *li-nuSf iqaama* | لنصف إقامة |
| Does the price include …? | *hal yashmil as-sAHr* | هل يشمل السعر …؟ |
| breakfast | *al-fuToor* الفطور | |
| sales tax [VAT] | *aD-Dareeba* الضريبة | |
| Do I have to pay a deposit? | *hal aHtaaj li-dafAH AHraboon* | هل أحتاج لدفع عربون؟ |
| Is there a discount for children? | *hal hunaak takhfeeD lil-aTfaal* | هل هناك تخفيض للأطفال؟ |

## Decision القرار

| | | |
|---|---|---|
| May I see the room? | *mumkin ara al-ghurfa* | ممكن أرى الغرفة؟ |
| That's fine. I'll take it. | *Hasanan. sa-aakhud-haa* | حسنا. سآخذها. |
| It's too … | *innahaa … jiddan* | أنها … جدا. |
| dark/small | *muZlima/Sagheera* مظلمة/صغيرة | |
| noisy | *Daajja* ضاجة | |
| Do you have anything …? | *hal AHndak shay* | هل عندك شيئ …؟ |
| bigger/cheaper | *akbar/arkhaS* أكبر/أرخص | |
| quieter/lighter | *ahda'/aktar inaara* أهدأ/أكثر إنارة | |
| No, I won't take it. | *laa, lan aakhud-haa* | لا، لن آخذها. |

## Problems مشاكل

| | |
|---|---|
| The ... doesn't work. | ... laa yAHmal. ... لا يعمل |
| air conditioning | takyeef al-hawaa<br>تكييف الهواء |
| fan | al-marwaHa المروحة |
| heating | at-tadfi'a التدفئة |
| light | aD-Dau النور |
| I can't turn the heat [heating] on/off. | laa astaTeeAH tashgheel/iTfaa' at-tadfi'a<br>لا أستطيع تشغيل/إطفاء التدفئة. |
| There is no hot water. | laa yoojad maa' saakhin<br>لا يوجد ماء ساخن. |
| There is no toilet paper. | laa yoojad waraq al-Hammam<br>لا يوجد ورق الحمام |
| The faucet [tap] is dripping. | al-Hanafeeya tunnaqiT<br>الحنفية تنقط. |
| The sink is blocked. | al-maghsal masdood<br>المغسل مسدود. |
| The window/door is jammed. | ash-shibbaak/al-baab maznooq<br>الشباك/الباب مزنوق. |
| My room has not been made up. | ghurfatee lam turattab<br>غرفتي لم ترتب. |
| The ... is broken. | ... maksoor. مكسور ... |
| blind/lamp | ash-sheesh/al-miSbaaH<br>الشيش /المصباح |
| lock/switch | al-qifl/miftaaH an-noor القفل/مفتاح النور |
| There are insects in our room. | hunaak Hasharaat fee ghurfatnaa<br>هناك حشرات في غرفتنا |

## Action تصرف

| | |
|---|---|
| Could you have that seen to? | mumkin tuAHaalij haazihil mushkila<br>ممكن تعالج هذه المشكلة؟ |
| I'd like to move to another room. | awadd al-intiqaal ilaa ghurfa ukhra<br>أود الانتقال إلى غرفة أخرى. |
| I'd like to speak to the manager. | awadd at-taHaddas mAHal mudeer<br>أود التحدث مع المدير. |

25

# General requirements
## طلبات عامة

In most Middle Eastern countries the current is 220 volts, but there are variations. There are many different types of sockets and plugs in use, so it is best to take a universal adaptor.

In some countries, you could experience power cuts and may want to take a flashlight [torch] and/or candles for emergencies.

## About the hotel عن الفندق

|  |  |  |
|---|---|---|
| Where's …? | ayn … ? | أين ... ؟ |
| the bar | al-baar | البار |
| the bathroom | al-Hammaam | الحمام |
| the dining room | Hujrat aT-TAHaam | حجرة الطعام |
| the elevator [lift] | al-miSAHad | المصعد |
| the parking lot [car park] | garaaj as-sayyaaraat | كراج السيارات |
| the sauna | ghurfat as-sauna | غرفة السونا |
| the shower | ad-dush | الدش |
| the swimming pool | al-masbaH | المسبح |
| the tour operator's bulletin board | lauhat maktab as-siyaaHa | لوحة مكتب السياحة |
| Where are the bathrooms [toilets]? | ayn al-Hammaamaat | أين الحمامات؟ |
| What time is the front door locked? | matta yuqfal al-baab ar-ra'eesee | متى يقفل الباب الرئيسي؟ |
| What time is breakfast served? | matta yuqaddam al-ifTaar | متى يقدم الفطور؟ |
| Is there room service? | AHndakum khidmaat lil-ghuraf | عندكم خدمات للغرف؟ |

|  |  |
|---|---|
| لمكنات الحلاقة فقط | razors [shavers] only |
| مخرج للطوارئ | emergency exit |
| باب حريق | fire door |
| الرجاء عدم الإزعاج | do not disturb |
| لخط خارجي اطلب رقم ... | for an outside line dial … |

# Personal needs طلبات شخصية

| | |
|---|---|
| The key to room ..., please. | al-miftaaH lil-ghurfa raqm ..., lau samaHt المفتاح للغرفة رقم.. ، لو سمحت |
| I've lost my key. | aDAHt miftaaHee أضعت مفتاحي. |
| I've locked myself out of my room. | aghlaqt al-baab wal-miftaaH daakhil al-ghurfa أغلقت الباب والمفتاح داخل الغرفة. |
| Could you wake me at ... ? | mumkin tuSaHHeenee as-SaaAH ممكن تصحيني الساعة ...؟ |
| I'd like breakfast in my room. | ureed al-ifTaar fee ghurfatee أريد الفطور في غرفتي. |
| Can I leave this in the safe? | mumkin atruk haaza feel khazeena ممكن أترك هذا في الخزينة؟ |
| Could I have my things from the safe? | mumkin aakhud ashyaa'ee min al-khazeena ممكن آخذ أشيائي من الخزينة؟ |
| Where is our tour guide? | ayn mandoobna as-siyaaHee أين مندوبنا السياحي؟ |
| May I have an extra ...? | mumkin aakhud ... iDaafee ممكن آخذ ... إضافي؟ |
| bath towel | minshafa منشفة |
| blanket | baTaaniya بطانية |
| hanger | AHlaaqa علاقة |
| pillow | wisaada وسادة |
| soap | Saaboon صابون |
| Is there any mail for me? | hal hunaak bareed lee هل هناك بريد لي؟ |
| Are there any messages for me? | hal hunaak rasaa'il lee هل هناك رسائل لي؟ |

*BREAKFAST ➤ 43; CHANGING MONEY ➤ 138*

# Renting الإيجار

| | |
|---|---|
| We've reserved an apartment/cottage in the name of ... | Hajaznaa shaqqa/shaalay bism ...<br>حجزنا شقة/شاليه باسم ... |
| Where do we pick up the keys? | min ayn sa-nakhud al-mafaateeH<br>من أين سنأخذ المفاتيح؟ |
| Where is ...? | ayn ...?  أين ...؟ |
| the electricity meter | AHddaad al-kahrabaa  عداد الكهرباء |
| the fuse box | AHilbat Sammamaat al-kahrabaa'<br>علبة صمامات الكهرباء |
| the valve [stopcock] | al-maHbas (aS-Samaam)  المحبس (الصمام) |
| the water heater | sakh-khaan al-maa  سخان الماء |
| Are there any spare ...? | hal hunaak ... iDaafeeya<br>هل هناك ... إضافية؟ |
| fuses | Samaamaat al-kahrabaa<br>صمامات الكهرباء |
| gas bottles | anaabeeb al-ghaaz  أنابيب الغاز |
| sheets | milaayaat  ملاءات |
| Which day does the maid come? | ayy yaum ya'tee AHmilat an-naZaafa<br>أي يوم يأتي عاملة النظافة؟ |
| Where/When do I put out the trash [rubbish]? | ayn/matta ukhrij az-zibaala<br>أين/متى أخرج الزبالة؟ |

## Problems? مشاكل؟

| | |
|---|---|
| Where can I contact you? | ayn attaSil bik<br>أين اتصل بك؟ |
| How does the stove/water heater work? | kayf yAHmal al-furn/sakh-khaan al-maa'  كيف يعمل الفرن/سخان الماء؟ |
| The ... is/are dirty. | al-... wisikh/wiskha  الـ... وسخ/وسخة. |
| The ... has broken down. | al-... tAHTal  الـ... تعطل. |
| We have accidentally broken/lost the ... | bidoon qaSd kasarnaa/aDAHnaa al-...<br>بدون قصد كسرنا/أضعنا الـ... |
| That was already damaged when we arrived. | kaan taalif AHandamaa waSalnaa<br>كان تالفا عندما وصلنا. |

## Useful terms عبارات مفيدة

| | | |
|---|---|---|
| boiler | sakh-khaan | سخان |
| crockery | awaanee | أواني |
| freezer | fireezir | فريزر |
| frying pan | miqlaa | مقلاة |
| kettle | ghallaaya | غلاية |
| lamp | miSbaH | مصباح |
| refrigerator | tallaaja | تلاجة |
| saucepan | inaa' Sahgeer | إناء صغير |
| stove [cooker] | furn | فرن |
| toilet paper | waraq al-Hammaam | ورق الحمام |
| washing machine | ghasaalat al-malaabis | غسالة الملابس |

## Rooms غرف

| | | |
|---|---|---|
| balcony | shurfa | شرفة |
| bathroom | Hammaam | حمام |
| bedroom | ghurfat naum | غرفة نوم |
| dining room | ghurfat TAHaam | غرفة طعام |
| kitchen | maTbakh | مطبخ |
| living room | ghurfat juloos | غرفة جلوس |
| toilet | marHaaD | مرحاض |

## Youth hostel بيت الشباب

| | |
|---|---|
| Do you have any places left for tonight? | hal AHndakum amaakin li-layla هل عندكم أماكن لليلة؟ |
| Do you rent out bedding? | hal tu'ajjir aghTiyyat as-sareer هل تؤجّر أغطية السرير؟ |
| What time are the doors locked? | matta tuqfal al-abwaab متى تقفل الأبواب؟ |
| I have an International Student Card. | mAHaya baTaaqat Taalib AHlameeyya معي بطاقة طالب عالمية. |

# Camping التخييم

Campsites are found throughout the Arab world and are often in attractive locations, close to the sea. Camping outside official sites is not recommended and can lead to fines and even arrest.

## Reservations الحجز

Is there a campsite near here?
*hal hunaak mukhayyam qareeb*
هل هناك مخيم قريب؟

Do you have space for a tent/ trailer [caravan]?
*AHndak makaan li-khayma/ li-bayt mutanaqqil*
عندك مكان لخيمة/لبيت متنقل؟

What is the charge ...?
*maa huwa as-siAHr ...؟*
ما هو السعر ...؟

per day/week
*li-yaum/li-usbooAH*
ليوم/لأسبوع

for a tent/a car
*li-khayma/li-sayyaara*
لخيمة/لسيارة

for a trailer [caravan]
*li-bayt mutanaqqil*
لبيت متنقل

## Facilities خدمات

Are there cooking facilities on site?
*hal hunaak lawaazim liT-Tabkh feel makaan*
هل هناك لوازم للطبخ في المكان؟

Are there any electric outlets [power points]?
*hal hunaak mawaaqiAH li-akhd al-kahrabaa*
هل هناك مواقع لأخذ الكهرباء؟

Where is/are ...?
*ayn ...؟*
أين ...؟

the drinking water
*maa' ash-shurb*
ماء الشرب

the trash can [dustbin]
*Sundooq iz-zibaala*
صندوق الزبالة

the laundry facilities
*al-maghsala*
المغسلة

the showers
*ad-dush*
الدش

Where can I get some butane gas?
*ayn astaTeeAH al-HuSool AHla ghaaz il-biyootaan*
أين أستطيع الحصول على غاز البيوتان؟

---

| | |
|---|---|
| ممنوع التخييم | no camping |
| ماء الشرب | drinking water |
| ممنوع إشعال النار/الشواء | no fires/barbecues |

## Complaints شكاوى

It's too sunny/shady here.
*innahu mushmis/
muZallal jiddan hunaa*
إنه مشمس/مظلل جدا هنا.

It's too crowded here.
*innahu muzdaHim jiddan
hunaa*
إنه مزدحم جدا هنا.

The ground's too hard/uneven.
*al-arD qaasya jiddan/
ghayr mustaweya*
الأرض قاسية جدا/غير مستوية.

Do you have a more level spot?
*hal AHndak biqAHa mustaweya*
هل عندك بقعة مستوية؟

You can't camp here.
*laa tastaTeeAH an tukhayyim hunaa.*
لا تستطيع أن تخيم هنا.

## Camping equipment أدوات التخييم

| | | |
|---|---|---|
| butane gas | *ghaaz al-biyootaan* | غاز البيوتان |
| campbed | *sareer safar* | سرير سفر |
| charcoal | *faHm* | فحم |
| flashlight [torch] | *baTaareeyat jayb* | بطارية جيب |
| groundcloth [groundsheet] | *HaSeera* | حصيرة |
| guy rope | *Habl il-khayma* | حبل الخيمة |
| hammer | *miTraqa* | مطرقة |
| kerosene [primus] stove | *mauqad il-bareemoos* | موقد البريموس |
| knapsack | *Haqeebat iZ-Zahr* | حقيبة الظهر |
| mallet | *miTraqa khashabeeya* | مطرقة خشبية |
| matches | *kibreet* | كبريت |
| mattress | *martaba* | مرتبة |
| paraffin | *baaraafeen* | بارافين |
| penknife | *miTwaa* | مطواة |
| sleeping bag | *Haqeebat lil-naum* | حقيبة للنوم |
| tent | *khayma* | خيمة |
| tent pegs | *autaad il-khayma* | أوتاد الخيمة |
| tent pole | *AHamood il-khayma* | عامود الخيمة |

## Checking out المغادرة

| | |
|---|---|
| What time do we need to vacate the room? | *matta nukhlee il-ghurfa*<br>متى نخلي الغرفة؟ |
| Could we leave our baggage here until ... p.m.? | *hal nastaTeeAH tark HaQaa'ibnaa hunaa Hatta as-sAHa ... bAHd aZ-Zuhr*<br>هل نستطيع ترك حقائبنا هنا حتى الساعة ... بعد الظهر؟ |
| I'm leaving now. | *ana mughaadir al-aan.*<br>أنا مغادر الآن. |
| Could you order me a taxi, please? | *mumkin tuTlub lee taaksee, lau samaHt*<br>ممكن تطلب لي تاكسي، لو سمحت؟ |
| It's been a very enjoyable stay. | *kaanit iqaama mumtiAH.*<br>كانت إقامة ممتعة. |

## Paying الدفع

Tipping is usual for most personal services in the Arab world, except perhaps Yemen where it is not customary. Hotel and restaurant staff, as well as taxi drivers, porters, parking lot/toilet attendants, etc., expect a tip at a level suitable to the service rendered. Tipping often supplements low basic wages and is an essential part of many people's income. Make sure you have the appropriate money easily accessible at all times.

| | |
|---|---|
| May I have my bill, please? | *mumkin tAHTeenee al-Hisaab, lau samaHt*<br>ممكن تعطيني الحساب، لو سمحت؟ |
| I think there's a mistake in the bill. | *AHtaqid an hunaak khaTa feel Hisaab*<br>أعتقد أن هناك خطأ في الحساب. |
| I've made ... telephone calls. | *itaSalt ... marra bit-tileefoon*<br>اتصلت ... مرة بالتليفون. |
| I've taken ... from the mini-bar. | *akhadt ... min al-baar aS-Sagheer*<br>أخذت ... من البار الصغير. |
| Can I have an itemized bill? | *mumkin taAHTeenee qaa'ima mufaSSala bil-Hisaab*<br>ممكن تعطيني قائمة مفصلة بالحساب؟ |
| Could I have a receipt, please? | *mumkin taAHTeenee al-waSl, lau samaHt*<br>ممكن تعطيني الوصل، لو سمحت؟ |

# Eating Out

## Restaurants المطاعم

Food has always been one of the central features of the tradition of hospitality in the Arab world. For this reason, you will still find some of the best meals are home-cooked. However, there is also a large variety of restaurants, fast-food outlets, and stalls offering various snacks.

You may have difficulty finding restaurants that offer no-smoking areas, but as much of the seating is outside or in air-conditioned rooms you should not find this too much of a problem.

### مطعم maTAHm
Restaurant. Ranging from the very expensive to the budget end of the market. Often offering a mixture of western and Middle-Eastern dishes.

### قهوة qahwa
Coffee shop. Mainly for drinking coffee and tea, and smoking **sheesha** (water pipes ➤ 51), but you may be able to eat a sandwich or other snacks.

### محل فول وفلافل maHall fool wa falaafil
Bean and falafel stall. One of the most popular snacks (➤ 40).

### حلواني halawaanee
Shop selling desserts from rice pudding to sweet sticky cakes.

### كأس عرق ومزة kaas AHraq wa mazza
Lebanese restaurant serving **mezza** (➤ 43) and the local aniseed drink, **araq.**

33

# Meal times أوقات الوجبات

Generally meals are later than in North America or Northern Europe. However, whenever you get hungry you will generally find something open day or night.

### الفطور al-futoor
Breakfast is served between 6 and 10 a.m. in most hotels.

### الغداء al-ghada
Lunch is the main meal of the day, usually eaten between 1 and 3:30 p.m.

### العشاء al-AHsha
Dinner is usually eaten between 8 and 11 p.m. (or even later) and can be a lighter version of lunch or a snack, such as **faTeer** (pancake ➤ 40).

# Arabic cuisine المطبخ العربي

Middle-Eastern cooking is broadly Mediterranean in nature but displays a variety of influences. Lebanese cooking, itself influenced by Greek and Turkish cuisine, is popular throughout the region. A typical meal would consist of **mazza** (appetizers ➤ 43) with the local bread **khubz** (also known as **AHysh**, meaning "life"). This would be followed by the main course of fish or meat, accompanied by vegetables and/or salad. Dessert usually consists of fruit, sweet milk puddings, or small sticky cakes.

# Ramadan رمضان

The month of Ramadan is the Muslim month of fasting and lasts for approximately 28 days. As the Muslim calendar is a lunar one, Ramadan moves through the seasons year by year. Your travel agent should be able to tell you the likely dates for a specific year.

During Ramadan many Muslims refrain from eating, drinking or smoking between sunrise and sunset as a communal display of religious faith. Eating habits and meal times change accordingly. The main meals of the day are **suHoor**, a pre-dawn snack, and **iftaar**, the sunset main meal which breaks the fast. There are specific drinks and dishes consumed during Ramadan. One of the most famous drinks is **qamar id-deen**, a type of thick juice made from dried apricot paste. You will find that many international hotels offer both **iftaar** at sunset and then dinner later during Ramadan. Generally cities come to life at night during Ramadan and people go out until the early hours of the morning. Shops are also often open very late.

If you are visiting a Muslim country during Ramadan you will usually be able to find places to eat during the day that cater for tourists or non-Muslims. Out of courtesy, however, you should try to avoid eating or smoking in public places during daylight hours.

| | |
|---|---|
| A table for ..., please. | *maa'ida li ..., lau samaHt*<br>مائدة لـ...، لو سمحت. |
| 1/2/3/4 (people) | *shakhS/shakhSayn/talaat*<br>*ashkhaaS/arbAH ashkhaaS*<br>شخص/شخصين/٣ أشخاص/٤ أشخاص |
| Thank you. | *shukran* شكراً. |
| I'd like to pay. | *ureed an adfAH* أريد أن أدفع. |

## Finding a place to eat التفتيش عن مكان لنأكل

| | |
|---|---|
| Can you recommend a good restaurant? | *mumkin tinSaHnaa bi-maTAHm jayyid*<br>ممكن تنصحنا بمطعم جيد؟ |
| Is there a ... restaurant near here? | *hal hunaak maTAHm ... qareeb*<br>هل هناك مطعم ... قريب؟ |
| traditional local restaurant | *taqleedee maHallee* تقليدي محلي |
| Lebanese | *lubnaanee* لبناني |
| Chinese | *Seenee* صيني |
| fish | *samak* سمك |
| Italian | *eeTaalee* إيطالي |
| inexpensive | *rakheeS* رخيص |
| vegetarian | *nabaateeyeen* نباتيين |
| Where can I find a(n) ... ? | *ayn ajid ...*<br>أين أجد ...؟ |
| burger stand | *kushk "burger"* كشك برغر |
| café/restaurant | *maqha/maTAHm* مقهى/مطعم |
| fast food restaurant | *maTAHm wajbaat sareeAHa*<br>مطعم وجبات سريعة |
| ice-cream parlor | *maHall aayis kreem* محل آيس كريم |
| pizzeria | *maHall beetza* محل بيتزا |
| steak house | *maTAHm laHm steek* مطعم لحم ستيك |

DIRECTIONS ➤ 94

## Reserving a table حجز مائدة

| | |
|---|---|
| I'd like to reserve a table for ... | *ureed hajz maa'da li*<br>أريد حجز مائدة لـ... |
| For this evening/tomorrow at ... | *li-haazihil layla/lil-ghad as-saAHa*<br>لهذه الليلة/للغد الساعة ... |
| We'll come at 8. | *sa-na'tee as-saAHa tamaanya*<br>سنأتي الساعة ٨. |
| A table for 2, please. | *maa'da li-shakhSayn, lau samaHt*<br>مائدة لشخصين، لو سمحت. |
| We have a reservation. | *AHndina Hajz*<br>عندنا حجز. |

| | |
|---|---|
| ما هو الاسم، لو سمحت؟ | What's the name, please? |
| آسف. المطعم مشغول/كامل العدد. | We're very busy/full up. I'm sorry. |
| ستتوفر مائدة بعد ... دقائق. | We'll have a free table in ... minutes. |
| رجاء عودوا بعد ... دقائق. | Please come back in ... minutes. |

## Where to sit أين نجلس

| | |
|---|---|
| Could we sit ...? | *mumkin najlis ...?* ممكن نجلس ...؟ |
| over there | *hunaak* هناك |
| outside | *feel khaarij* في الخارج |
| in a non-smoking area | *feel manTiqa mamnooAH feehaa at-tadkheen*<br>في منطقة ممنوع فيها التدخين |
| by the window | *bi-qurb ash-shubaak* بقرب الشباك |
| Smoking or non-smoking? | *tadkheen au AHdam at-tadkheen*<br>تدخين أو عدم التدخين؟ |

> – *ureed Hajz maa'da li-haazihil layla.*
> – *li-kam shakhS?*
> – *li-arbaAH ashkhaaS.*
> – *matta sa-ta'toon?*
> – *sa-na'tee as-sAHa at-tamaanya.*
> – *wa maa huwal ism, lau samaHt?*
> – *smith.*
> – *Hasanan. ashoofkum.*

# Ordering الطلب

| | |
|---|---|
| Waiter!/Waitress! | yaa garsoon/yaa aanisa |
| | ياجرسون!/يا آنسة! |
| Do you have a set menu? | hal ladaykum Tabaq al-yaum |
| | هل لديكم طبق اليوم؟ |
| Can you recommend some typical local dishes? | hal tinSaHnaa bi-aklaat taqleedeeya maHalleeya |
| | هل تنصحنا بأكلات تقليدية محلية؟ |
| Could you tell me what ... is? | mumkin tiqool lee maaza yakoon |
| | ممكن تقول لي ماذا يكون ...؟ |
| What's in it? | maaza bi-daakhiluh؟ ماذا بداخله |
| What kind of ... do you have? | ayy nauAH min ... AHandak |
| | أي نوع من ... عندك؟ |
| I'd like | ureed ... أريد |
| I'll have ... | sa-aakhud ... سآخذ |
| a bottle/glass/carafe of ... | zujaajat/koob/ibreeq min |
| | زجاجة/كوب/إبريق من ... |

| | |
|---|---|
| جاهز لتطلب؟ | Are you ready to order? |
| ماذا تحب؟ | What would you like? |
| هل تفضل طلب المشروبات أولا؟ | Would you like to order drinks first? |
| أنصحكم بـ... | I recommend ... |
| لا يوجد عندنا ... | We don't have ... |
| هذا سيستغرق ... دقائق. | That will take ... minutes. |
| صحتين. | Enjoy your meal. |

– jaahiz li taTlub?
– hal tinSaHnaa bi-aklaat maHalleeya?
– naAHm. anSaHkum bil-kufta.
– muwaafiq, sa-aakhud haaza maAH salaTa, lau samaHt.
– bit-ta'keed. wa maaza tureed an tishrab.
– koob min AHSeer manga, lau samaHt.
– bit-ta'keed.

DRINKS ➤ 49; MENU READER ➤ 52

## المتممات Accompaniments

| | |
|---|---|
| Could I have ... without ...? | mumkin tAHTeenee ... bidoon ... ممكن تعطيني ... بدون ...؟ |
| With a side order of ... | mAHa Talb jaanibee min ... مع طلب جانبي من ... |
| Could I have salad instead of vegetables, please? | mumkin aakhud salaTa badal al-khuDaar, lau samaHt ممكن آخذ سلطة بدل الخضار، لو سمحت؟ |
| Does the meal come with vegetables/rice? | hal al-wajba ta'tee mAHa khuDaar/ruzz هل الوجبة تأتي مع خضار/رز؟ |
| Do you have any sauces? | AHndakum SalSa عندكم صلصة؟ |
| Would you like ... with that? | hal tureed ... mAHah هل تريد ... معه؟ |
| vegetables/salad | khuDaar/salaTa خضار/سلطة |
| potatoes/French fries | baTaaTis/baTaaTis maqleeya بطاطس/بطاطس مقلية |

| | |
|---|---|
| sauce | SalSa صلصة |
| ice | talj ثلج |
| May I have some ...? | mumkin aakhud ... ؟ ممكن آخذ ... |
| bread | khubz خبز |
| butter | zibda زبدة |
| chili | shaTTa شطة |
| lemon | leemoon ليمون |
| mustard | musTarda مسطردة |
| pepper | filfil فلفل |
| salt | malH ملح |
| sugar | sukkar سكر |
| artificial sweetener | sukkar SinaAH-ee سكر صناعي |
| vinaigrette [French dressing] | SalSat al-khall صلصة الخل |

MENU READER ➤ 52

## General questions أسئلة عامة

| Could I have a clean …, please? | mumkin taAHTeenee … naDeef[a], lau samaHt |
| | ممكن تعطيني ... نظيف[ة]، لو سمحت؟ |
| cup/glass | finjaan/koob |
| | فنجان/كوب |
| fork/knife | shauka/sikkeen |
| | شوكة/سكين |
| serviette [napkin]/ashtray | mindeel al-maa'ida/manfaDat sajaayir |
| | منديل المائدة/منفضة سجاير |
| plate/spoon | SaHn/malAHaqa |
| | صحن/ملعقة |
| I'd like some more …, please. | ureed al-mazeed min …, lau samaHt |
| | أريد المزيد من ...، لو سمحت. |
| Nothing more, thanks. | haaza kifaaya, shukran |
| | هذا كفاية، شكرا. |
| Where are the bathrooms [toilets]? | ayn al-Hammaamaat |
| | أين الحمامات؟ |

## Special requirements طلبات خاصة

| I mustn't eat food containing … | ana laa aakul TAHaam feeh |
| | أنا لا آكل طعاما فيه ... |
| flour/fat | TaHeen/duhn |
| | طحين/دهن |
| salt/sugar | milH/sukkar |
| | ملح/سكر |
| Do you have meals/drinks for diabetics? | AHndak wajbaat/mashroobaat li-marDa as-sukkaree |
| | عندك وجبات/مشروبات لمرضى السكري؟ |
| Do you have vegetarian meals? | AHndak wajbaat lin-nabaatiyeen |
| | عندك وجبات للنباتيين؟ |

## For the children للأطفال

| Do you serve children's portions? | hal tuqaddimoo maqaadeer lil-aTfaal? |
| | هل تقدمون مقادير للأطفال؟ |
| Could we have a child's seat, please? | mumkin taAHTeenee kursee lil-Tifl, lau samaHt |
| | ممكن تعطيني كرسي للطفل، لو سمحت؟ |
| Where can I change the baby? | ayn ughayyeer al-fuwaT liT-Tifl |
| | أين أغيير الفوط للطفل؟ |

CHILDREN ➤ 113

# Fast food وجبات سريعة

Fast food is a Middle-Eastern specialty, with all sorts of stalls and small shops offering tasty and cheap meals. Arabic bread filled with **fool** (baked fava beans) or **falaafil** (fried crushed chickpeas) are particularly popular. It is best to stick to cooked vegetables or pickles rather than fresh salad if eating off the street. In addition, most major cities will also feature a large number of American-style fast food outlets.

| | |
|---|---|
| Coffee/Tea, please. | *qahwa/shaay, min faDlak* قهوة/شاي، من فضلك. |
| with milk/black | *bil-Haleeb/saada* بالحليب/سادة |
| I'd like a glass of juice. | *ureed koob min al-AHSeer* أريد كوب من العصير. |
| I'd like two of those. | *ureed itnayn min haaza* أريد اثنين من هذا. |
| burger/fries | *"burger"/baTaaTis maqleeya* برغر/بطاطس مقلية |
| (bean/falafel) sandwich | *sandawitsh (fool/falaafil)* سندويتش (فول/فلافل) |
| (vanilla/chocolate/mango) ice cream | *aayis kreem (faneela/shokoolaata/manga)* آيس كريم (فنيلا/شكولاتة/منجا) |
| rice pudding | *ruzz bi-Haleeb/ruzz bi-laban* رز بحليب/رز بلبن |
| A ... portion, please. | *miqdaar ..., lau samaHt* مقدار ...، لو سمحت. |
| small/large | *Sagheer/kabeer* صغير/كبير |
| It's to go [take away]. | *sa-aakhuduh mAHaya* سآخذه معي. |
| That's all, thanks. | *haaza kull maa ureed, shukran* هذا كل ما أريد، شكرا. |

### كشري *kosharee*
A mixture of pasta, lentils, fried onions, and rice with a garlic sauce.

### شاورمة *shawaarma*
Spit-roasted meat, sliced and put into bread with salad, **humoos**, or **taheena**.

### فطير *faTeer*
Thin, rolled savory or sweet pancakes. Watching the pancakes being made is an entertainment in itself.

– maaza tureed?
– itnayn qahwa, lau samaHt.
– bil-Haleeb au saada?
– bil-Haleeb, lau samaHt.
– ta'kul shay'?
– haaza kull maa ureed, shukran.

## Complaints شكاوى

| | |
|---|---|
| I have no knife/fork/spoon. | laysa AHndee sikkeen/shauka/milAHqa. ليس عندي سكين/شوكة/ملعقة. |
| There must be some mistake. | AHtaqid an hunaak khaTa أعتقد أن هناك خطأ. |
| That's not what I ordered. | haaza laysa maa Talabtuh هذا ليس ما طلبته. |
| I asked for … | ana Talabt … أنا طلبت … |
| I can't eat this. | laa astaTeeAH an aakul haaza لا أستطيع أن آكل هذا. |
| The meat is … | al-laHm … اللحم … |
| overdone/underdone | kateer as-siwaa/qaleel as-siwaa كثير السوا/قليل السوا |
| too tough | AHseer al-maDgh عسير المضغ |
| This is too … | haaza … jiddan هذا … جدا. |
| bitter/sour | murr/Haaziq مر/حاذق |
| The food is cold. | aT-TAHaam baarid. الطعام بارد. |
| This isn't fresh/clean. | haaza ghayr Taazij/naZeef هذا غير طازج/نظيف. |
| How much longer will our food be? | kam min al-waqt yajib intiZaar aklinaa كم من الوقت يجب انتظار أكلنا؟ |
| We can't wait any longer. We're leaving. | laa nastaTeeAH al-intiZaar aktar. sa-nughaadir لا نستطيع الانتظار أكثر. سنغادر. |
| I'd like to speak to the head waiter/manager. | ureed at-takallum mAHal mitr/mudeer أريد التكلم مع المتر/المدير. |

# الدفع Paying

Tipping is generally expected if you are happy with the service.
ten percent is usually fine, although you might want to tip the
main waiter and the assistants separately.

| | |
|---|---|
| I'd like to pay. | *ureed an adfAH.* أريد أن أدفع. |
| The bill, please. | *al-Hisaab, lau samaHt.* الحساب، لو سمحت. |
| We'd like to pay separately. | *nureed an nidfAH munfaSileen* نريد أن ندفع منفصلين. |
| It's all together, please. | *Hisaab waaHid, lau samaHt* حساب واحد، لو سمحت. |
| I think there's a mistake in this bill. | *AHtaqid an hunaak khaTa feel Hisaab* اعتقد أن هناك خطأ في الحساب. |
| What is this amount for? | *maa hazaal mablagh?* ما هذا المبلغ؟ |
| I didn't have that. I had … | *maa akhadt haaza. akhadt* ما أخذت هذا. أخذت … |
| Is service included? | *hal al-khidma Dimn al-Hisaab* هل الخدمة ضمن الحساب؟ |
| Can I pay with this credit card? | *mumkin adfAH bi-biTaaqat al-itimaan haazihi?* ممكن أدفع ببطاقة الائتمان هذه؟ |
| I've forgotten my wallet. | *naseet maHfaZtee.* نسيت محفظتي. |
| I don't have enough money. | *laysa AHndee fuloos kifaaya* ليس عندي فلوس كفاية. |
| Could I have a receipt, please? | *mumkin taAHTeenee al-waSl, lau samaHt* ممكن تعطيني الوصل، لو سمحت؟ |
| That was a very good meal. | *kaanat wajba mumtaaza.* كانت وجبة ممتازة. |

---

– garsoon! mumkin tAHTeenee al-Hisaab, lau samaHt?
– bit-ta'keed. tafaDDal.
– hal il-khidma Dimn al-Hisaab?
– naAHm.
– mumkin adfAH bi-biTaaqat al-itimaan haazihi?
– TabAHan.
– shukran. kaanat wajba mumtaaza.

# Course by course

## Breakfast الفطور

A typical Arabic breakfast would consist of tea, **fool** and
**falaafil** (> 40), eggs, olives, cheese, and bread.
Many hotels will offer this and more Western-style dishes as well.

| | |
|---|---|
| I'd like … | *ureed* … أريد |
| bread/butter | *khubz/zibda* خبز/زبدة |
| a boiled egg | *bayDa maslooqa* بيضة مسلوقة |
| fried/scrambled eggs | *bayD maqlee/mamzooj* بيض مقلي/ممزوج |
| fruit juice | *AHseer fawaakih* عصير فواكه |
| orange/grapefruit | *burtuqaal/ greeb froot* برتقال/كريب فروت |
| honey/jam | *AHsal/murabba* عسل/مربى |
| milk | *Haleeb* حليب |
| roll | *khubz sagheer* خبز صغير |
| toast | *khubz muHammaS* خبز محمص |

## Appetizers [Starters] (المشهيات) المقبلات

Appetizers, or **mazza,** are an important part of an Arabic meal. A mixture
of appetizers is usually placed in the middle of the table and shared by
everyone. Here are some of the most popular:

### باباغنوج *babaghannooj*
A dip made with eggplant [aubergine] and tahini paste.

### حمص بالطحينة *HumooS bi-TaHeena*
A dip made of ground chickpeas and sesame paste.

### كفتة *kofta*
Fried or grilled balls/fingers of minced meat.

### جبنة بيضاء بالطماطم *jibna bayDa biT-TamaaTim*
White, soft cheese (similar to Greek feta cheese) mashed with
tomatoes, and herbs.

### طحينة *TaHeena*
A dip made of sesame paste with olive oil, lemon, and cumin.
Particularly popular in Egypt.

### ورق عنب *waraq AHinab*
Rolled vine leaves stuffed with rice, sometimes mixed with minced meat.

### بطارخ *baTaarikh*
Egyptian smoked grey mullet roe.

## Soups شوربة

Soups are popular in winter and tend to be rich. They are always accompanied by bread and sometimes include noodles. There is a huge variety of soups based on beans, vegetables, and meat. Here are some of the most popular:

| | | |
|---|---|---|
| شوربة عدس | *shoorbit AHds* | lentil soup |
| شوربة فراخ | *shoorbit firaakh* | chicken soup |
| شوربة خضار | *shoorbit khuDaar* | vegetable soup |
| شوربة لحم | *shoorbit laHm* | meat soup |
| شوربة طماطم | *shoorbit TamaaTim* | tomato soup |
| شوربة سمك | *shoorbit samak* | fish soup |

### ملوخية *mulookheeya*
Thick Egyptian soup made of finely chopped **mulookheeya** leaves (a green vegetable similar to spinach), cooked with rabbit, chicken, or meat. Often poured onto pieces of torn-up bread or rice.

### شوربة كوارع *shoorbit kawaariAH*
Thick gelatinous soup made from calves hoofs.

## Egg dishes أطباق البيض

| | | |
|---|---|---|
| بيضة مسلوقة | *bayDa maslooqa* | boiled eggs |
| بيض مقلي | *bayD maqlee* | fried eggs |
| بيض ممزوج | *bayD mamzooj* | scrambled eggs |
| عجة | *AHjja* | omelet |
| بيض بالبسطرمة | *bayD bil-basTurma* | eggs with cured beef |
| بيض بالفول | *bayD bil-fool* | eggs with fava beans |
| بيض بالبلوبيف | *bayD bil-buloobeef* | eggs with corned beef |

## Pastries and pies الفطائر

Savory pastries and pies are a favorite in many parts of the
Arab world, particularly North Africa. Here are a few you
might want to sample in addition to the pancakes
(**faTeer** ➤ 40):

سنبوسك *sanboosak*
Half-moon-shaped pastries filled with cheese or meat.

بريك *breek*
Fried Tunisian filo pastry parcels, with a variety of fillings.

بستلة *bastilla*
Moroccan pigeon pie, often baked for special occasions.

طاجن *Taajin*
Baked Tunisian meat pie with string [haricot] beans and cinnamon.

لحم بعجين *laHm bi-AHjeen*
Syrian baked, open-faced minced-meat pies.

## Fish and seafood أسماك و مأكولات بحرية

In coastal areas, take advantage of the wonderful variety of fresh fish and
seafood. You'll find the fish is often laid out fresh on ice or even alive in
tanks for you to take your pick. You'll recognize **toona** and **sardeen**.

Other types of fish are regional and often have several different names,
making it difficult to provide a comprehensive list.

Fish is usually eaten whole, either grilled (**mashwee**) or fried (**maqlee**),
although fish kebabs (**kabaab samak**) are also popular.

| | | |
|---|---|---|
| كابوريا | *kaaboorya* | crab |
| استاكوزا | *istaakooza* | lobster |
| بوري/سلطان إبراهيم | *booree/sulTaan ibraaheem* | mullet |
| بلح البحر | *balaH al-baHr* | mussels |
| أخطبوط | *akhTabooT* | octopus |
| محار | *maHHaar* | oyster |
| جمبري/قريدس | *jambaree/quraydis* | shrimp [prawn] |
| سمك موسى | *samak moosa* | sole |
| سبيط | *subbayT* | squid |

# Meat and poultry اللحم والدواجن

Traditionally "meat" (**al-laHm**) in the Middle East meant lamb or mutton as cattle was not reared and pork is forbidden by Islamic law. Although lamb is still probably the most widely available meat, beef is now also popular and chicken, turkey, duck, pigeon, and some other small birds are also staples of Arabic cuisine. In some areas goat, rabbit, and camel meat are also eaten. However, pork (**laHm al-khinzeer**) is not generally available, except in some Christian areas.

I'd like some...        *ureed* ... أريد

| | | |
|---|---|---|
| لحم بقري | *laHm baqaree* | beef |
| ضاني | *Daanee* | lamb |
| بتلو | *bitilloo* | veal |
| أرانب | *araanib* | rabbit |
| دجاج | *dajaaj* | chicken |
| حمام | *Hamaam* | pigeon |
| ديك رومي | *deek roomee* | turkey |
| بط | *baTT* | duck |
| كبدة | *kibda* | liver |
| كلاوي | *kalaawee* | kidney |
| سجق | *sujuq* | sausage |
| فيليه | *feelayh* | steak |
| اسكالوب | *iskaaloob* | veal cutlet |
| كفتة | *kufta* | meatballs |
| مخ | *mukh* | brains |

### كبة نية *kibba nayya*
Raw minced meat with spices. A kind of Lebanese steak tartar.

### طاجن *Taajin*
North African lamb stew baked in clay pots with fruit and honey.

### فتة *fatta*
Boiled mutton with rice and bread soaked in broth, vinegar, and garlic.

### كبيبة *kubayba*
Minced meat and cracked wheat, either in balls or flat in a tray.

### سليق *saleeq*
Lamb cooked in spiced milk and served on rice. A Bedouin specialty.

### حمام محشٍ *Hamaam maHshee*
Pigeon stuffed with cracked wheat or rice.

# Vegetables خضار

Vegetables are more often found stuffed, stewed, or pickled than boiled. A wide range is generally available, and some vegetables, e.g., eggplant [aubergine], have seemingly endless variations.

| | | |
|---|---|---|
| باذنجان | *baazinjaan* | eggplant [aubergine] |
| كرنب/ملفوف | *kurunb/malfoof* | cabbage |
| بصل | *baSal* | onion |
| بسلة | *bisilla* | peas |
| فاصوليا خضراء | *faSoolya khaDra* | green beans |
| خس | *khass* | lettuce |
| بطاطس | *baTaaTis* | potatoes |
| فلفل أخضر | *filfil akhDar* | green pepper |
| بامية | *bamya* | okra [ladies' fingers] |
| كوسة | *koosa* | zucchini [courgette] |
| جزر | *jazar* | carrots |
| ذرة | *dura* | corn |
| خيار | *khiyaar* | cucumber |
| طماطم | *TamaaTim* | tomatoes |

### محشي *maHshee*
Vegetables stuffed with a mixture of rice, onion, minced meat, and herbs. Stuffed vine leaves (**waraq AHinab** ➤ 43) are one of the most popular **maHshee**. Others are stuffed eggplant [aubergine], cabbage, tomato, pepper, and zucchini [courgette]. They can be eaten hot or cold.

### بامية بالموزة *bamya bil-mauza*
Okra [ladies' fingers] stewed with lamb knuckles.

### تبولة *tabboola*
Lebanese salad made with cracked wheat and very finely chopped onion, tomato, parsley, mint, olive oil, and lemon.

### طرشي *Torshee*
Pickled vegetables – carrots, cucumbers, etc. – which are sometimes a distinctive red color due to a red cabbage dye.

## Cereals and beans الحبول والبقول

Rice is the staple cereal but cracked wheat, lentils, beans and chickpeas are also popular. A specialty of North Africa is couscous (**kuskus**). This is steamed cracked wheat served hot with meat, vegetables, and the broth from the meat.

| | | |
|---|---|---|
| رز | *ruzz* | rice |
| عدس | *AHds* | lentils |
| مكرونة | *makaroona* | pasta |
| حمص | *HumuS* | chickpeas |
| فول | *fool* | brown (fava) beans |
| برغل | *burghul* | cracked wheat |

## Cheese جبنة

| | | |
|---|---|---|
| جبنة بيضاء | *jibna bayDa* | white (feta) cheese |
| جبنة رومي | *jibna roomee* | hard cheese, similar to Parmesan |
| لبنة | *labna* | curd cheese |
| جبنة مالحة | *jibna malHa* | salted curd cheese |

## Dessert الحلو

Most Arabs have a sweet tooth and tend to eat very sugary desserts, but in small portions, together with fruit (➤ 49). The most popular desserts are syrupy pastries or milk-based puddings.

### مهلبية *maHallabeeya*
Smooth rice or corn-flour pudding.

### أم علي *umm AHlee*
A type of sweet hot milk pudding with nuts and raisins.

### قطايف *qaTaayif*
Pastry filled with nuts and soaked in syrup.

### لقمة القاضي *luqmit al-QaaDee*
Small fried dough balls soaked in syrup. Literally means "the judge's morsel."

### بسبوسة *basboosa*
Semolina cake soaked in syrup.

### كعب الغزال *kAHb al-ghazaal*
North African speciality. Horn-shaped pastries filled with almonds and flavored with orange-flower water.

# Fruit فواكه

| | | |
|---|---|---|
| برقوق | *barqooq* | plums |
| تين | *teen* | figs |
| فراولة | *faraawla* | strawberries |
| رمان | *rummaan* | pomegranates |
| أناناس | *anaanaas* | pineapples |
| بلح | *balaH* | dates |
| تفاح | *tufaaH* | apples |
| مشمش | *mishmish* | apricots |
| بطيخ | *baTTeekh* | watermelon |
| جوافة | *jawaafa* | guavas |
| خوخ | *khookh* | peaches |
| برتقال | *burtuqaal* | oranges |
| موز | *mauz* | bananas |
| منجا | *manga* | mangos |
| عنب | *AHinab* | grapes |

# Drinks مشروبات

## Alcoholic drinks مشروبات كحولية

Alcohol is strictly forbidden to Muslims under Islamic law, and in some Arab countries, notably Saudi Arabia, it is illegal. However, in many other countries alcohol is relatively available in tourist areas and hotels. Lebanon and Egypt have a long history of wine and beer production, and local brews are worth sampling – and are much cheaper than imported brands. A local specialty of Lebanon and the Levant is **AHraq**, an aniseed drink similar to the Greek ouzo or the French pastis. Most other alcoholic drinks are known by their original names: **weeskee**, **rum**, **beera**, etc.

| | | |
|---|---|---|
| I'd like a bottle of … | *ureed zujaajit …* | أريد زجاجة … |
| local beer | *beera maHalleeya* | بيرة محلية |
| imported beer | *beera mustawrada* | بيرة مستوردة |
| white wine | *nabeet abyaD* | نبيذ أبيض |
| red wine | *nabeet aHmar* | نبيذ أحمر |
| I'd like a glass of araq. | *ureed koob AHraq.* | أريد كوب عرق. |
| with ice/without ice | *bi-talj/bidoon talj* | بثلج/بدون ثلج |

49

## Non-alcoholic drinks مشروبات بدون كحول

Freshly squeezed juices and bottles of international and local soft drinks are popular throughout the region. You will find juice bars serving a large variety of delicious fruit juices and cocktails squeezed in front of you. Soft drinks often have to be drunk on the spot and the bottles returned. Non-alcoholic beers and wines are also becoming widely available, and there are several international and local brands on the market.

You may also find **karkaday**, a drink made from the flowers of the fuchsia plant that can be drunk hot or cold, and tamarind or sugar-cane juice (see below).

| | |
|---|---|
| I'd like a bottle of … | *ureed zujaajit* … أريد زجاجة |
| I'd like a/an … | *ureed* … أريد |
| apricot juice | *AHSeer mishmish* عصير مشمش |
| carrot juice | *AHSeer jazar* عصير جزر |
| grape juice | *AHSeer AHinab* عصير عنب |
| guava juice | *AHSeer jawaafa* عصير جوافة |
| lemon juice | *AHSeer laymoon* عصير ليمون |
| mango juice | *AHSeer manga* عصير منجا |
| orange juice | *AHSeer burTuqaal* عصير برتقال |
| pomegranate juice | *AHSeer rummaan* عصير رمان |
| strawberry juice | *AHSeer faraawla* عصير فراولة |
| sugar-cane juice | *AHSeer qaSab* عصير قصب |
| tamarind juice | *tamr hindee* تمر هندي |
| mineral water | *miyaah mAHdaneeya* مياه معدنية |
| non-alcoholic beer/wine | *beera/nabeet bidoon kuHool* بيرة/نبيذ بدون كحول |

# Tea and coffee شاي وقهوة

Tea and coffee are popular throughout the Middle East, drunk both in the traditional way – strong, sweet, and black – and increasingly also in the Western style. You can find Western-style cafés within hotels and in the larger towns, or you can try out a local coffee house (**al-qahwa**).

Going to an Arab coffee house is more than just refreshment. It's tradition. Inside or on the terrace you can entertain yourself by watching the local street life.

Tea is served in a glass, black with sugar and sometimes mint. Coffee is served in espresso-sized glasses or cups and is very strong and black. The coffee beans are roasted and cardamon is added for flavoring. You can order it regular, extra sweet, or without sugar.

You can also order a **sheesha** (or **naarjeela**), the famous Arab water pipe. You need to specify whether you want **tumbaak**, a natural coarse tobacco, or **maa AHsil**, a lighter tobacco mixed with molasses. You may also like to play backgammon or dominoes.

Unfortunately, it's almost exclusively men who patronize coffee houses, and if you go as an unaccompanied woman you could feel ill at ease.

| | |
|---|---|
| I'd like a glass/cup of … | *ureed koob/finjaan* |
| | أريد كوب/فنجان … |
| tea | *shaay* … شاي |
| mint tea | *shaay bi-nAHnAH* شاي بنعنع |
| (Arabic) coffee | *qahwa* قهوة |
| regular (Arabic) coffee | *qahwa maZbooT* قهوة مظبوط |
| extra-sweet (Arabic) coffee | *qahwa ziyaada* قهوة زيادة |
| (Arabic) coffee without sugar | *qahwa saada* قهوة سادة |
| instant coffee | *naskaafay* نسكافيه |
| I'd like a water pipe. | *ureed sheesha (naarjeela)* |
| | أريد شيشة (نارجيلة). |
| We'd like a backgammon board/some dominoes, please. | *nureed Taawlat az-zahr/doomeenoo, min faDlak* |
| | نريد طاولة الزهر/دومينو، من فضلك. |

# Menu Reader

This Menu Reader gives listings under main food headings. You will see that the Arabic script is shown in large type. This is to help you to identify, from a menu that has no English, at least the basic ingredients making up a dish.

## Meat and poultry

| | | |
|---|---|---|
| لحم | laHm | meat (general) |
| بقري | baqaree | beef |
| ضاني | Daanee | lamb/mutton |
| دجاج | dajjaaj | chicken |
| بطّ | baTT | duck |
| ديك رومي | deek roomee | turkey |
| حمام | Hamaam | pigeon |
| كبدة | kibda | liver |
| سجق | sujuq | sausages |
| مخ | mukh | brain |
| شوربة | shoorba | soup |

# Fish and seafood

| | | |
|---|---|---|
| سمك | samak | fish (general) |
| كابوريا | kaaboorya | crab |
| استاكوزا | istaakooza/ | lobster |
| بوري/ سلطان إبراهيم | booree/ sulTaan ibraheem | mullet |
| بلح البحر | balaH al-baHr | mussels |
| أخطبوط | akhTabooT | octopus |
| محار | maHHaar | oysters |
| جمبري/قريدس | jambaree/quraydis | shrimp [prawn] |
| سمك موسى | samak moosa | sole |
| سبيط | subbayT | squid |
| قاروس | qaaroos | sea bass |
| تونة | toona | tuna |
| قرش | qirsh | shark |

## Vegetables

| خضار | khuDaar | vegetables (general) |
|---|---|---|
| ثوم | toom | garlic |
| سبانخ | sabaanikh | spinach |
| بطاطس | baTaaTis | potatoes |
| طماطم | TamaaTim | tomatoes |
| خس | khass | lettuce |
| خيار | khiyaar | cucumber |
| كوسة | koosa | zucchini [courgette] |
| بامية | bamya | okra [ladies' fingers] |
| جزر | jazar | carrots |
| بصل | baSal | onions |
| ذرة | dura | corn |
| باذنجان | baadinjaan | eggplant [aubergine] |

# Fruit

| فواكه | fawaakih | fruit (general) |
|---|---|---|
| تفّاح | tuffaaH | apples |
| برتقال | burtuqaal | oranges |
| موز | mauz | bananas |
| عنب | AHinab | grapes |
| تين | teen | figs |
| منجا | mangaa | mangos |
| فراولة | faraawla | strawberries |
| بلح | balaH | dates |
| مشمش | mishmish | apricots |
| بطيخ | batteekh | watermelon |
| شمام | shammaam | cantaloupe |
| تين شوكي | teen shaukee | prickly pears |

## Staples: bread, rice, pasta, etc.

| خبز | khubz | bread |
|---|---|---|
| رزّ | ruzz | rice |
| برغل | burghul | cracked wheat |
| مكرونة | makaroona | pasta |
| عدس | AHds | lentils |
| فول | fool | brown (fava) beans |
| حمص | HummuS | chickpeas |

## Basics

| ملح | malH | salt |
|---|---|---|
| فلفل | filfil | pepper |
| خل | khall | vinegar |
| زيت زيتون | zayt zaytoon | olive oil |

# Herbs and spices

| | | |
|---|---|---|
| شطّة | *shaTTa* | chili |
| بقدونس | *baqdoonis* | parsley |
| زعتر | *zAHtar* | thyme |
| كرفس | *karafs* | celery |
| حب الهان | *Habb al-haan* | cardamon |
| قرفة | *qirfa* | cinnamon |
| كزبرة | *kuzbara* | coriander |
| كمون | *kammoon* | cumin |
| قرنفل | *qurunfil* | clove |
| حار | *Haar* | hot (chili) |
| طازج | *Taazij* | fresh |
| مجفف | *mujaffaf* | dried |

| محشٍ | maHshee | stuffed |
|---|---|---|
| مشوٍ | mashwee | grilled |
| مقلٍ | maqlee | fried |
| مدخّن | mudakhkhan | smoked |
| مسلوق | maslooq | boiled |
| متبّل | mutabbal | marinated |
| في الفرن | feel furn | baked |
| مهروس | mahroos | creamed |
| مكعّبات | mukAHabaat | diced |
| مخلّل | muKHallal | pickled |
| ني | nayy | raw |
| بالتقلية | bit-taqleeya | flavored with coriander and garlic |

# Classic dishes

| | | |
|---|---|---|
| كفتة | kofta | kofta<br>*fried or grilled meat balls* |
| كباب | kabaab | shish kebab<br>*grilled lamb chunks* |
| ورق عنب | waraq AHinab | stuffed vine leaves |
| طاجن | Taajin | *North African lamb stew* |
| كبيبة | kubayba | *balls of minced meat and cracked wheat* |
| فول مدمّس | fool mudammis | fava beans<br>*slow baked fava beans* |
| فلافل | falaafil | falafel<br>*fried crushed chick peas* |
| ملوخية | mulookheeya | *soup made of green-leaf plant* |
| كسكس | kuskus | couscous<br>*steamed cracked wheat* |
| فطير | faTeer | *savory or sweet dough-based pancakes* |
| شاورمة | shawarma | *sliced, spit-roasted meat* |

## Drinks

| | | |
|---|---|---|
| مشروبات | *mashroobaat* | drinks (general) |
| ماء | *maa'* | water |
| حليب | *Haleeb* | milk |
| شاي | *shaay* | tea |
| شاي بنعناع | *shaay bi-nAHnaAH* | mint tea |
| قهوة | *qahwa* | (Arabic) coffee |
| نسكافيه | *naskaafayh* | instant coffee |
| كركديه | *karkadayh* | tea made from fuchsia flowers, *drunk hot or cold* |
| بيرة | *beera* | beer |
| نبيذ | *nabeet* | wine |
| مياه معدنية | *miyaah mAHdaneeya* | mineral water |

# Juices

| عصير | AHSeer | juice |
|---|---|---|
| عصير برتقال | AHSeer burtuqaal | orange juice |
| عصير ليمون | AHSeer laymoon | lemon juice |
| تمر هندي | tamr hindee | tamarind juice |
| عصير قصب | AHSeer qaSab | sugar-cane juice |
| عصير منجا | AHSeer manga | mango juice |
| عصير جزر | AHSeer jazar | carrot juice |
| عصير مشمش | AHSeer mishmish | apricot juice |
| عصيرجوافة | AHSeer jawaafa | guava juice |
| عصير أناناس | AHSeer anaanaas | pineapple juice |
| عصير فراولة | AHSeer faraawla | strawberry juice |

| بطاطس مقلية | baTaaTis maqleeya | French fries [chips] |
|---|---|---|
| برغر | burghur | burger |
| بسكوت | baskoot | cookies [biscuits] |
| كعكة | kAHka | cake |
| سندويتش | sandwitsh | sandwich |
| شبس | shibs | potato chips [crisps] |
| فول سوداني | fool soodaanee | peanuts |
| لبّ | libb | dried melon seeds |
| عين جمل | AHyn jamal | walnuts |
| فستق | fuzduq | pistachios |
| شوكولاتة | shookoolaata | chocolate |
| ذرة مشوية | dura mashweeya | grilled corn |

# Dairy products

| | | |
|---|---|---|
| جبنة | jibna | cheese |
| لبن زيادي | laban zabaadee | yogurt |
| قشطة | qishTa | cream |
| زبدة | zibda | butter |
| حليب | Haleeb | milk |
| لبنة | labna | curd cheese |
| جبنة قديمة | jibna qadeema | matured cheese |
| جبنة بيضاء | jibna bayDaa | feta cheese |
| بيض | bayD | eggs |
| سمنة | samna | ghee *clarified butter* |
| شنكليش | shankaleesh | curd cheese *with olive oil* |

## Desserts

|  |  |  |
|---|---|---|
| رز بحليب | *ruzz bi-Haleeb* | rice pudding |
| آيس كريم | *aayis kreem* | ice cream |
| سلطة فواكه | *salaTat fawaakih* | fruit salad |
| كريم كرامل | *kreem karamil* | crème caramel |
| مهلبية | *muHallabeeya* | *smooth cold milk pudding* |
| بسبوسة | *basboosa* | semolina cake |
| قطايف | *qaTaayif* | *filled sweet pastries* |
| أمّ علي | *umm AHlee* | *sweet hot milk pudding* |
| كعب الغزال | *kAHb al-ghazaal* | North-African pastries |
| عجوة | *AHjwa* | dried dates |
| كنافة | *kunaafa* | vermicelli cake |

# Travel

## ESSENTIAL

| | | |
|---|---|---|
| 1/2/3 ticket(s) to … | waaHid/itnayn/talaata tazaakir ilaa | ١/٢/٣ تذاكر إلى … |
| To …, please. | ilaa …, lau samaHt | إلى … ، لو سمحت. |
| one-way [single] | zahaab | ذهاب |
| round-trip [return] | zahaab wa eeyaab | ذهاب وإياب |
| How much …? | bikam …? | بكم …؟ |

## Safety السلامة

| | | |
|---|---|---|
| Would you accompany me to …? | mumkin turaafiqnee ilaa | ممكن ترافقني إلى …؟ |
| the bus stop | mauqaf il-ootoobees | موقف الأوتوبيس |
| my hotel | al-funduq | إلى الفندق |
| I don't want to … on my own. | laa ureed an … waHdee | لا أريد أن … وحدي. |
| stay here | abqaa hunaa | أبقى هنا |
| walk home | amshee lil-bayt | أمشي للبيت |
| I don't feel safe here. | laa aHiss bil-amaan hunaa | لا أحس بالأمان هنا. |

# Arrival الوصول

Visas are needed to enter most Middle-Eastern countries, but the cost and criteria vary. Sometimes visas can be bought at the point of entry, but you will need to check as this varies from country to country and from year to year. Check with your travel agent or with the relevant consulate. Usually it is better to obtain your visa from your own country prior to travel.

Generally it is easier to obtain visas to countries with a tradition of tourism – Egypt, Jordan, Morocco, Tunisia, etc. – than it is to Saudi Arabia or some of the Gulf states. You could experience difficulties obtaining a visa if you have evidence of a visit to Israel on your passport.

It is best generally to avoid bringing videotapes, camcorders, or electronic goods into the country as you could experience a delay, or could even have items confiscated, while the material is checked out by customs.

Saudi Arabia prohibits the import of alcohol or pork products.

## Passport control مراقبة جوازات السفر

| | |
|---|---|
| We have a joint passport. | mAHana jawaaz mushtarak |
| | معنا جواز مشترك. |
| The children are on this passport. | al-aulaad AHla hazal jawaaz |
| | الأولاد على هذا الجواز. |
| I'm here on vacation [holiday]/ business. | ana huna fee ijaaza/fee riHlit AHmal |
| | أنا هنا في إجازة/في رحلة عمل. |
| I'm just passing through. | ana huna fee muroor |
| | أنا هنا في مرور. |
| I'm going to ... | ana zaahib ilaa |
| | أنا ذاهب إلى ... |
| I'm ... | ana ... أنا |
| on my own | waHdee وحدي |
| with my family | mAHa AHiltee مع عائلتي |
| with a group | mAHa majmooAH مع مجموعة |

WHO ARE YOU WITH? ➤ 120

## Customs الجمرك

| | |
|---|---|
| I have only the normal allowances. | mAHaya al-mukhaSSaS al-AHdee faqaT |
| | معي المخصص العادي فقط. |
| It's a gift. | innahaa hadeeya. إنها هدية. |
| It's for my personal use. | haaza li-istiAHmaalee ash-shakhsee |
| | هذا لاستعمالي الشخصي. |

| | |
|---|---|
| هل عندك شيء للإعلان عنه؟ | Do you have anything to declare? |
| يجب دفع رسوم على هذا. | You must pay duty on this. |
| أين اشتريت هذا؟ | Where did you buy this? |
| من فضلك افتح هذه الحقيبة. | Please open this bag. |
| هل معك حقائب أخرى؟ | Do you have any more baggage? |

| | |
|---|---|
| I would like to declare … | ureed al-iAHlaan AHn … |
| | أريد الإعلان عن … |
| I don't understand. | laa afham. لا أفهم. |
| Does anyone here speak English? | hunaaka aHad yitkallam injileezee |
| | هناك أحد يتكلم إنجليزي؟ |

| | |
|---|---|
| مراقبة جوازات السفر | passport control |
| معبر الحدود | border crossing |
| الجمارك | customs |
| لاشيء للإعلان عنه | nothing to declare |
| بضائع للإعلان عنها | goods to declare |
| بضائع السوق الحرة | duty-free goods |

## Duty-free shopping مشتريات السوق الحرة

| | |
|---|---|
| What currency is this in? | bi-ayy al-AHumlaat hazaa |
| | بأي العملات هذا؟ |
| Can I pay in … | mumkin adfAH bil… ممكن أدفع بالـ… |
| dollars | dolaar دولار |
| marks | mark مارك |
| pounds (Sterling) | junayh (isterleenee) جنيه (إسترليني) |

## الطائرة Plane

Because of the distances involved and difficulties in traveling
overland, flying is often the best option for moving around
the region. Many countries have established airlines –
EgyptAir, Saudia, Kuwait Air, etc. – and extensive internal
networks. The services tend to be frequent and reliable.

## Tickets and reservations التذاكر والحجز

| | | |
|---|---|---|
| When is the ... flight to ...? | *matta ar-riHla ... ilaa ?* | متى الرحلة ... إلى ... ؟ |
| first/next/last | *al-oolaa/al-qaadima/al-akheera* | الأولى/القادمة/الأخيرة |
| I'd like 2 ... tickets. | *ureed tazkaratayn* | أريد تذكرتين ... |
| one-way [single] | *zahaab (faqaT)* | ذهاب (فقط) |
| round-trip [return] | *zahaab wa eeyaab* | ذهاب وإياب |
| first class | *ad-daraja al-oolaa* | الدرجة الأولى |
| business class | *darajit rijaal al-AHmaal* | درجة رجال الأعمال |
| economy class | *ad-daraja as-siyaaHiyya* | الدرجة السياحية |
| How much is a flight to ...? | *bikam ar-riHla ilaa ... ?* | بكم الرحلة إلى ... ؟ |
| Are there any supplements/reductions? | *hal hunaak ayy iDaafaat/takhfeeDaat* | هل هناك أي إضافات/تخفيضات؟ |
| I'd like to ... my reservation for flight number 526. | *ureed ... al-Hajz lil-riHla raqm 526* | أريد ... الحجز للرحلة رقم ٥٢٦. |
| cancel | *ilhgaa'* | إلغاء |
| change | *tahgyeer* | تغيير |
| confirm | *ta'keed* | تأكيد |

## Inquiries about the flight استعلامات عن الرحلة

| | | |
|---|---|---|
| What time does the plane leave? | *matta tuqliAH aT-Taa'ira* | متى تقلع الطائرة؟ |
| What time will we arrive? | *matta sa-naSil?* | متى سنصل؟ |
| What time do I have to check in? | *matta yajib an atsajjal feel maTaar* | متى يجب أن أتسجل في المطار؟ |

NUMBERS ➤ 216; TIME ➤ 220

## Checking in التسجيل

| | |
|---|---|
| Where is the check-in desk for flight …? | *ayn maktab at-tasjeel lir-riHla*<br>أين مكتب التسجيل للرحلة…؟ |
| I have … | *mAHaya* … معي … |
| 3 cases to check in | *talat Haqaa'ib lit-tasjeel*<br>٣ حقائب للتسجيل |
| 2 pieces of hand baggage | *Haqeebatayn lil-yad*<br>حقيبتين لليد |

| | |
|---|---|
| تذكرتك/جواز سفرك، لو سمحت. | Your ticket/passport, please. |
| تريد مقعدا بجانب الشباك أم بقرب الممر؟ | Would you like a window or an aisle seat? |
| للمدخنين أم لغير المدخنين؟ | Smoking or non-smoking? |
| اذهب إلى قاعة الرحيل، لو سمحت. | Please go through to the departure lounge. |
| كم حقيبة معك؟ | How many pieces of baggage do you have? |
| معك أمتعة زيادة. | You have excess baggage. |
| لازم تدفع مبلغ إضافي بقدر … ريال. | You'll have to pay a supplement of … Riyals |
| هذا ثقيل/كبير جدا لحقيبة يد. | That's too heavy/large for hand baggage. |
| هل حزمت هذه الحقائب بنفسك؟ | Did you pack these bags yourself? |
| هل تحتوي على مواد حادة أو كهربائية؟ | Do they contain any sharp or electronic items? |

| | |
|---|---|
| الوصول | arrivals |
| الرحيل | departures |
| الأمن | security check |
| لا تترك أمتعة وحدها. | Do not leave bags unattended. |

BAGGAGE ➤ 71

## Information المعلومات

| | |
|---|---|
| Is there any delay on flight …? | *hal hunaak ta'kheer AHla ar-riHla …?* |
| | هل هناك تأخير على الرحلة …؟ |
| How late will it be? | *kam muddit at-ta'kheer?* |
| | كم مدة التأخير؟ |
| Has the flight from … landed? | *hal waSalt ar-riHla min …* |
| | هل وصلت الرحلة من …؟ |
| Which gate does flight … leave from? | *min ayy bawwaaba tughaadir ar-riHla raqm* |
| | من أي بوابة تغادر الرحلة رقم …؟ |

## Boarding/In-flight الصعود/أثناء الطيران

| | |
|---|---|
| Your boarding card, please. | *baTaaqat aS-SuAHood, lau samaHt* |
| | بطاقة الصعود، لو سمحت. |
| Could I have a drink/something to eat, please? | *mumkin tAHTeenee mashroob/bAHD aT-TAHaam, lau samaHt* |
| | ممكن تعطيني مشروبا/بعض الطعام، لو سمحت؟ |
| Please wake me for the meal. | *arjook ayqiZnee lil-wajba* |
| | أرجوك أيقظني للوجبة. |
| What time will we arrive? | *matta sa-naSil?* متى سنصل؟ |

## Arrival الوصول

| | |
|---|---|
| Where is/are …? | *ayn …?* أين …؟ |
| the currency exchange | *maktab aS-Sarf* مكتب الصرف |
| the buses | *al-ootoobeesaat* الأوتوبيسات |
| the car rental [hire] | *sayyaara lil-isti'jaar* سيارة للاستئجار |
| the exit | *al-makhraj* المخرج |
| the taxis | *at-takseeyaat* التكسيات |
| Is there a bus into town? | *hal hunaak ootoobees ilaa wasT al-madeena* |
| | هل هناك أوتوبيس إلى وسط المدينة؟ |
| How do I get to the … Hotel? | *kayf aSil ilaa funduq …* |
| | كيف أصل إلى فندق …؟ |

## Baggage أمتعة

Porters at airports and railway stations usually expect a tip (➤ 32).

| | |
|---|---|
| Porter! Excuse me! | shayyaal! lau samaHt<br>شيال! لو سمحت! |
| Could you take my baggage to …? | mumkin tusaaAHidnee fee Haml Haqaa'ibee ilaa<br>ممكن تساعدني في حمل حقائبي إلى …؟ |
| the taxi/bus | at-taaksee/al-ootoobees التاكسي/الأوتوبيس |
| Where is/are the …? | ayn …؟ أين …؟ |
| luggage carts [trolleys] | AHarabit al-Haqaa'ib عربة الحقائب |
| luggage lockers | khazaa'in al-Haqaa'ib خزائن الحقائب |
| luggage check [left-luggage office] | maktab al-amaanaat مكتب الأمانات |
| baggage reclaim | istirdaad al-Haqaa'ib استرداد الحقائب |
| Where is the baggage from flight …? | ayn al-Haqaa'ib min ar-riHla …؟<br>أين الحقائب من الرحلة …؟ |

## Loss, damage, and theft فقدان، تلف وسرقة

| | |
|---|---|
| I've lost my baggage. | faqadt Haqaa'ibee. فقدت حقائبي. |
| My baggage has been stolen. | suriqat Haqaa'ibee. سرقت حقائبي. |
| My suitcase was damaged. | talifat Haqeebtee. تلفت حقيبتي. |
| Our baggage has not arrived. | Haqaa'ibnaa lam taSil. حقائبنا لم تصل. |

| | |
|---|---|
| ما شكل أمتعتك؟ | What does your baggage look like? |
| هل معك بطاقة الاسترداد؟ | Do you have the claim check [reclaim tag]? |
| أمتعتك … | Your baggage … |
| ربما بعثت إلى… | may have been sent to … |
| ربما تصل في أي وقت اليوم. | may arrive later today |
| أرجوك أن تعود غدا. | Please come back tomorrow. |
| اتصل بهذا الرقم لمراجعة ما إذا كانت الأمتعة قد وصلت. | Call this number to check if your baggage has arrived. |

POLICE ➤ 152; COLORS ➤ 143

# Train قطار

In contrast to the airline network, the rail network in the Middle East is patchy and sometimes decrepit. There are virtually no international services in operation, a notable exception being the Amman to Damascus route (part of the famous Hijaaz railway line). In some tourist areas there are good quality services running between cities, such as the Cairo to Luxor overnight service which departs from Ramses station. Where such services exist, they can be a relaxing alternative to traveling by bus or airplane and a good way of seeing some of the countryside.

## To the station إلى المحطة

| | |
|---|---|
| How do I get to the (main) train station? | kayf aSil ilaa maHaTTat il-qiTaar (ar-ra'eeseeya) |
| | كيف أصل إلى محطة القطار (الرئيسية)؟ |
| Does the train to Aswan leave from ... Station? | hal al-qiTaar ilaa aswaan yaqoom min maHaTTat |
| | هل القطار إلى أسوان يقوم من محطة ...؟ |
| How far is it? | kam tabAHod? كم تبعد؟ |
| Can I leave my car there? | mumkin atruk sayyaartee hunaak |
| | ممكن أترك سيارتي هناك؟ |

## At the station في المحطة

| | |
|---|---|
| Where is/are ...? | ayn ...? أين ...؟ |
| the information desk | maktab al-istiAHlaamaat مكتب الاستعلامات |
| the baggage check | maktab tasjeel al-amtiAHa مكتب تسجيل الأمتعة |
| the lost-and-found [lost property office] | maktab al-mafqoodaat مكتب المفقودات |
| the luggage lockers | khazaa'in al-amtiAHa خزائن الأمتعة |
| the platforms | al-arsifa الأرصفة |
| the snack bar | maTAHm snaak مطعم سناك |
| the ticket office | shibbaak at-tazaakir شباك التذاكر |
| the waiting room | Saalit il-intiZaar صالة الانتظار |

72

مدخل entrance
مخرج exit
إلى الأرصفة to the platforms
معلومات information
الحجز reservations
الوصول arrivals
الرحيل departures

## Tickets and reservations التذاكر والحجز

Inter-rail passes, available for 30-day train travel in participating European countries, are also valid in Morocco. Student discounts are also often available if you have an International Student Card.

| | |
|---|---|
| I'd like a … ticket to Cairo. | *ureed tazkara … ilaal qaaHira* |
| | أريد تذكرة ... إلى القاهرة. |
| one-way [single] | *zahaab (faqaT)* |
| | ذهاب (فقط) |
| round-trip [return] | *zahaab wa eeyaab* |
| | ذهاب وإياب |
| first/second class | *daraja oolaa/tanya* |
| | درجة أولى/ثانية |
| concessionary | *bi-takhfeeD* |
| | بتخفيض |
| I'd like to reserve a seat. | *ureed Hajz maqAHd* |
| | أريد حجز مقعد. |
| aisle seat | *qurb al-mamarr* قرب الممر |
| window seat | *qurb ash-shibbaak* قرب الشباك |
| Is there a sleeper car? | *hal hunaak AHarabit naum* |
| | هل هناك عربة نوم؟ |
| I'd like a … berth. | *ureed sareer* |
| | أريد سرير .... |
| upper/lower | *AHlwee/sufla* علوي/سفلى |

DIRECTIONS ➤ 94

## Price ثمن

Be sure to check out ticket prices in advance at the station of departure. Finding out about and buying the correct tickets could take some time – and you don't want to do it five minutes before the train is due to leave!

| | |
|---|---|
| How much is that? | kam tamanuh؟ كم ثمنه |
| Are there discounts for ...? | hunaak takhfeeDaat lil هناك تخفيضات للـ...؟ |
| children/families | aTfaal/AH'ilaat أطفال/عائلات |
| senior citizens | musinneen مسنين |
| students | Tullaab طلاب |
| Do you offer a cheap same-day round-trip [return] fare? | hunaak takhfeeDaat lil-AHauda fee nafs al-yaum هناك تخفيضات للعودة في نفس اليوم؟ |

## استفسارات Queries

| | |
|---|---|
| Do I have to change trains? | laazim ughayyir al-qiTaar لازم أغير القطار؟ |
| Is it a direct train? | hal huwa qiTaar mubaashir هل هو قطار مباشر؟ |
| You have to change at ... | laazim tughayyir AHand ... لازم تغير عند ... |
| How long is this ticket valid for? | maa hiya muddit SalaaHeeyit hazihit tazkara؟ ما هي مدة صلاحية هذه التذكرة؟ |
| Can I take my bicycle on to the train? | mumkin aakhud ad-darraaja feel qiTaar ممكن آخذ الدرّاجة في القطار؟ |
| Can I return on the same ticket? | mumkin arjAH bi-nafs at-tazkara ممكن أرجع بنفس التذكرة؟ |
| In which car [coach] is my seat? | maqAHdee fee ayy maqToora مقعدي في أي مقطورة؟ |
| Is there a dining car on the train? | hal hunaak ghurfit TAHaam feel qiTaar هل هناك غرفة طعام في القطار؟ |

## Train times مواعيد القطارات

| | |
|---|---|
| Could I have a timetable, please? | mumkin tAHTeenee jadwal al-mawaaAHeed, lau samaHt |
| | ممكن تعطيني جدول المواعيد، لو سمحت؟ |
| When is … train to Luxor? | matta yaqoom al-qiTaar … ilaal uqSur |
| | متى يقوم القطار ... إلى الأقصر؟ |
| the first/next/last | al-awall/al-qaadim/al-akheer |
| | الأول/القادم/الأخير |
| How frequent are the trains to …? | kam AHadad al-qiTaaraat ilaa |
| | كم عدد القطارات إلى...؟ |
| once/twice a day | marra/marratayn feel yaum |
| | مرة / مرتين في اليوم |
| 5 times a day | khamas marraat feel yaum |
| | ٥ مرات في اليوم |
| every hour | kull SaAHa |
| | كل ساعة |
| What time do they leave? | matta taqoom al-qiTaaraat |
| | متى تقوم القطارات؟ |
| What time does the train stop at …? | matta yaqif al-qiTar AHnd |
| | متى يقف القطار عند ...؟ |
| What time does the train arrive in …? | matta yaSil al-qiTar ilaa |
| | متى يصل القطار إلى ...؟ |
| How long is the trip? | kam muddit ir-riHla كم مدة الرحلة؟ |
| Is the train on time? | hal al-qiTaar fee mauAHiduh |
| | هل القطار في موعده؟ |

## Departures رحيل

| | |
|---|---|
| Which platform does the train to … leave from? | min ayy raSeef yaqoom al-qiTaar ilaa<br>من أي رصيف يقوم القطار إلى ...؟ |
| Where is platform 4? | ayn ar-raSeef raqm arbAHa<br>أين الرصيف رقم ٤؟ |
| over there | hunaak هناك |
| on the left/right | AHla al-yasaar/al-yameen<br>على اليسار/اليمين |
| Where do I change for …? | ayn ughayyir al-qiTaar li<br>أين أغير القطار لـ ...؟ |
| How long will I have to wait for a connection? | kam Tool fatrat intiZaar al-muwaaSla<br>كم طول فترة انتظار المواصلة؟ |

## Boarding الصعود

| | |
|---|---|
| Is this the right platform for the train to …? | hal haaza huwa raSeef al-qiTaar ilaa<br>هل هذا هو رصيف القطار إلى ...؟ |
| Is this the train to …? | hal haazal qiTaar ilaa<br>هل هذا القطار إلى ...؟ |
| Is this seat taken? | hal haazal maqAHd maHjooz<br>هل هذا المقعد محجوز؟ |
| I think that's my seat. | aZunn an haaza makaanee<br>أظن أن هذا مكاني. |
| Here's my reservation. | haaza Hajzee. هذا حجزي. |
| Are there any seats/ berths available? | hal hunaak maqaaAHid/asirra farigha<br>هل توجد مقاعد/أسرة فارغة؟ |
| Do you mind if …? | hal AHndak maaniAH an<br>هل عندك مانع أن ...؟ |
| I sit here | ajlis hunaa أجلس هنا |
| I open the window | aftaH ash-shibbaak<br>أفتح الشباك |

## On the journey أثناء الرحلة

How long are we stopping here for?
*kam sa-natwaqqaf hunaa*
كم سنتوقف هنا؟

When do we get to ...?
*matta naSil ilaa*
متى نصل إلى ...؟

Have we passed ...?
*hal futnaa* هل فتنا ...؟

Where is the dining/sleeper car?
*ayn AHrabit aT-TAHaam/an-naum*
أين عربة الطعام/النوم؟

Where is my berth?
*ayn sareeree* أين سريري؟

I've lost my ticket.
*faqadt tazkartee.* فقدت تذكرتي.

| | |
|---|---|
| فرامل الطوارئ | emergency brake |
| أداة الإنذار | alarm |
| باب أوتوماتيكي | automatic door |

## Long-distance bus [Coach] أوتوبيس رحلات

Long-distance buses are a popular means of transportation in the region and cover far more destinations than the rail network. They are usually cheap and fairly reliable, but can be crowded. You may have to book in advance to ensure you get a seat.

Where is the bus [coach] station?
*ayn maHaTTit il-ootoobees*
أين محطة الأوتوبيس؟

When's the next bus [coach] to ...?
*matta yaqoom al-ootoobees al-qaadim ilaa*
متى يقوم الأوتوبيس القادم إلى ...؟

Which bay does it leave from?
*min ayy mawqaf sa-yantaliq*
من أي موقف سينطلق؟

Where are the bus [coach] bays?
*ayn mawaaqif al-ootoobees*
أين مواقف الأوتوبيس؟

Does the bus [coach] stop at ...?
*hal yaqif al-ootoobees AHnd*
هل يقف الأوتوبيس عند ...؟

How long does the trip take?
*kam min al-waqt ta'khud ar-riHla*
كم من الوقت تأخذ الرحلة؟

TIME ➤ 220

## تاكسي جماعي (سرفيس) Shared taxi

Another popular means of long-distance travel is the shared taxi or microbus (**servees**), which is the middle ground between long-distance buses and private taxis. These run between towns from known starting points and usually seat seven to ten people paying a fixed fare. Each **servees** will wait until it is full and then depart. If the wait is very long, it is possible for the existing passengers to agree to share the cost of the empty places.

| | |
|---|---|
| From where does the shared taxi to … leave? | *min ayn yughaadir as-sarfees ilaa*<br>من أين يغادر السرفيس إلى ...؟ |
| How much is the fare to …? | *kam al-ujra ilaa … ؟*<br>كم الأجرة إلى ... ؟ |

## أوتوبيس/ترام Bus/Tram

Buses and sometimes trams are a cheap way to travel around cities, but avoid them during the crowded rush hours. You might find the bus number in Western figures, but the destination is often written only in Arabic script, so you'll need to ask around to find the correct bus.

| | |
|---|---|
| Where is the bus station/terminus? | *ayn maHaTTit al-ootoobees/al-mawqaf*<br>أين محطة الأوتوبيس/الموقف؟ |
| Where can I get a bus/tram to …? | *ayn mumkin aakhud al-ootoobees/at-traam ilaa*<br>أين ممكن آخذ الأوتوبيس/الترام إلى ...؟ |
| What time is the bus to …? | *matta yaqoom al-ootoobees ilaa*<br>متى يقوم الأوتوبيس إلى ...؟ |

| | |
|---|---|
| تحتاج إلى هذا الموقف هناك/<br>في آخر الشارع. | You need that stop over there/down the road. |
| تحتاج إلى الأوتوبيس رقم ... | You need bus number … |
| لازم تغير الأوتوبيس عند ... | You must change buses at … |

| | |
|---|---|
| موقف الأوتوبيس | bus stop |
| طلب التوقف | request stop |
| ممنوع التدخين | no smoking |
| مخرج (طوارئ) | (emergency) exit |

## Buying tickets شراء تذاكر

Where can I buy tickets?

*ayn ashtaree at-tazaakir*

أين أشتري التذاكر؟

A ... ticket, please.

*tazkara ..., lau samaHt*

تذكرة ...، لو سمحت.

one-way [single]

*zahaab (faqaT)*

ذهاب (فقط)

round-trip [return]

*zahaab wa eeyaab*

ذهاب وإياب

one-day/weekly/monthly

*yaumeeya/usbooAHeeya/shahreeya*

يومية/أسبوعية/شهرية

A booklet of tickets, please.

*kutayb min at-tazaakir, lau samaHt*

كتيب من التذاكر، لو سمحت.

How much is the fare to ...?

*bikam at-tazkara ilaa*

بكم التذكرة إلى ...؟

## Traveling السفر

Is this the right bus/tram to ...?

*hal haaza huwa al-ootoobees/
at-traam ilaa*

هل هذا هو الأوتوبيس/الترام إلى ...؟

Can you tell me when to
get off?

*mumkin taqool lee matta anzil, min
faDlak*

ممكن تقول لي متى أنزل، من فضلك؟

Do I have to change buses?

*hal yajib an ughayyir al-ootoobees*

هل يجب أن أغير الأوتوبيس؟

How many stops are there to ...?

*kam maHaTTa qabl ...*

كم محطة قبل ...؟

Next stop, please!

*al-maHaTTa al-qaadima, lau samaHt*

المحطة القادمة، لو سمحت!

---

– lau samaHt. hal haaza huwa al-ootoobees
ilaa mabnal muHaafZa?
– naAHm, raqm tamanya.
– waHda ilaa mabnal muHaafZa, lau samaHt.
– haaza itnayn junayh.
– mumkin taqool lee matta anzil, min faDlak?
– arbaAH maHaTTaat min huna.

---

# Subway [Metro] (أنفاق) مترو

Cairo has a modern subway [metro] which opened in the late 1980s. The single line runs for over 40 kilometers from the southern suburb of Helwan, through the center and out to the northeast suburbs. Further extensions are planned. It is an efficient, clean, and cheap way to travel.

## General inquiries استعلامات عامة

| | |
|---|---|
| Where's the nearest subway [metro] station? | *ayn aqrab maHaTTit metro*<br>أين أقرب محطة مترو؟ |
| Where can I buy a ticket? | *ayn ashtaree tazkara*<br>أين أشتري تذكرة؟ |
| Could I have a map of the subway [metro]? | *mumkin tAHTeenee khareeTit al-metro*<br>ممكن تعطيني خريطة المترو؟ |

## Traveling التنقل

| | |
|---|---|
| Is this the right train for …? | *hal haaza huwa al-qiTaar ilaa*<br>هل هذا هو القطار إلى …؟ |
| Which stop is it for …? | *ayy maHaTTa li*<br>أي محطة لـ …؟ |
| How many stops is it to …? | *kam maHaTTa qabl*<br>كم محطة قبل …؟ |
| Is the next stop …? | *hal al-maHaTTa al-qaadima hiya*<br>هل المحطة القادمة هي …؟ |
| Where are we? | *ayn naHnu*<br>أين نحن؟ |
| Where do I change for …? | *ayn sa-ughayyir ilaa*<br>أين سأغير إلى …؟ |
| What time is the last train to …? | *matta aakhir qiTaar ilaa*<br>متى آخر قطار إلى …؟ |

> to other lines    إلى خطوط أخرى

# Ferry المعدية

There are numerous ferries operating to and between Middle-Eastern countries, across the Mediterranean, the Red Sea, and the Persian Gulf. Taking a ferry is usually an economical choice, as well as being a good way of avoiding trouble spots on land.

A cruise down the Nile is a perennial favorite. Many ships operate between Luxor and Aswan. Check with your travel agent or the Egyptian tourist office for details about cruises currently available.

| When is the ... car ferry? | matta mAHdeeyat as-sayyaaraat ... |
| | متى معدية السيارات ...؟ |
| first/next/last | al-oolaa/al-qaadima/al-akheera |
| | الأولى/القادمة/الأخيرة |
| A round-trip [return] ticket for ... | tazkara zahaab wa eeyaab ilaa |
| | تذكرة ذهاب وإياب إلى ... |
| 1 car and 1 trailer [caravan] | sayyaara wa bayt mutanaqqil |
| | سيارة وبيت متنقل |
| 2 adults and 3 children | itnayn kubaar wa talaat aTfaal |
| | ٢ كبار و٣ أطفال |
| I want to reserve a ... cabin. | ureed Hajz kaabeena |
| | أريد حجز كابينة ... |
| single/double | li-shakhS/li-shakhSayn لشخص/لشخصين |

| حزام النجاة | life preserver [life belt] |
| مركب النجاة | lifeboat |
| محطة الاجتماع | muster station |

## Boat trips رحلات بالمركب

| Is there a ...? | hal hunaak ... ؟ هل هناك ... |
| boat trip | riHla bil-markib رحلة بالمركب |
| river cruise | jaula feen nahr جولة في النهر |
| What time does it leave/return? | matta tuqliAH/tAHood متى تقلع/تعود؟ |
| Where can I buy tickets? | min ayn ashtaree at-tazaakir |
| | من أين أشتري التذاكر؟ |

TIME ➤ 220; BUYING TICKETS ➤ 73, 79

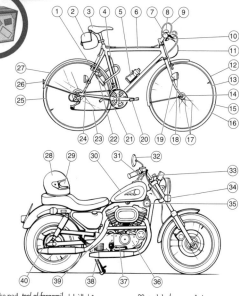

1 brake pad *teel al-faraamil* تيل الفرامل
2 bicycle bag *Haqeebit ad-darraaja* حقيبة الدراجة
3 saddle *sarj* سرج
4 pump *maDakhkha* مضخة
5 water bottle *qaneenit maa'* قنينة ماء
6 frame *iTaar* إطار
7 handlebars *maqwad ad-darraaja* مقود الدراجة
8 bell *jaras* جرس
9 brake cable *kabl al-faraamil* كيبل الفرامل
10 gear shift [lever] *ziraaH al-musanninaat* ذراع المسننات
11 gear/control cable *musanninaat/* *silk at-taHakkum* مسننات/ سلك التحكم
12 inner tube *anbooba daakhileeya* أنبوبة داخلية
13 front/back wheel *doolaab (AHjala)* *amaamee/khalfee* دولاب (عجلة) أمامي/خلفي
14 axle *miHwar ad-doolaab* محور الدولاب
15 tire [tyre] *doolaab (AHjala)* دولاب (عجلة)
16 wheel *doolaab (AHjala)* دولاب (عجلة)
17 spokes *barmaq* برمق
18 bulb *lamba* لمبة
19 headlamp *noor AHalee* نور عال

20 pedal *dawaasa* دواسة
21 lock *qifl* قفل
22 generator [dynamo] *muwallid* مولّد
23 chain *silsila* سلسلة
24 rear light *noor khalfee* نور خلفي
25 rim *Hafa* حافة
26 reflectors *AHaakis* عاكس
27 fender [mudguard] *rafraf ad-doolaab (al-AHjala)* رفرف الدولاب (العجلة)
28 helmet *khooza* خوذة
29 visor *muqadimat al-khooza* مقدمة الخوذة
30 fuel tank *tank al-batrool* تنك البترول
31 clutch lever *dibriyaaj* دبرياج
32 mirror *miraaya* مرآة
33 ignition switch *miftaH al-muHarrik* مفتاح المحرك
34 turn switch [indicator] *mu'ashshir* مؤشر
35 horn *aalat at-tanbeeh* آلة التنبيه
36 engine *muHarrik* محرك
37 gear stick [shift] *mubaddil as-surAHa* مبدل السرعة
38 kick [main] stand *sannaada wuqoof* سنادة وقوف
39 exhaust pipe *maasoorat al-AHdim* ماسورة العادم
40 chain guard *ghaTaa as-silsila* غطاء السلسلة

# Bicycle/Motorbike دراجة/دراجة نارية

Bicycles can be rented in many tourist resorts and are often
a fun and cheap alternative to taxis. Look for rental
places in the street or ask your guide or at your hotel.

| | |
|---|---|
| I'd like to rent a … | *ureed isti'jaar* … أريد استئجار … |
| 3-/10-speed bicycle | *darraaja bi-talaat/ bi-AHshar musanninaat* دراجة بثلاثة/بعشرة مسننات |
| moped/motorbike | *darraaja naareeya Sahgeera/darraaja naareeya* دراجة نارية صغيرة/دراجة نارية |
| How much does it cost per day/week? | *kam tukallif bil-yaum/bil-usbooAH* كم تكلف باليوم/بالأسبوع؟ |
| Do you require a deposit? | *hal taHtaaj ilaa AHrboon* هل تحتاج إلى عربون؟ |
| The brakes don't work. | *al-faraamil laa tAHmil.* الفرامل لا تعمل. |
| There is/are no lights. | *laa yoojad anwaar* لا يوجد أنوار. |
| The front/rear tire [tyre] has a flat [puncture]. | *al-AHjala al-amaameeya/ al-khalfeeya feehaa thuqb* العجلة الأمامية/الخلفية فيها ثقب. |

# Hitchhiking طلب توصيل

People do hitchhike around the region but it is not recommended,
particularly for women. Often the truck or car providing the lift will
expect to be paid anyway, in which case you might as well have taken a
bus or a shared taxi (➤ 78).

| | |
|---|---|
| Where are you heading? | *ilaa ayn tazhab* إلى أين تذهب؟ |
| I'm heading for … | *azhab ilaa* … أذهب إلى … |
| Could you drop me off …? | *mumkin tunazzilnee* …؟ ممكن تنزلني …؟ |
| here | *hunaa* هنا |
| at the next exit | *AHnd al-makhraj al-qaadim* عند المخرج القادم |
| downtown | *fee wasT al-balad* في وسط البلد |
| Thanks for the lift. | *shukran AHla tawSeelee.* شكرا على توصيلي. |

DIRECTIONS ➤ 94; NUMBERS ➤ 216

## تاكسي Cab [Taxi]

| Where can I get a taxi? | ayn mumkin aakhud taaksee |
| | أين ممكن آخذ تاكسي؟ |
| Do you have the number for a taxi? | AHndak nimrit tileefoon taaksee |
| | عندك نمرة تليفون تاكسي؟ |

| I'd like a taxi ... | ureed taaksee ... |
| | أريد تاكسي ... |
| now | al-aan |
| | الآن |
| in an hour | bAHd saAHa |
| | بعد ساعة |
| for tomorrow at 9:00 | ghadan as-saAHa at-taasiAHa |
| | غدا الساعة التاسعة |

| The address is ... . | al-AHunwaan huwa ... |
| | العنوان هو ... |
| I'm going to ... . | azhab ilaa ... |
| | أذهب إلى ... |

للتأجير for hire

| Please take me to ... | min faDlak, waSSilnee ilaa |
| | من فضلك، وصلني إلى ... |
| the airport | al-maTaar المطار |
| the train station | maHaTTat al-qiTaar محطة القطار |
| this address | hazaal AHunwaan هذا العنوان |
| How much will it cost? | kam sa-tukallif? كم ستكلف؟ |
| How much is that? | bikam hazaa? بكم هذا؟ |
| You said ... pounds. | anta qult ... junayh |
| | أنت قلت ... جنيه. |
| On the meter it's ... . | inaahaa ... AHlal AHdaad |
| | إنها ... على العداد. |
| Keep the change. | iHtafiZ bil-baaqee احتفظ بالباقي. |

– mumkin tuwaSSilnee ilaal maHaTTa, lau samaHt?
  – bit-ta'keed.
– shukran ... kam sa-tukallif?
  – AHshara junayh.
– tafaDDal. iHtafiz bil-baaqee

# Car/Automobile سيارة

Having your own car can be an advantage in some parts of the Middle East, for example Saudi Arabia and the Gulf states, but driving presents several problems, and you might find it easier to use other available means of transportation.

Driving between towns is reasonable by day, but obtaining permits and finding a feasible route may not be – especially if this involves crossing borders.

You will need an International Driver's license for all countries in the region. Minimum driving ages vary, and regulations can be difficult to fathom or non-existent. Unless you have sufficient time to get used to the local driving conditions, you might want to opt for a local driver.

One general feature of driving in the area is the frequent use of the horn, which Western visitors should try to understand. This is often interpreted as impatience – and sometimes it is – but it is also the most usual way of alerting a car in front to your presence when, for example, passing. Many vehicles do not make use of rearview mirrors and will expect you to give a couple of short blasts on the horn when you are about to pass. They will probably also move over to give you more room.

## Conversion chart

Kilometers are the standard measure of distance in the Arab world. Here is a conversion chart to convert distance and speed:

| km | 1 | 10 | 20 | 30 | 40 | 50 | 60 | 70 | 80 | 90 | 100 | 110 | 120 | 130 |
|---|---|---|---|---|---|---|---|---|---|---|---|---|---|---|
| miles | 0.62 | 6 | 12 | 19 | 25 | 31 | 37 | 44 | 50 | 56 | 62 | 68 | 74 | 81 |

## Road network

Main roads in Arab countries, often desert roads, are generally reliable, and you will sometimes find signs in both English and Arabic. However, these roads can be dangerous at night as they have no barriers and other vehicles can be traveling at high speeds.

Finding your way within towns, especially the older cities, can be a major problem. Streets may not have names, and many traffic signs are written only in Arabic. It is therefore easy to get completely lost. You will be more comfortable with a driver.

## Car rental تأجير سيارة

Renting a car is possible in most towns, but it is often expensive. It may be possible to rent a car with an English-speaking driver, either through your hotel or a travel agent.

| | |
|---|---|
| Where can I rent a car? | ayn astaTeeAH isti'jaar sayyaara<br>أين أستطيع استئجار سيارة؟ |
| I'd like to rent ... | ureed isti'jaar ...<br>أريد استئجار ... |
| a 2-/4-door car | sayyaara bi-baabayn/bi-arbAHa abwaab<br>سيارة ببابين/بأربع أبواب |
| an automatic | otomateek<br>أوتوماتيك |
| a car with 4-wheel drive | sayyaara bid-dafAH ar-rubaaAHee<br>سيارة بالدفع الرباعي |
| a car with air conditioning | sayyaara bit-takyeef.<br>سيارة بالتكييف. |
| I'd like it for a day/week. | ureedha li-muddit yaum/usbooAH<br>أريدها لمدة يوم/أسبوع. |
| How much does it cost per day/week? | kam sa-tukallif bil-yaum/bil-usbooAH<br>كم ستكلف باليوم/بالأسبوع؟ |
| Is mileage/insurance included? | hal al-massafa/at-ta'meen mashmool<br>هل المسافة/التأمين مشمول؟ |
| Are there special weekend rates? | hunaak asAHaar khaaSSa bi-nihaayat al-usbooAH<br>هناك أسعار خاصة بنهاية الأسبوع؟ |
| Can I return the car at ...? | mumkin urajjiAH as-sayyaara AHnd ...<br>ممكن أرجّع السيارة عند ...؟ |
| What sort of fuel does it take? | maa nauAH al-wuqood alazee tatzawwad bih<br>ما نوع الوقود الذي تتزود به؟ |
| Where is the high [full]/ low [dipped] beam? | ayn aD-Dau' al-AHalee/al-munkhafiD<br>أين الضوء العالي/المنخفض؟ |
| Could I have full insurance? | mumkin aakhud ta'meen shaamil<br>ممكن آخذ تأمين شامل؟ |

# Gas [Petrol] station محطة البنزين

| | |
|---|---|
| Where's the next gas [petrol] station, please? | ayn maHaTTa al-banzeen at-taaleeya, lau samaHt<br>أين محطة البنزين التالية، لو سمحت؟ |
| Is it self-service? | hal hiya khidma zaateeya<br>هل هي خدمة ذاتية؟ |
| Fill it up, please. | imlaa'haa, lau samaHt. املأها، لو سمحت. |
| ... liters of gasoline [petrol], please. | ... litraat banzeen, lau samaHt<br>... لترات بنزين، لو سمحت. |
| premium [super]/regular | mumtaaz/AHadee ممتاز/عادي |
| lead-free/diesel | doon raSaaS/deezil دون رصاص/ديزل |
| Pump number ... | al-maDakhkha raqm ... المضخة رقم ... |
| Where is the air pump/water? | ayn maDakhkhat al-hawaa/al-maa'<br>أين مضخة الهواء/الماء؟ |

> price per liter ثمن اللتر

## Parking الركن

Parking is usually a question of survival of the fittest and double parking is common – although most town centers do have restrictions. Often you can find people in the street who, for a modest tip, will find you a parking place and look after your car while you're gone. Many of the larger hotels will have their own parking lots [car parks] for the use of the guests.

| | |
|---|---|
| Is there a parking lot [car park] nearby? | hal hunaak makaan rakn sayyaaraat qareeb<br>هل هناك مكان ركن سيارات قريب؟ |
| What's the charge per hour/per day? | kam al-Hisaab fees saAHa/feel yaum<br>كم الحساب في الساعة/في اليوم؟ |
| Do you have some change for the parking meter? | AHndak Sarraafa li-AHdaad ar-rakn<br>عندك صرافة لعداد الركن؟ |
| My car has been booted [clamped]. Who do I call? | sayyaaratee rubiTat bi-mulzim.<br>bi-man attaSil<br>سيارتي رُبطت بملزم. بمن أتصل؟ |

## Breakdown تعطل

If you break down in a populated area, you can usually find a local mechanic who can at least temporarily repair your car. Otherwise you will have to flag down a passing car or truck to take you to a garage. In more remote areas you should try to travel in a convoy with at least one more vehicle. The various international recovery services do not cover most of the region.

| | |
|---|---|
| Where is the nearest garage? | *ayn aqrab garaaj* أين أقرب كراج؟ |
| My car broke down. | *AHndee AHTl* عندي عطل. |
| Can you send a mechanic/ tow [breakdown] truck? | *mumkin tibAHat meekaaneekee/al-winsh* ممكن تبعث ميكانيكي/الونش؟ |
| I belong to ... recovery service. | *ana antamee ilaa ... li-khidmaat al-AHTaal* أنا أنتمي إلى ... لخدمات الأعطال. |
| My registration number is ... | *raqm as-sayyaara huwa ...* رقم السيارة هو ... |
| The car is ... | *as-sayyaara ...* السيارة ... |
| on the main highway | *AHlaaT Tareeq ar-ra'eesee* على الطريق الرئيسي |
| 2 km from ... | *itnayn keeloo min ...* ٢ كم من ... |
| How long will you be? | *kam sa-tastaghriq?* كم ستستغرق؟ |

## What is wrong? ما هي المشكلة؟

| | |
|---|---|
| My car won't start. | *sayyaaratee laa tureed an tabdaa* سيارتي لا تريد أن تبدأ. |
| The battery is dead. | *al-baTaareeya faargha.* البطارية فارغة. |
| I've run out of gas [petrol]. | *nafaz minee al-banzeen* نفذ مني البنزين. |
| I have a flat [puncture]. | *AHndee thuqb* عندي ثقب. |
| There is something wrong with ... | *hunaak shay khaTa fee ...* هناك شيء خطأ في ... |
| I've locked the keys in the car. | *qafalt AHlal miftaaH daakhil as-sayyaara* قفلت على المفتاح داخل السيارة. |

## Repairs تصليح

| | |
|---|---|
| Do you do repairs? | *hal tuSalliH* هل تصلح؟ |
| Can you repair it (temporarily)? | *hal mumkin tuSalliHhaa (mu'aqqatan)* هل ممكن تصلحها (مؤقتا)؟ |
| Please make only essential repairs. | *ar-rajaa taSleeH aD-Darooreeyaat faqaT* الرجاء تصليح الضروريات فقط. |
| Can I wait for it? | *mumkin antaZirhaa* ممكن أنتظرها؟ |
| Can you repair it today? | *mumkin tuSalliHhaa al-yaum* ممكن تصلحها اليوم؟ |
| When will it be ready? | *matta sa-takoon jaahiza* متى ستكون جاهزة؟ |
| How much will it cost? | *kam sa-tukallif* كم ستكلف؟ |
| That's outrageous! | *haaza junoonee* هذا جنوني! |
| Can I have a receipt for my insurance? | *mumkin aakhuz al-waSl li-ajl sharikat at-ta'meen* ممكن آخذ الوصل لأجل شركة التأمين؟ |

| | |
|---|---|
| الـ ... لا يعمل. | The ... isn't working. |
| ما عندي قطع الغيار المطلوبة. | I don't have the necessary parts. |
| لازم أطلب قطع الغيار. | I will have to order the parts. |
| ممكن أصلحها مؤقتا. | I can only repair it temporarily. |
| لا يوجد أمل من تصليح سيارتك. | Your car is beyond repair. |
| لا يمكن تصليحها | It can't be repaired. |
| ستكون جاهزة ... | It will be ready ... |
| بعدين | later today |
| غدا | tomorrow |
| بعد ... أيام | in ... days |

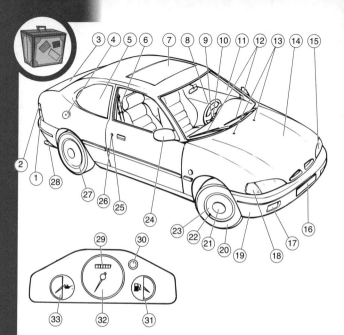

1 taillights [back lights] *aDwaa' khalfeeya*
أضواء خلفية

2 brakelights *aDwaa' al-faraamil* أضواء الفرامل

3 trunk [boot] *Sundooq as-sayyaara* صندوق السيارة

4 gas tank door [petrol cap] *ghaTaa baab (Haud) al-banzeen*
غطاء باب (حوض) البنزين

5 window *shibbaak* شباك

6 seat belt *Hazaam al-amaan* حزام الأمان

7 sunroof *saqf munzaliq* سقف منزلق

8 steering wheel *AHjalat al-qiyaada* عجلة القيادة

9 ignition *mushaghghil* مشغل

10 ignition key *miftaaH mushaghghil* مفتاح مشغل

11 windshield [windscreen] *az-zujaaj al-amaamee*
الزجاج الأمامي

12 windshield [windscreen] wipers *massaaHaat az-zujaaj*
مساحات الزجاج

13 windshield [windscreen] washer *maghsalat az-zujaaj*
مغسلة الزجاج

14 hood [bonnet] *ghaTaa al-muHarrik* غطاء المحرك

15 headlights *al-aDwaa' al-amaameeya*
الأضواء الأمامية

16 license [number] plate *lauHat raqm as-sayyaara*
لوحة رقم السيارة

17 fog lamp *Dau' aD-Dabaab* ضوء الضباب

18 turn signal [indicator] *al-mu'ashshir* المؤشر

19 bumper *maSadd (mukhaffif aS-Sadma)*
مصد (مخفف الصدمة)

20 tires [tyres] *iTaaraat* إطارات

21 hubcap *ghaTaa al-AHjala* غطاء العجلة

22 valve *Sammaam* صمام

23 wheels *AHjalaat* عجلات

24 outside [wing] mirror *al-miraya al-jaanibeeya*
المرآة الجانبية

25 central locking *qafl markazee* قفل مركزي

26 lock *qifl* قفل

27 wheel rim *iTaar mAHdanee* إطار معدني

28 exhaust pipe *anboob al-AHdim* أنبوب العادم

29 odometer [milometre] *AHdaad al-masaafa*
عداد المسافات

90

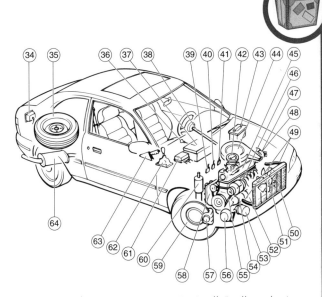

30 warning light *Dau' al-inzaar* ضوء الإنذار

31 fuel gauge/pump *mu'ashshir/miDakhkhat al-banzeen* مؤشر/مضخة البنزين

32 speedometer *AHdaad as-surAHa* عداد السرعة

33 oil gauge *mu'ashshir az-zayt* مؤشر الزيت

34 back-up [reversing] lights *Dau ar-rujooAH* ضوء الرجوع

35 spare wheel *AHjala iHtiyaaTeeya* عجلة احتياطية

36 choke *sharaaqa* شراقة

37 heater *sakhkhaan* سخان

38 steering column *AHmood al-qiyaada* عامود القيادة

39 accelerator *dawaasat al-banzeen* دواسة البنزين

40 pedal *dawaasa* دواسة

41 clutch *dibriyaaj* دبرياج

42 carburetor *mukarbin* مكربن

43 battery *baTaareeya* بطارية

44 alternator *munauba* منوبة

45 camshaft *AHmood al-Hudbaat* عمود الحدبات

47 distributor *muwazziAH* موزع

48 points *ru'oos* رؤوس

49 radiator hose *kharToom khazana al-maa'* خرطوم خزان الماء

50 radiator *khazaan al-maa'* خزان الماء

51 fan *marwaHa* مروحة

52 engine *muHarrik* محرك

53 oil filter *miSfaat az-zayt* مصفاة الزيت

54 starter motor *mushaghghil al-muHarrik* مشغل المحرك

55 fan belt *Hizaam al-marwaHa* حزام المروحة

56 horn *aalat at-tanbeeh* آلة التنبيه

57 brake pads *teel al-faraamil* تيل الفرامل

58 transmission [gearbox] *AHulbat at-turoos* علبة التروس

59 brakes *faraamil* فرامل

60 shock absorbers *mumtaSS aS-Sadamaat* ممتص الصدمات

61 fuses *Sammaamaat kahrabaa'eeya* صمامات كهربائية

62 gear shift [lever] *ziraaAH at-turoos* ذراع التروس

63 handbrake *faraamil al-yad* فرامل اليد

64 muffler [silencer] *mukhammid aS-Saut* مخمد الصوت

CAR REPAIRS ➤ 89

# حوادث Accidents

If you have an accident, you should go to the nearest police station and report it rather than wait for the police to come to you. Try not to get into a dispute about blame as this could end you up in an argument with more people than you had bargained for. If the car is rented, contact the rental company as soon as you can with the details. They can give you further instructions.

| | | |
|---|---|---|
| There has been an accident. | *hunaak Haadis.* | هناك حادث. |
| It's … | *innahu …* | إنه … |
| on the highway [main road] | *AHlaT Tareeq ar-ra'eesee* | على الطريق الرئيسي |
| near … | *qareeb min …* | قريب من … |
| Where's the nearest telephone? | *ayn aqrab tilifoon?* | أين أقرب تلفون؟ |
| Call … | *ittaSil bi …* | اتصل بـ … |
| the police | *ash-shurTa* | الشرطة |
| an ambulance | *sayyaarat isAHaaf* | سيارة إسعاف |
| a doctor | *doktoor* | دكتور |
| the fire department [brigade] | *al-maTaafi'* | المطافئ |
| Can you help me, please? | *mumkin tusaAHidnee, lau samaHt* | ممكن تساعدني، لو سمحت؟ |

## إصابات Injuries

| | | |
|---|---|---|
| There are people injured. | *hunaak naas muSaaboon* | هناك ناس مصابون. |
| No one is hurt. | *lam yu'azza aHad.* | لم يؤذَ أحد. |
| He is seriously injured. | *AHnduh iSaabaat khaTeera* | عنده إصابات خطيرة. |
| She's unconscious. | *hiya faaqidat al-wAHee.* | هي فاقدة الوعي. |
| He can't breathe/move. | *huwa laa yastaTeeAH at-tanaffus/ al-Haraka.* | هو لا يستطيع التنفس/الحركة. |
| Don't move him. | *laa tuHarrikuh.* | لا تحرّكه. |

# Legal matters أمور قانونية

| | |
|---|---|
| What's your insurance company? | *maa hiya sharikat ta'meenak?*<br>ما هي شركة تأمينك؟ |
| What's your name and address? | *maa huwa ismak wa AHunwaanak?*<br>ما هو اسمك وعنوانك؟ |
| He ran into me. | *huwa Sadamnee.*<br>هو صدمني. |
| She was driving too fast/<br>too close. | *kaanat tasooq bi-surAHa/qareeb jiddan minnee.*<br>كانت تسوق بسرعة/قريبة جدا مني. |
| I had the right of way. | *kaan AHndee Haqq al-muroor*<br>كان عندي حق المرور. |
| I was only driving at … km/h. | *kunt asooq AHlaa … kiloo fess-saAHa.*<br>كنت أسوق على ... ك م في الساعة. |
| I'd like an interpreter. | *ureed mutarjim.*<br>أريد مترجم. |
| I didn't see the sign. | *lam ara al-laafita.*<br>لم أرى اللافتة. |
| He/She saw it happen. | *huwa shaahid/hiya shaahdat al-Haadis.*<br>هو شاهد/هي شاهدت الحادث. |
| The registration number was … | *raqm as-sayyaara kaan …*<br>رقم السيارة كان ... |

| | |
|---|---|
| ممكن أرى ... رجاء؟ | Can I see your …, please. |
| شهادة السواقة | driver's license |
| شهادة التأمين. | insurance card |
| أوراق السيارة | vehicle registration document |
| متى حدثت؟ | What time did it happen? |
| أين حدثت؟ | Where did it happen? |
| في شخص ثاني متورط؟ | Was anyone else involved? |
| هناك أي شهود؟ | Are there any witnesses? |
| كنت تسوق بسرعة. | You were speeding. |
| الأضواء لا تعمل. | Your lights aren't working. |
| لازم تدفع غرامة (فورا). | You'll have to pay a fine (on the spot). |
| نريدك أن نأخذ أقوالك في المركز. | We need you to make a statement at the station. |

TIME ➤ 220

# Asking directions
أسئلة عن الاتجاهات

| Excuse me, please. | lau samaHt. | لو سمحت. |
| How do I get to …? | kayf aSil ilaa …? | كيف أصل إلى …؟ |
| Where is …? | ayn …? | أين …؟ |
| Can you show me on the map where I am? | mumkin tareenee ayn ana AHlaal khareeTa | ممكن تريني أين أنا على الخريطة؟ |
| I've lost my way. | ana tuht. | أنا تهت. |
| Can you repeat that, please? | mumkin tukarir maa qultuh lau samaHt | ممكن تكرّر ما قلته، لو سمحت؟ |
| More slowly, please. | bi-buT', lau samaHt. | ببطء، لو سمحت. |
| Thanks for your help. | shukran AHlaal musaaAHda | شكرا على المساعدة. |

## Traveling by car   التنقل بالسيارة

| Is this the right road for …? | hal haaza aT-Tareeq aS-SaHeeH ilaa … | هل هذا الطريق الصحيح إلى …؟ |
| How far is it to … from here? | kam al-masaafa ilaa … min hunaa | كم المسافة إلى … من هنا؟ |
| Where does this road lead? | ilaa ayn yu'addee haazaT Tareeq | إلى أين يوّدي هذا الطريق؟ |
| What's the next town called? | maa ism al-madeena at-taaleeya | ما اسم المدينة التالية؟ |
| How long does it take by car? | kam ta'khud bis-sayyaara | كم تأخذ بالسيارة؟ |

---

– lau samaHt, kayf aSil ilaa maHattat al-qiTaar?
– khud ash-sharriAH at-taalit AHlaal yasaar, wa min hunaak AHlaa Tool.
at-taalit AHlaal yasaar. hal huwa bAHeed?
– AHshara daqaa'iq – masheeyan.
– shukran AHlaal musaaAHda.
– AHfwan.

## موقع Location

| | |
|---|---|
| إنه ... | It's ... |
| على طول | straight ahead |
| على اليسار | on the left |
| على اليمين | on the right |
| في آخر الطريق | at the end of the street |
| على الزاوية | on the corner |
| حول الزاوية | around the corner |
| باتجاه ... | in the direction of ... |
| خلف ... /مقابل ... | behind ... /opposite ... |
| بعد ... /بجانب ... | after ... /next to ... |
| اذهب إلى ... | Go down the ... |
| الطريق الجانبي/الطريق الرئيسي. | side street/main street |
| اعبر ... | Cross the ... |
| الميدان/الجسر | square/bridge |
| خذ المنعطف الثالث إلى اليمين. | Take the third right. |
| انعطف إلى اليسار ... | Turn left ... |
| بعد أول إشارة مرور | after the first traffic lights |
| عند نقطة التقاطع الثانية | at the second intersection [crossroad] |

## By car بالسيارة

| | |
|---|---|
| إنها ... من هنا. | It's ... of here. |
| شمال/جنوب | north/south |
| شرق/غرب | east/west |
| خذ الطريق إلى ... | Take the road for ... |
| أنت على طريق خاطئ. | You're on the wrong road. |
| لازم ترجع إلى ... | You'll have to go back to ... |
| اتبع اللافتات إلى ... | Follow the signs for ... |

## How far? كم تبعد؟

| | |
|---|---|
| إنها ... | It's ... |
| قريبة/بعيدة جدا | close/a long way |
| خمس دقائق ماشيا | 5 minutes on foot |
| ١٠ دقائق بالسيارة | 10 minutes by car |
| قرابة ١٠٠متر على هذا الطريق | about 100 meters down the road |
| تبعد ١٠ كيلو مترات تقريبا | about 10 kilometers away |

TIME ➤ 220; NUMBERS ➤ 216

# علامات الطريق Road signs

| | |
|---|---|
| للدخول فقط | access only |
| طريق مؤقت | alternate route |
| تحويل | detour [diversion] |
| أبقى في الممر | stay in lane |
| أعطي الأولوية | yield [give way] |
| جسر منخفض | low bridge |
| طريق باتجاه واحد | one-way street |
| طريق مسدود | road closed |
| مدرسة | school |
| استعمل الأضواء الأمامية | use headlights |

## خريطة المدينة Town plans

| | |
|---|---|
| مطار | airport |
| مسلك الأوتوبيس | bus route |
| موقف الأوتوبيس | bus stop |
| كنيسة | church |
| مكتب الاستعلامات | information office |
| الشارع الرئيسي | main [high] street |
| جامع | mosque |
| سينما | movie theater [cinema] |
| مدينة قديمة | old town |
| حديقة عامة | park |
| موقف السيارات | parking lot [car park] |
| ممر المشاة | pedestrian crossing |
| منطقة المشاة | pedestrian zone [precinct] |
| أرض الملعب | playing field [sports ground] |
| مركز الشرطة | police station |
| مكتب البريد | post office |
| بناء للعامة | public building |
| محطة | station |
| مدرج | stadium |
| نفق | underpass |
| موقف تاكسي | taxi stand [rank] |
| مسرح | theater |
| أنت هنا | you are here |

# *Sightseeing*

## Tourist information office مكتب السياحة

In major tourist areas you will probably find tourist offices downtown with information about attractions, special events, etc. You may also be able to find special tours, for example of pharaonic sites or crusader castles, with English-speaking guides.

| | |
|---|---|
| Where's the tourist office? | ayn maktab as-siyyaaHa |
| | أين مكتب السياحة؟ |
| What are the main points of interest? | maa hiya al-mAHaalim al-athreeya al-muhimma ما هي المعالم الأثرية المهمة؟ |
| We're here for … | naHnu hunaa li-muddat |
| | نحن هنا لمدة … |
| only a few hours | saAHaat faqaT |
| | ساعات فقط |
| a day | yaum waaHid واحد يوم |
| a week | usbooAH waaHid أسبوع واحد |
| Can you recommend …? | hal tastaTeeAH an tinSaHnaa bi |
| | هل تستطيع أن تنصحنا بـ …؟ |
| a sightseeing tour | jaula li-ziyaarat al-mAHaalim |
| | جولة لزيارة المعالم |
| an excursion | jaula siyyaaHeeya munaZZama |
| | جولة سياحية منظمة |
| a boat trip | riHla bil-markib رحلة بالمركب |
| Do you have any information on …? | AHndak ayy mAHloomaat AHn |
| | عندك أي معلومات عن …؟ |
| Are there any trips to …? | hal hunaak riHlaat ilaa |
| | هل هناك رحلات إلى …؟ |

## Excursions جولات سياحية

| How much does the tour cost? | kam tukallif ar-riHla |
| | كم تكلف الرحلة؟ |
| Is lunch included? | hal al-ghadaa mashmool |
| | هل الغداء مشمول؟ |
| Where do we leave from? | min ayn sa-nughaadir |
| | من أين سنغادر؟ |
| What time does the tour start? | matta tabda' ar-riHla |
| | متى تبدأ الرحلة؟ |
| What time do we get back? | matta sa-narjAH |
| | متى سنرجع؟ |
| Do we have free time in ...? | hal AHndanaa waqt Hurr fee |
| | هل عندنا وقت حر في ...؟ |
| Is there an English-speaking guide? | hal hunaak murshid yatkallam injileezee |
| | هل هناك مرشد يتكلم إنجليزي؟ |

## On tour خلال الجولة

| Are we going to see ...? | hal sa-nushaahid ... ؟ | هل سنشاهد ...؟ |
| We'd like to have a look at the ... | nureed ilqaa' naZra AHlaa | |
| | نريد إلقاء نظرة على ... | |
| Can we stop here ...? | mumkin naqif huna | |
| | ممكن نقف هنا ...؟ | |
| to take photographs | liltiqaaT Suwar | لالتقاط صور |
| to buy souvenirs | li-shiraa' tizkaar | لشراء تذكار |
| to use the bathrooms [toilets] | lil-Hammaamaat | للحمامات |
| Would you take a photo of us, please? | mumkin ta'khud linaa Soora, lau samaHt | |
| | ممكن تأخذ لنا صورة، لو سمحت؟ | |
| How long do we have here/in ...? | kam mAHnaa min al-waqt huna/fee | |
| | كم معنا من الوقت هنا/في ...؟ | |
| Wait! ... isn't back yet | intaZir! ... lam yAHud bAHd | |
| | انتظر! ... لم يعد بعد. | |

# Sights معالم

| | |
|---|---|
| Where is the …? | ayn …؟ أين |
| art gallery | mAHraD al-funoon |
| | معرض الفنون |
| battle site | mawqiAH al-mAHraka موقع المعركة |
| botanical garden | Hadeeqat an-nabaat حديقة النبات |
| castle | al-qalAHa القلعة |
| cemetery | al-maqbara المقبرة |
| church | al-kaneesa الكنيسة |
| downtown area | wasT al-madeena وسط المدينة |
| fountain | an-naafoora النافورة |
| market | as-sooq السوق |
| monastery | ad-dayr الدير |
| mosque | al-jaamiAH الجامع |
| museum | al-matHaf المتحف |
| old town | al-madeena al-qadeema المدينة القديمة |
| opera house | darr al-oobraa دار الأوبرا |
| palace | al-qaSr القصر |
| park | al-Hadeeqa al-AHama الحديقة العامة |
| parliament building | mabnaa al-barlamaan مبنى البرلمان |
| ruins | al-aTlaal الأطلال |
| statue | at-timthaal التمثال |
| theater | al-masraH المسرح |
| temple | al-mAHbad المعبد |
| tower | al-burj البرج |
| town hall | daar al-baladeeya دار البلدية |
| viewpoint | makaan murtafiAH lil-mushaahada |
| | مكان مرتفع للمشاهدة |
| Can you show me on the map? | mumkin tureenee AHlal khareeTa |
| | ممكن تريني على الخريطة؟ |

## Admission الدخول

Museums are usually closed on Fridays and on important holidays (► 219). Check in advance for individual opening times.

| | |
|---|---|
| Can we look around? | mumkin nalqee naZra ممكن نلقي نظرة؟ |
| What are the opening hours? | maa hiya al-muwaaAHeed ما هي المواعيد؟ |
| When does it close? | matta tughliq متى تغلق؟ |
| Is ... open on Fridays? | hal ... maftooH yaum al-jumAha هل ... مفتوح يوم الجمعة؟ |
| When's the next guided tour? | matta al-jaula at-taaleeya mAHal murshid متى الجولة التالية مع المرشد؟ |
| Do you have you a guide book (in English)? | hal mAHak daleel (bil-injileezee) هل معك دليل (بالإنجليزي)؟ |
| Can I take photos? | mumkin uSawwir ممكن أصوّر؟ |
| Is there access for the disabled? | hal hunaak madkhal lil-muAHaaqeen هل هناك مدخل للمعاقين؟ |

## Paying/Tickets الدفع/التذاكر

| | |
|---|---|
| How much is the entrance fee? | bi-kam ad-dukhool بكم الدخول؟ |
| Are there any discounts for ...? | hal hunaak takhfeeD lil-... هل هناك تخفيض للـ ...؟ |
| children | ATfaal أطفال |
| the disabled | muAHaaqeen معاقين |
| senior citizens | kubaar as-sinn كبار السن |
| students | Tullaab طلاب |
| 1 adult ticket and 3 children, please. | tazkara wa talaat aTfaal, lau samaHt تذكرة و٣ أطفال، لو سمحت. |
| I've lost my ticket. | faqadt tazkartee فقدت تذكرتي. |

– arbAHa tazaakir, lau samaHt.
AHndak takhfeeDaat?
– naAHm. khamsa junayh lil-aTfaal
wal-kubaar fees-seen.
– tazkirtayn wa talaata aTfaal, lau samaHt.
– khamsa wa talaateen junayh, lau samaHt.

| | |
|---|---|
| الدخول مجاني | admission free |
| مغلق | closed |
| محل هدايا | gift shop |
| آخر موعد للدخول الساعة ٥ مساء. | latest entry at 5 p.m. |
| الجولة القادمة الساعة ... | next tour at ... |
| ممنوع الدخول | no entry |
| ممنوع التصوير | no flash photography |
| مفتوح | open |
| مواعيد الزيارة | visiting hours |

## Impressions انطباعات

| It's ... | innahu ... ... إنه |
|---|---|
| amazing | mudhish مدهش |
| awful | murAHib مرعب |
| beautiful | jameel جميل |
| boring | mumill ممل |
| great fun | mumtiAH jiddan ممتع جدا |
| incredible | raa'iAH رائع |
| interesting | mutheer lil-ihtimaam مثير للاهتمام |
| magnificent | jameel jiddan جميل جدا |
| strange | ghareeb غريب |
| stunning | muzhil مذهل |
| superb | mumtaaz ممتاز |
| terrible | faZeeAH فظيع |
| ugly | bashiAH بشع |
| I like it. | uHibbuh. أحبه. |
| I don't like it. | laa uHibbuh. لا أحبه. |

| قلعة | qalAHa | castle/citadel |
|---|---|---|
| كنيسة | kaneesa | church |
| مسجد | masjid | mosque |
| متحف | matHaf | museum |
| واحة | waaHa | oasis |
| مدينة قديمة | madeena qadeema | old city |
| قصر | qaSr | palace |
| هرم | haram | pyramid |
| معبد | mAHbad | temple |
| مقبرة | maqbara | tomb |
| برج | burj | tower |
| أطلال | aTlaal | ruins |
| شاطئ | shaaTi' | beach |
| حديقة | Hadeeqa | park |

| | | |
|---|---|---|
| دراسة الآثار | *diraasat al-aathaar* | archaeology |
| فن العمارة | *fann al-Ahimaara* | architecture |
| الفن | *al-fann* | art |
| الخط | *al-khaTT* | calligraphy |
| الخزف | *al-khazaf* | ceramics/pottery |
| الصناعات اليدوية | *aS-SinaaAHaat al-yadaweeya* | handicrafts |
| الهيروغليفية | *al-heerooghleefeeya* | hieroglyphics |
| التاريخ | *at-taareekh* | history |
| الفن الإسلامي | *al-fann al-islaamee* | Islamic art |
| الرسم | *ar-rasm* | painting |
| الدين | *ad-deen* | religion |
| النحت | *an-naHt* | sculpture |

103

## من/ماذا/متى؟ Who/What/When?

| | | |
|---|---|---|
| What's that building? | *maa hazaal binaa* | ما هذا البناء؟ |
| When was it built? | *matta buniya* | متى بني؟ |
| Who was the artist/architect? | *man kaan al-fanaan/ al-muhandis al-mAHmaaree* | من كان الفنان/المهندس المعماري؟ |

Some of the sightseeing highlights of a region rich in history and architecture:

## Egypt
Pyramids at Giza; Islamic Cairo; Coptic Christian Cairo; Egyptian Museum; pharaonic temples and tombs at Luxor, Aswan, and Abu Simbel; Mount Sinai and St. Catherine's Monastery.

## Lebanon
Ruined Roman temple at Baalbek; Saladin's restored palace at Ash-shouf; Bibli~al cedar tree forests near Bsherri.

## Jordan
Ruined Nabataean capital at Petra; Roman ampitheater in Amman.

## Syria
Medieval crusader castles; Islamic architecture of Damascus and Aleppo; Roman ruins at Palmyra.

## Saudi Arabia
Ancient Islamic cities of Mecca and Medina (only accessible to Muslims); Nabataean ruins of Mada'in Salih in the north of the country; ruins of original Saud capital city of ad-Dir'iyah near Riyadh.

## Other countries
Old walled city of San'a, Yemen; medieval forts built by local rulers and Portuguese occupiers in Oman and Bahrain; "Queen of Sheeba's palace" – ancient ruins and fortifications at Ras al-Khaima in the United Arab Emirates.

## Places of worship دور العبادة

The Arab world is predominantly Muslim. However, other religions are represented as well – there are large Christian populations in Lebanon and Egypt. Muslims pray five times a day and gather in the mosques for Friday prayers. In some areas, non-Muslims may not be able to enter mosques, and you should ask for permission first. If allowed, you should remove your shoes, cover your legs and arms, and women should cover their hair.

| church | *kaneesa* كنيسة |
| mosque | *jaamiAH* جامع |
| What time is/are prayers/mass? | *ayy saAHa aS-Salaat/ al-qaddaas* |

أي ساعة الصلاة/القداس ...

## History التاريخ

### Early civilizations (5000–30 B.C.)

Details are sketchy about the very earliest civilizations. In 3100 B.C., Menes united Upper and Lower Egypt to form a kingdom that lasted over 2000 years. From the eighth century B.C. Egypt went through periods of rule by the Nubians, Assyrians, Persians and Greeks until it's final conquest in 30 B.C. by the Roman Emperor Augustus. About 500 B.C. the Nabataeans also established themselves in present-day Jordan.

### Eastern Roman (Byzantine) Empire (400 B.C.–700 A.D.)

By the time Augustus conquered Egypt, the Romans were dominant in most of Asia Minor, the Levant, and Egypt. A Persian dynasty, the Sassanians, ruled further to the East. The Byzantine Empire gradually declined through the Middle Ages until its final demise in 1453.

### Early Islam (610–932)

The prophet Mohammed lived from 570–632 in western Arabia. In the 100 years after his death his followers conquered a huge area from Spain to India. Early Islamic history is dominated by two dynasties: the Umayyads, based in Damascus, and the later Abbasids, based in Baghdad.

### The Middle Ages (932–1520)

The early medieval period was dominated by the Papal Crusades and the Mogul invasions of Genghis Khan. For nearly 300 years, beginning in 1250, much of the region was ruled by the Mamelukes, self-styled soldier monarchs.

### Ottoman Empire (1520–1914)

In 1453, the Islamic Ottomans took Constantinople, ending Byzantine rule. They then expanded their empire to include most of the Middle East. In the nineteenth century the empire declined in the face of the European powers. The Ottoman sultan finally sealed the fate of the empire by siding with Germany in the First World War.

### The Twentieth Century

For the period between the wars, most of the Middle East was under the direct or indirect control of the European colonial powers. After the Second World War this influence gradually declined and the different countries of the region followed their own separate courses.

## In the countryside/desert

### في الريف/الصحراء

| | | |
|---|---|---|
| I'd like a map of ... | ureed khareeTa li ... | أريد خريطة لـ ... |
| this region | haazihil minTaqa | هذه المنطقة |
| walking routes | Turuq as-sayr | طرق السير |
| desert tracks | Turuq aS-SaHraa' | طرق الصحراء |
| How far is it to ...? | kam al-masaafa ilaa | كم المسافة إلى ...؟ |
| Is there a right of way? | hal AHndanaa Haqq al-muroor | هل عندنا حق المرور؟ |
| Is there a desert route to ... | hal hunaak Tareeq SaHraawee ilaa | هل هناك طريق صحراوي إلى ...؟ |
| Can you show me on the map? | mumkin tureenee AHlal khareeTa | ممكن تريني على الخريطة؟ |
| I'm lost. | ana tuht. | أنا تهت. |

## Organized treks رحلات السير منظمة

| | | |
|---|---|---|
| When does the trek start? | matta tabda' ar-riHla | متى تبدأ الرحلة؟ |
| When will we return? | matta sa-narjAH | متى سنرجع؟ |
| What is the trek like? | kayf kaanat ar-riHla | ما هي طبيعة الرحلة؟ |
| gentle/medium/tough | sahla/mutwassiTa/SaAHba jiddan | سهلة/متوسطة/صعبة جدا |
| I'm exhausted. | ana munhak. | أنا منهك. |
| How long are we resting here? | maa hiya muddat al-istiraaHa hunaa | ما هي مدة الاستراحة هنا؟ |
| What kind of ... is that? | min ayy nauAH hazaa | من أي نوع هذا ...؟ |
| animal/bird | al-Hayawaan/aT-Tayr | الحيوان/الطير |
| flower/tree | az-zahra/ash-shajara | الزهرة/الشجرة |

# Geographic features معالم جغرافية

| | |
|---|---|
| bridge | جسر *jisr* |
| cave | كهف *kahf* |
| cliff | منحدر *munHadar* |
| coast | ساحل *saaHil* |
| date palms | نخيل *nakheel* |
| desert | صحراء *SaHraa'* |
| farm | مزرعة *mazrAHa* |
| field | حقل *Haql* |
| forest/wood | غابة *ghaaba* |
| hill | تل *tall* |
| lake | بحيرة *buhayra* |
| mountain | جبل *jabal* |
| mountain pass | ممر جبلي *mamarr jabalee* |
| mountain range | سلسلة جبلية *silsila jabaleeya* |
| oasis | واحة *waaHa* |
| park | حديقة عامة *Hadeeqa AHama* |
| peak | قمة *qimma* |
| pond | بركة *birka* |
| river | نهر *nahr* |
| sand dune | كثيب رملي *kuthayb ramlee* |
| sea | بحر *baHr* |
| stream | جدول *jadwal* |
| swamp | مستنقع *mustanqAH* |
| valley | وادٍ *waadee* |
| village | قرية *qarya* |
| waterfall | شلال *shallaal* |

# Leisure

## Events الأنشطة

At your hotel or in the tourist information centers you'll often find publications listing local attractions, or you can consult the English-language newspapers.

Television programs are mostly in Arabic, but news and foreign films are also broadcast in English – and some countries have a separate English-language channel.

Most major hotels have English-language cable and satellite TV.

| | |
|---|---|
| Do you have a program of events? | hal AHandak barnaamij al-anshiTa |
| | هل عندك برنامج الأنشطة؟ |
| Can you recommend a good ...? | mumkin tinSaHnaa bi ... jayyid |
| | ممكن تنصحنا بـ ... جيد؟ |
| ballet/concert | baaleyh/Hafla mooseeqeeya |
| | باليه/حفلة موسيقية |
| movie [film] | feelm seenamaa'ee فيلم سينمائي |
| opera | oobraa أوبرا |

## Availability التوفر

| | |
|---|---|
| When does it start? | matta yabda' متى يبدأ؟ |
| When does it end? | matta yantahee متى ينتهي؟ |
| Are there any seats for tonight? | hal hunaak amaakin li-haazihil layla |
| | هل هناك أماكن لهذه الليلة؟ |
| Where can I get tickets? | ayn ashtaree at-tazaakir |
| | أين أشتري التذاكر؟ |

## Tickets تذاكر

| | |
|---|---|
| How much are the tickets? | bikam at-tazaakir |
| | بكم التذاكر؟ |
| Do you have anything cheaper? | AHndak shay' arkhaS |
| | عندك شيء أرخص؟ |
| I'd like to reserve ... | ureed Hajz ... |
| | أريد حجز ... |
| for Sunday evening | li-yaum al-aHad masaa'an |
| | ليوم الأحد مساءً |

| | |
|---|---|
| ما ... بطاقة الائتمان؟ | What's your credit card ...? |
| رقم | number |
| نوع | type |
| تاريخ الانتهاء | expiration [expiry] date |
| الرجاء أخذ التذاكر ... | Please pick up the tickets ... |
| قبل الساعة ... بعد الظهر. | by ... p.m. |
| عند مكتب الحجز | at the reservations desk |

| | |
|---|---|
| May I have a program, please? | mumkin aakhud al-barnaamij, lau samaHt |
| | ممكن آخذ البرنامج، لو سمحت؟ |
| Where's the coatcheck [cloakroom]? | ayn Hujrat al-mAHaaTif |
| | أين حجرة المعاطف؟ |

– mumkin usaAHidak?
– ureed talaat tazaakir li-Haflat al-layla.
– bit-ta'keed.
– mumkin adfAH bi-biTaaqat al-itimaan?
– naAHm, yaa seedee.
– izaa, sa-astAHmil "VISA".
– shukran ... tauqeeAHak huna, lau samaHt.

| | |
|---|---|
| حجز مسبق | Advance reservations |
| العدد كامل | Sold out |
| تذاكر لليوم | Tickets for today |

NUMBERS ➤ 216

## Movies [Cinema] سينما

Foreign films are usually shown in their original language with Arabic subtitling. However, some popular films may be dubbed, so check in advance.

| | |
|---|---|
| Is there a movie theater [cinema] near here? | *hal hunaak seenimaa qareeba*<br>هل هناك سينما قريبة؟ |
| What's playing at the movies [on at the cinema] tonight? | *maaza tAHraD as-seenimaa al-layla*<br>ماذا تعرض السينما الليلة؟ |
| Is the film dubbed/subtitled? | *hal al feelm madablaj/mutarjam*<br>هل الفيلم مدبلج/مترجم؟ |
| Is the film in the original English? | *hal al feelm naaTiq bil-injileezeeya*<br>هل الفيلم ناطق بالإنجليزية؟ |
| A ... please. | *ureed ... lau samaHt*<br>أريد ... لو سمحت. |
| packet of roasted seeds | *kees lubb* كيس لب |
| chocolate ice cream [choc-ice] | *ayes kreem shookoolaata*<br>آيس كريم شوكولاتة |
| hot dog | *sandwitsh sujuq* ساندويتش سجق |
| juice/soft drink | *AHSeer/kaazooza* عصير/كازوزة |
| small/regular/large | *Sahgeer/mutawassiT/kabeer*<br>صغير/متوسط/كبير |

## Theater مسرح

| | |
|---|---|
| What's the play at the ... Theater? | *maa al-masraHeeya fee masraH ...*<br>ما المسرحية في مسرح ...؟ |
| Who's the playwright? | *man kaatib al-masraHeeya*<br>من كاتب المسرحية؟ |
| Do you think I'd enjoy it?<br>I don't know much Arabic. | *taZunn annanee sa-AHjab bihaa.*<br>*ana laa ujeed al-AHrabeeya*<br>تظن أنني سأعجب بها؟ أنا لا أجيد العربية. |

110

## Opera/Ballet/Dance أوبرا/باليه/رقص

| | |
|---|---|
| Where's the opera house? | *ayn daar al-oobraa*<br>أين دار الأوبرا؟ |
| Who is the composer/soloist? | *man huwal mu'allif/*<br>*al-AHazif al-munfarid*<br>من هو المؤلف/العازف المنفرد؟ |
| Who's dancing? | *man ar-raaqiS*<br>من الراقص؟ |

## Music/Concerts موسيقى/حفلات موسيقية

| | |
|---|---|
| Where's the concert hall? | *ayn qaAHat al-Hafla al-mooseeqeeya*<br>أين قاعة الحفلة الموسيقية؟ |
| Which orchestra/band is playing? | *ayy oorkistraa/firqa sa-tAHzif*<br>أي أوركسترا/فرقة ستعزف؟ |
| What are they playing? | *maaza sa-yAHzifoon*<br>ماذا سيعزفون؟ |
| Who is the conductor/soloist? | *man huwa qaa'id al-firqa/*<br>*al-aazif al-munfarid*<br>من هو قائد الفرقة/العازف المنفرد؟ |
| Who is the singer? | *man al-mughannee* من المغني؟ |
| I really like ... | *ana uHibb ... kateeran*<br>أنا أحب ... كثيراً |
| Arabic music | *al-mooseeqaa al-AHrabeeya*<br>الموسيقى العربية |
| jazz | *al-jaaz* الجاز |
| rock/pop music | *mooseeqaa ar-rook/al-boob*<br>موسيقى الروك/البوب |
| Have you ever heard of her/him? | *hal samiAHt bihaa/bih*<br>هل سمعت بها/به؟ |
| Are they popular? | *hal hum mash-hooroon*<br>هل هم مشهورون؟ |

## Nightlife الحياة الليلية

What is there to do in the evenings? — maaza yumkinana an nafAHal feel masaa ماذا يمكننا أن نفعل في المساء؟

Can you recommend a ... — mumkin tinSaHnaa bi ... ممكن تنصحنا بـ ...؟

Is there a ... in town? — hal hunaak ... feel madeena هل هناك ... في المدينة؟

bar/restaurant — baar/maTAHm بار/مطعم

casino — Saalat al-qumaar صالة القمار

discotheque — deeskoo ديسكو

nightclub — naadee laylee نادٍ ليلي

What type of music do they play? — maa nauAH al-mooseeqaa hunaak ما نوع الموسيقى هناك؟

How do I get there? — kayf aSil hunaak كيف أصل هناك؟

## Admission الدخول

What time does the show start? — matta yabda al-AHrD متى يبدأ العرض؟

Is evening dress required? — hal malaabis as-sahra maTlooba هل ملابس السهرة مطلوبة؟

Is there a cover charge? — hunaak Hisaab AHlal khidma هناك حساب على الخدمة؟

Is a reservation necessary? — yajib an naHjiz يجب أن نحجز؟

Do we need to be members? — yajib an nakoon AHDaa يجب أن نكون أعضاء؟

Is it customary to dine there? — hal min al-ma'loof an na'kul hunaak هل من المألوف أن نأكل هناك؟

How long will we have to stand in line [queue]? — kam min al-waqt yajib an naSTaff كم من الوقت يجب أن نصطف؟

I'd like a good table. — ureed maa'ida jayyida. أريد مائدة جيدة.

## Children الأطفال

Can you recommend something
for the children?

*mumkin tinSaHna*
*bi-shay' lil-aTfaal*

ممكن تنصحنا بشيء للأطفال؟

Are there changing facilities
here for babies?

*hal hunaak tas-heelaat*
*li-tahgyeer fuwaT aT-Tifl hunaa*

هل هناك تسهيلات لتغيير فوط الطفل هنا؟

Where are the bathrooms [toilets]?

*ayn al-maraaHeeD* أين المراحيض؟

amusement arcade

*qaAHat tasleeya* قاعة تسلية

fairground

*madeenat al-malaahee* مدينة الملاهي

kiddie [paddling] pool

*masbaH lil-aTfaal* مسبح للأطفال

playground

*malAHb* ملعب

play group

*majmooAHat lAHb*

مجموعة لعب

zoo

*Hadeeqat al-Hayawaanaat*

حديقة الحيوانات

## Babysitting الحضن

Can you recommend a reliable
babysitter?

*mumkin tinSaHnaa bi-HaaDina mausooq*
*bihaa*

ممكن تنصحنا بحاضنة موثوق بها؟

Is there constant supervision?

*hal hunaak ishraaf daa'im*

هل هناك إشراف دائم؟

Is the staff properly trained?

*hal al-musaaAHideen mudarraboon*
*jayyidan?*

هل المساعدون مدربون جيداً؟

When can I drop them off?

*matta astaTeeAH eeSaalhum*

متى أستطيع إيصالهم.

I'll pick them up at ...

*sa-akhudhum as-saAHa*

سآخذهم الساعة ...

We'll be back by ...

*sa-narjAH qabl ...* سنعود قبل ...

She's 3 and he's 18 months.

*AHumrahaa talaata wa AHumruh*
*tamantashar shahr*

عمرها ٣ وعمره ١٨ شهر.

# الرياضة Sports

The Arab world is mad about soccer. Going to watch a local game can be an experience and is something you can enjoy as a tourist without needing to know the language. Games are usually held on Fridays.

Basketball, volleyball, squash and horseback riding are also popular. Some countries, such as the United Arab Emirates, offer a huge variety of land and water-based sports as well as local specialties such as camel racing and falconry. Many of these you can take part in as well as being a spectator.

## المشاهدة Spectating

| | |
|---|---|
| Is there a soccer [football] game this Friday? | hal hunaak maatsh kurrat qadam hazaal jumAHa<br>هل هناك ماتش كرة قدم هذا الجمعة؟ |
| Which teams are playing? | ayy al-firaq sa-talAHb<br>أي الفرق ستلعب؟ |
| Can you get me a ticket? | mumkin taHSul lee AHla tazkara<br>ممكن تحصل لي على تذكرة؟ |
| What's the admission charge? | maa huwa rasm ad-dukhool<br>ما هو رسم الدخول؟ |
| Where's the racetrack [racecourse]? | ayn miDmaar as-sibaaq<br>أين مضمار السباق؟ |
| Is there camel racing near here? | hal hunaak sibaaq lil-jimaal qurayb min hunaa<br>هل هناك سباق للجمال قريب من هنا؟ |
| Are there any falconry expeditions? | hal hunaak riHlaat Sayd biS-Suqoor<br>هل هناك رحلات صيد بالصقور؟ |
| aerobics | tamreenaat riyaaDeeya تمرينات رياضية |
| angling | Sayd as-samak صيد السمك |
| athletics | alAHaab al-quwa ألعاب القوى |
| badminton | tanis ar-reesha تنس الريشة |
| baseball | al-baayisbool البايسبول |
| basketball | kurat as-salla كرة السلة |
| boxing | al-mulaakma الملاكمة |

| | |
|---|---|
| cycling | *rukoob ad-darraajaat* |
| | ركوب الدراجات |
| falconry | *SayD biS-Suqoor* |
| | صيد بالصقور |
| field hockey | الهوكي *al-hookee* |
| golf | الجولف *al-goolf* |
| horseracing | *sibaaq al-khayl* سباق الخيل |
| horseback riding | *rukoob al-khayl* ركوب الخيل |
| judo | الجودو *al-joodoo* |
| mountaineering | *tasalluq al-jibaal* تسلق الجبال |
| rowing | التجديف *at-tajdeef* |
| skiing | *at-tazaHluq AHlaal jaleed* |
| | التزحلق على الجليد |
| soccer [football] | *kurat al-qadam* كرة القدم |
| squash | الإسكواش *al-iskwaash* |
| swimming | السباحة *as-sibaaHa* |
| table tennis | *tanis aT-Taawla* تنس الطاولة |
| tennis | التنس *at-tanis* |
| volleyball | *al-kura aT-Taa'ira* الكرة الطائرة |

## Playing لعب

| | |
|---|---|
| Where's the nearest …? | *ayn aqrab* …؟ أين أقرب |
| golf course | *arD al-goolf* أرض الجولف |
| sports club | *nadee riyaaDee* نادٍ رياضي |
| Where are the tennis courts? | *ayn malaaAHib at-tanis* |
| | أين ملاعب التنس؟ |
| What's the charge per …? | *kam al-Hisaab li* …؟ كم الحساب لـ |
| day/round/hour | *yaum/jaula/saAHa* يوم/جولة/ساعة |

| | | |
|---|---|---|
| Where can I rent ...? | min ayn asta'jir ...? | من أين أستأجر ...؟ |
| boots | Hizaa | حذاء |
| clubs | maDaarib (goolf) | مضارب (جولف) |
| equipment | muAHiddaat | معدات |
| a racket | miDrab | مضرب |

Do I need to be a member?

hal yajib an akoon AHDoo

هل يجب أن أكون عضوا؟

Can I get lessons?

mumkin aakhud duroos

ممكن آخذ دروسا؟

Do you have a fitness room?

hal AHandakum ghurfa
lil-yaaqa al-badaneeya

هل عندكم غرفة للياقة البدنية؟

Can I join in?

mumkin ashtarik

ممكن أشترك؟

| | |
|---|---|
| آسف، كل شيء محجوز. | I'm sorry. We're booked up. |
| هناك عربون بمبلغ... | There is a deposit of ... |
| قياسك كم؟ | What size are you? |
| تحتاج لصورة بحجم جواز السفر. | You need a passport-size photo. |
| تغيير الملابس | changing rooms |
| ممنوع صيد السمك | no fishing |
| لحاملي التصاريح فقط | permit holders only |

## Horseback riding ركوب الخيل

Arab horses are famous the world over, and the desert is the ideal place to ride as long as you avoid the hottest part of the day. You will find stables all over over the Middle East where you can rent horses by the hour or day.

| | |
|---|---|
| I'm an experienced rider. | ana faaris mumtaaz. أنا فارس ممتاز. |
| I'm a beginner. | ana mubtadi'. أنا مبتدئ. |
| Do you have a Western [American]/English saddle? | hal AHandak sarj amreekee/ooroobee هل عندك سرج أمريكي/أوروبي؟ |

## At the beach على الشاطئ

Some resort beaches are supervised, but many are not – and you should take care to assess conditions before bathing, particularly where children are concerned.

In coral reef areas (the Red Sea, for example), wear plastic shoes to protect your feet when swimming – and be careful not to deliberately or accidently break off any of the coral, which is protected by law.

| | |
|---|---|
| Is the beach pebbly/sandy? | *hal as-saaHil Sakhree/ramlee*<br>هل الساحل صخري/رملي؟ |
| Is there a ... here? | *hal hunaak ... hunaa*<br>هل هناك ... هنا؟ |
| children's pool | *misbaH lil-aTfaal*<br>مسبح للأطفال |
| swimming pool | *Hammaam sibaaHa* حمام سباحة |
| indoor/open-air | *masqoof/makshoof* مسقوف/مكشوف |
| Is it safe to swim/dive here? | *hal hazza aamin lis-sibaaHa/lil-ghaTs*<br>هل هذا آمن للسباحة/للغطس؟ |
| Is it safe for children? | *hal huwa aamin lil-aTfaal*<br>هل هو آمن للأطفال؟ |
| Is there a lifeguard? | *hal hunaak munqiz?* هل هناك منقذ؟ |
| I want to rent a/some ... | *ureed isti'jaar ...* أريد استئجار ... |
| deck chair | *kursee ash-shaaTi'* كرسي الشاطئ |
| jetski | *darraaja maa'eeya* دراجة مائية |
| motorboat | *zauraq bukhaaree* زورق بخاري |
| scuba [skin-diving] equipment | *mAHiddaat al-ghaTs* معدات الغطس |
| umbrella [sunshade] | *maZalla (shamseeya)* مظلة (شمسية) |
| surfboard | *lauH rukoob al-mauj* لوح ركوب الموج |
| water skis | *lauh at-tazaHluq AHlaal maa'*<br>لوح التزحلق على الماء |
| For ... hours. | *li-muddit ... SaAHaat*<br>لمدة ... ساعات. |

# Making Friends

## Introductions التعارف

Arabic speakers usually have three names. These are their own first name, their father's first name, and their family name. For example, the son of Mohammed Yousef Shaheen would be Ashraf Mohammed Shaheen. If they are being less formal, they will drop the middle name: Mohammed Shaheen/Ashraf Shaheen. Note that this also applies to women, who retain their family name after marriage rather than adopting their husband's. So the daughter of Mohammed Yousef Shaheen would be Mona Mohammed Shaheen.

There are many different greetings and replies in Arabic depending on the situation. From the point of view of the tourist it is better to stick to one of the general greetings, such as **marHaban** (hello) or **ahlan** (Hi!). It's also usual to shake hands when you meet someone.

| | | |
|---|---|---|
| Hello. | *marHaban.* | مرحبا. |
| My name is ... | *ismee ...* | اسمي ... |
| May I introduce ...? | *mumkin uqaddim lak ...?* | ممكن أقدم لك ...؟ |
| Pleased to meet you. | *tasharrafnaa.* | تشرفنا. |
| What's your name? | *maa ismak* | ما اسمك؟ |
| How are you? | *kayf Haalak* | كيف حالك؟ |
| Fine, thanks. And you? | *bi-khayr, al-Hamdu lilaah. wa-anta* | بخير، الحمد لله. وأنت؟ |

> – *marHaban. kayf Haalak?*
> – *bi-khayr, shukran. wa-anta?*
> – *bi-khayr, al-Hamdu lilaah.*

## Where are you from? من أين أنت؟

| Where are you from? | *min ayn anta* | من أين أنت؟ |
| Where were you born? | *ayn wulidt* | أين ولدت؟ |
| I'm from ... | *ana min ...* | أنا من ... |
| Australia | *ostraalyaa* | استراليا |
| Britain | *bireeTaanya* | بريطانيا |
| Canada | *Kanadaa* | كندا |
| England | *injilteraa* | إنجلترا |
| Ireland | *irlandaa* | إرلندا |
| Scotland | *iskootlandaa* | اسكوتلندا |
| U.S. | *amreekaa* | أمريكا |
| Wales | *waylz* | ويلز |
| Where do you live? | *ayn taskun* | أين تسكن؟ |
| What part of ... are you from? | *anta min ayy manTiqa fee* | أنت من أي منطقة في ... ؟ |
| Egypt | *muSr* | مصر |
| Morrocco | *al-maghrib* | المغرب |
| the (Persian) Gulf | *al-khaleej* | الخليج |
| We come here every year. | *najee hunaa kull sana* | نجيء هنا كل سنة. |
| It's my/our first visit. | *innahaa awwal ziyaara lee/linaa* | إنها أول زيارة لي/لنا. |
| Have you ever been to ... | *zurt ... bi-Hayaatak* | زرت ... بحياتك؟ |
| Britain/the U.S. | *bireeTaanya/amreekaa* | بريطانيا/أمريكا |
| Do you like it here? | *hal anta sAHeed hunaa* | هل أنت سعيد هنا؟ |
| What do you think of ... | *maa ra'yak fee ...* | ما رأيك في ... ؟ |
| I love ... here. | *uHibb ... huna* | أحب ... هنا. |
| I don't really like ... here. | *laa uHibb ... hunaa* | لا أحب ... هنا. |
| the food/people | *al-akl/an-naas* | الأكل/الناس |

119

## Who are you with?/Family
### من معك؟/عائلة

| | | |
|---|---|---|
| Who are you with? | man mAHak | من معك؟ |
| I'm on my own. | ana waHdee | أنا وحدي. |
| I'm with a friend. | ana mAHa Sadeeq | أنا مع صديق. |
| I'm with ... | ana mAHa ... | أنا مع ... |
| my husband/wife | zaujee/zaujatee | زوجي/زوجتي |
| my family | AH'iltee | عائلتي |
| my children/parents | aulaadee/waalidayya | أولادي/والديّ |
| my boyfriend/girlfriend | SaaHbee/SaaHbatee | صاحبي/صاحبتي |
| my father/son | abee/ibnee | أبي/ابني |
| my mother/daughter | ummee/ibnatee | أمي/ابنتي |
| my brother/uncle | akhee/AHmee (khaalee) | أخي/عمي (خالي) |
| my sister/aunt | ukhtee/AHmatee (khaaltee) | أختي/عمتي (خالتي) |
| What's your son's/wife's name? | maa ism ibnak/zaujatak | ما اسم ابنك/زوجتك؟ |
| Are you married? | hal anta mutzawwij | هل أنت متزوج؟ |
| I'm ... | ana ... | أنا ... |
| married/single | mutzawwij/AHaazib | متزوج/عازب |
| divorced/separated | muTallaq/munfaSil | مطلق/منفصل |
| engaged | khaaTib | خاطب |
| We live together. | naskun mAHa bAHD | نسكن مع بعض. |
| Do you have any children? | AHandak aulaad | عندك أولاد؟ |
| a boy and a girl | walad wa bint | ولد وبنت. |
| How old are they? | AHmaarhum kam? | أعمارهم كم؟ |
| 10 and 12 years old | AHshara wa itnaAHshar sana | عشرة واثنا عشر سنة. |

## What do you do? بماذا تعمل؟

| | |
|---|---|
| What do you do? | bi-maaza tAHmal |
| | بماذا تعمل؟ |
| What line are you in? | fee ayy majaal tAHmal |
| | في أي مجال تعمل؟ |
| What are you studying? | mazaa tadrus؟ ماذا تدرس |
| I'm studying … | adrus … أدرس |
| I'm in … | ana fee … أنا في |
| business | tijaara تجارة |
| engineering | handasa هندسة |
| retail | baa'iAH tajzi'a بائع تجزئة |
| sales | mabeeAHaat مبيعات |
| Who do you work for? | li-Hisaab man tAHmil؟ لحساب من تعمل |
| I work for … | AHmil li-Hisaab … أعمل لحساب |
| I'm a/an … | ana … أنا |
| accountant | muHaasib محاسب |
| housewife | rabbat manzil ربة منزل |
| student | Taalib طالب |
| retired | mutaqaAHid متقاعد |
| self-employed | SaaHib mihna Hurra صاحب مهنة حرة |
| between jobs | bayn waZeeftayn بين وظيفتين |
| What are your interests/hobbies? | maa hiya hiwaayaatak؟ ما هي هواياتك |
| I like … | uHibb … أحب |
| music | al-mooseeqa الموسيقى |
| reading | al-qiraa'a القراءة |
| sports | ar-riyaaDa الرياضة |
| I play … | alAHb … ألعب |
| Would you like to play …? | tuHibb talAHb …؟ تحب تلعب |
| cards | kootsheena كوتشينة |
| chess | shaTranj شطرنج |

## What weather! ‫ما هذا الطقس!‬

| | | |
|---|---|---|
| What a lovely day! | al-jau mumtaaz al-yaum! | ‫الجو ممتاز اليوم!‬ |
| What awful weather! | al-jau shaneeAH al-yaum | ‫الجو شنيع اليوم!‬ |

Isn't it cold/hot today!　　　alaysa al-jau baarid/Harr al-yaum
‫أليس الجو باردًا/حارًا اليوم!‬

Is it usually this warm?　　　hal al-jau AHadatan Harr li-haazihid
daraja ‫هل الجو عادة حار لهذه الدرجة؟‬

Do you think it's going　　　hal tAHtaqid innahaa ... ghadan
to ... tomorrow ?　　　　　‫هل تعتقد أنها ... غدًا؟‬

be a fine day　　　　　　　sa-yakoon yaum jameel ‫سيكون يومًا جميلا‬

rain　　　　　　　　　　　sa-tumTir ‫ستمطر‬

What is the weather forecast?　maa hiya tanabu'aat al-jau
‫ما هي تنبؤات الجو؟‬

It's ...　　　innahu ... ‫إنه ...‬

cloudy　　　ghaa'im ‫غائم‬

sunny　　　mushmis ‫مشمس‬

stormy　　　raAHid ‫راعد‬

windy　　　mazroo bir-riyaaH ‫مذرو بالرياح‬

Has the weather been like　　hal al-jau AHlaa haazihil
this for long?　　　　　　　Haal min mudda Taweela
‫هل الجو على هذه الحال من مدة طويلة؟‬

What's the pollen count?　　maa hiya nisbat ghubaar aT-TalAH
‫ما هي نسبة غبار الطلع؟‬

high/medium/low　　　　　murtafiAH/mutwassiTa/munkhafiDa
‫مرتفعة/متوسطة/منخفضة‬

---

weather forecast　‫تنبؤات الجو‬

122

# Enjoying your trip? مستمتع بالرحلة؟

| | |
|---|---|
| أنت في عطلة؟ | Are you on vacation? |
| كيف وصلت إلى هنا؟ | How did you get/ travel here? |
| أين تقيم؟ | Where are you staying? |
| منذ متى وأنت هنا؟ | How long have you been here? |
| كم ستبقى؟ | How long are you staying? |
| ماذا فعلت حتى الآن؟ | What have you done so far? |
| أين ستذهب من بعد هنا؟ | Where are you going next? |
| مستمتع بالعطلة؟ | Are you enjoying your vacation [holiday]? |

| | | |
|---|---|---|
| I'm here on ... | ana hunaa fee ... | أنا هنا في ... |
| a business trip | riHlat AHmal | رحلة عمل |
| vacation [holiday] | ijaaza | إجازة |
| We came ... | waSalnaa ... | وصلنا ... |
| by train/by bus/by plane | bil-qiTaar/bil-ootoobees/biT-Taa'ira | بالقطار/بالأوتوبيس/بالطائرة |
| by car/by ferry | bis-sayyaara/bil-mAHdeeya | بالسيارة/بالمعدية |
| I have a rental [hire] car. | mAHaya sayyaara mu'ajjara | معي سيارة مؤجرة. |
| We're staying in ... | nuqeem fee ... | نقيم في ... |
| an apartment | shaqqa | شقة |
| a hotel/campsite | funduq/mukhayyam | في فندق/مخيَّم |
| with friends | mAHa aSdiqaa | مع أصدقاء |
| Can you suggest ...? | mumkin taqtariH ...? | ممكن تقترح ...؟ |
| things to do | ashyaa' nAHmilhaa | أشياء نعملها |
| places to eat | amaakin lil-akl | أماكن للأكل |
| places to visit | amaakin liz-ziyaara | أماكن للزيارة |
| We're having a great/awful time. | naqDee waqt raa'iAH/shaneeAH | نقضي وقتاً رائعاً/شنيعاً. |

## Invitations دعوى

| | |
|---|---|
| Would you like to have dinner with us on …? | *tuHibb tatAHshshaa mAHaana yaum*<br>تحب تتعشى معنا يوم …؟ |
| May I invite you to lunch? | *mumkin adAHook lil-ghadaa*<br>ممكن أدعوك للغداء؟ |
| We are having a party.<br>Can you come? | *AHndanaa Hafla. taqdar taHDar*<br>عندنا حفلة. تقدر تحضر؟ |
| May we join you? | *mumkin nushaarik-kum* ممكن نشاركّكم؟ |
| Would you like to join us? | *tuHibb tushaarik-naa* تحب تشاركنا؟ |

## Going out الخروج

| | |
|---|---|
| What are your plans for …? | *mazza sa-tafAHal fee*<br>ماذا ستفعل في …؟ |
| today/tonight | *al-yaum/al-layla* اليوم/الليلة |
| tomorrow | *al-ghad* الغد |
| Are you free this evening? | *hal anta faaDee al-layla*<br>هل أنت فاضٍ الليلة؟ |
| Would you like to …? | *tuHibb* تحب …؟ |
| go dancing | *nurqus* نرقص |
| go out for a meal | *na'kul feel-khaarij* نأكل في الخارج |
| go for a walk | *natmashshaa* نتمشى |
| go shopping | *natsawwaq* نتسوق |
| I'd like to go to … | *uHibb an azhab ilaa*<br>أحب أن أذهب إلى … |
| I'd like to see … | *uHibb an ushaahid*<br>أحب أن أشاهد … |
| Do you enjoy …? | *hal tastamtiAH bi*<br>هل تستمتع بـ …؟ |

## Accepting/Declining قبول/رفض

| | |
|---|---|
| Thank you. I'd love to. | mumtaaz. sa-yusharrifnee |
| | ممتاز. سيشرفني. |
| Thank you, but I'm busy. | shukran, laakinee mashghool |
| | شكرا، لكني مشغول. |
| May I bring a friend? | mumkin uHDir Sadeeq? |
| | ممكن أحضر صديقاً؟ |
| Where shall we meet? | ayn sa-naltaqee? |
| | أين سنلتقي؟ |
| I'll meet you … | sa-ulaaqeek … |
| | سألاقيك … |
| in front of your hotel | amaam funduqak |
| | أمام فندقك |
| I'll call for you at 8. | sa-aatee li-aakhudak as-saAHa tamanya |
| | سآتي لآخذك الساعة ٨. |
| Could we make it a bit later/earlier? | mumkin badree/mutakhkhar aktar |
| | ممكن بدري/متأخر أكثر؟ |
| That will be fine. | hazaa mumtaaz |
| | هذا ممتاز. |

## Dining out/in الأكل خارج البيت/في البيت

Hospitality is taken very seriously in the Middle East. If you are invited out to a meal in a restaurant you would not be expected to pay, nor should you try! If you are invited to a meal in someone's home you should take a gift – a cake, chocolates, or something for the house.

Expect to have your plate piled high and to be bombarded with constant encouragements to have more. A polite way of refusing is to say **dayman** or "always," which roughly means "may you always be in a position to provide such a sumptuous meal."

| | |
|---|---|
| Let me buy you a drink. | dAHnee ashtaree lak mashroob |
| | دعني أشتري لك مشروبا. |
| Do you like …? | hal tuHibb …? هل تحب … ؟ |
| What are you going to have? | mazaa sa-ta'khud? ماذا ستأخذ؟ |
| That was a lovely meal. | kaanat wajba raa'iAHa |
| | كانت وجبة رائعة. |

# Encounters لقاءات بالصدفة

| | |
|---|---|
| Do you mind if ...? | AHandak maaniAH izaa |
| | عندك مانع إذا ...؟ |
| I sit here/I smoke | ajlis hunaa/udakhkhin أجلس هنا/أدخن |
| Can I get you a drink? | mumkin ajeeb lak mashroob |
| | ممكن أجيب لك مشروباً؟ |
| I'd love to have some company. | yasAHadnee muraafaqtak |
| | يسعدني مرافقتك. |
| Why are you laughing? | li-mazaa taDHak لماذا تضحك؟ |
| Is my Arabic that bad? | hal lughatee al-AHrabeeya sayy'ia li-hazihid daraja |
| | هل لغتي العربية سيئة لهذه الدرجة؟ |
| Shall we go somewhere quieter? | tuHibb nazhab ilaa makaan ahda |
| | تحب نذهب إلى مكان أهدأ؟ |
| Leave me alone, please! | utruknee waHdee, lau samaHt |
| | اتركني وحدي، لو سمحت! |
| You look great! | shaklak Hilw! شكلك حلو! |
| Would you like to come back with me? | tuHibb tirjAH mAHaya |
| | تحب ترجع معي؟ |
| I'm not ready for that. | ana lastu jaahiz li-kull haaza |
| | انا لست جاهزاً لكل هذا. أ |
| Unfortunately we've got to leave now. | lil-asaf yajib an nimshee al-aan |
| | للأسف يجب أن نمشي الآن. |
| Thanks for the evening. | shukran AHlas sahra |
| | شكرا على السهرة. |
| It was great. | kaanat AHZeema. كانت عظيمة. |
| Can I see you again tomorrow? | mumkin ashoofak marra taanya ghadan |
| | ممكن أشوفك مرة ثانية غدا؟ |
| See you soon. | ilaal liqaa. إلى اللقاء. |
| May I have your address? | mumkin tAHTeenee AHunwaanak |
| | ممكن تعطيني عنوانك؟ |

# Telephoning الاتصالات بالتلفون

The major cities of the Arab World are rapidly becoming part
of the international telephone network. You can often call
home direct or use international calling cards. Outside the major
cities, however, you may still have to go to a post office or telephone
bureau to make international calls. You will be directed to a booth and
connected by an operator. Find out the rates per minute in advance.

Telephone cards for use in public phones are still not common, although
some Gulf states have introduced them on a limited basis.

| | |
|---|---|
| Can I have your telephone number? | *mumkin aakhud raqm tilifoonak* ممكن آخذ رقم تلفونك؟ |
| Here's my number. | *hazaa raqmee.* هذا رقمي. |
| Please call me. | *ittaSil bee lau samaHt.* اتصل بي لو سمحت. |
| I'll give you a call. | *sa-attaSil bik* سأتصل بك. |
| Where's the nearest telephone booth? | *ayn aqrab tilifoon AHamm* أين أقرب تلفون عام؟ |
| May I use your phone? | *mumkin astAHmil tilifoonak* ممكن أستعمل تلفونك؟ |
| It's an emergency. | *Haala Taari'a.* حالة طارئة. |
| I'd like to call someone in England. | *ureed an attaSil bi-shakhS fee injiltaraa* أريد أن أتصل بشخص في إنجلترا. |
| What's the area [dialling] code for …? | *maa raqm an-nidaa' ad-daulee li* ما رقم النداء الدولي لـ …؟ |
| Which booth shall I use? | *sa-astAHmil ayy kushk* سأستعمل أي كشك؟ |
| What's the number for Information [Directory Enquiries]? | *maa huwa raqm daleel at-tilifoonaat* ما هو رقم دليل التلفونات؟ |
| What's the number for … | *maa ar-raqm li …* ما الرقم لـ …؟ |
| I'd like the number for … | *ureed ar-raqm li …* أريد الرقم لـ …؟ |
| I'd like to reverse the charges/ call collect. | *ureed taHweel ujrat al-mukaalma AHlal mustalim* أريد تحويل أجرة المكالمة على المستلم. |

## Speaking التكلم

| | |
|---|---|
| Hello. This is … | aloo. ana … ألو. أنا … |
| I'd like to speak to … | ureed at-takallum mAHa أريد التكلم مع … |
| extension … | imtidaad … امتداد |
| Speak louder/speak more slowly, please. | irfAH Sautak/takallam bi-buT', lau samaHt ارفع صوتك/تكلم ببطء، لو سمحت. |
| Could you repeat that, please? | mumkin tukarrir hazaa, lau samaHt ممكن تكرر هذا، لو سمحت؟ |
| Can you hear me clearly? | hal tasmAHnee bi-wuDooH هل تسمعني بوضوح؟ |
| I'm afraid he's not in/ she's not in. | mutassif. huwa ghayr maujood/ hiya ghayr maujooda متأسف. هو غير موجود/هي غير موجودة. |
| You have the wrong number. | ar-raqm ghalaT الرقم غلط. |
| Just a moment. | intaZir laHZa انتظر لحظة. |
| Hold on, please. | laHZa, lau samaHt لحظة، لو سمحت. |
| We were cut off! | al-khaTT inqaTAH الخط انقطع! |
| When will he/she be back? | matta sa-yaAHood/sa-tAHood متى سيعود/ستعود؟ |
| Will you tell him/her that I called? | mumkin taqool luh/lahaa annanee attaSalt ممكن تقول له/لها أنني اتصلت؟ |
| My name is … | ismee … اسمي … |
| Would you ask him/her to call me? | mumkin taTlub minuh/minhaa an yattaSil/tattaSil bee ممكن تطلب منه/منها أن يتصل/تتصل بي؟ |
| I'll be in touch. | sa-attaSil qareeban. سأتصل قريباً. |
| Bye. | mAHas salaama. مع السلامة. |

# Stores & Services

Although there are large shopping malls and supermarkets in the region, the most interesting way to shop is still in the many local markets (**sooq**). These sell everything from perfumes and spices to gold and carpets. You will be expected to bargain (▶ 156), but make sure you don't overdo it and end up making an insulting offer.

## ESSENTIAL

| | | |
|---|---|---|
| I'd like ... | *ureed* ... | أريد ... |
| Do you have ...? | *hal AHndak* ...؟ | هل عندك ...؟ |
| How much is that? | *bikam haaza* | بكم هذا؟ |
| Thank you. | *shukran.* | شكرا. |

| | |
|---|---|
| مفتوح | open |
| مغلق | closed |
| تخفيضات | sale |

# Stores and services محلات وخدمات

## أين الـ ...؟ Where is ...?

| | | |
|---|---|---|
| Where's the nearest ...? | ayn aqrab ... | أين أقرب ...؟ |
| Where's there a good ...? | ayn yoojad ... jayyid | أين يوجد ... جيد؟ |
| Where's the main shopping mall [centre]? | ayn al-markaz at-tijaaree ar-ra'eesee | أين المركز التجاري الرئيسي؟ |
| Is it far from here? | hal huwa bAHeed min hunaa | هل هو بعيد من هنا؟ |
| How do I get there? | kayf aSil hunaak | كيف أصل هناك؟ |

## Stores محلات

| | | |
|---|---|---|
| antique store | maHall anteekaat | محل أنتيكات |
| bakery | makhbaz | مخبز |
| bank | bank | بنك |
| bookstore | maktaba | مكتبة |
| butcher | jazzaar | جزار |
| camera store | maHall kaameeraat | محل كاميرات |
| cigarette kiosk [tobacconist] | kushk sajaa'ir | كشك سجائر |
| clothing store [clothes shop] | maHall malaabis | محل ملابس |
| delicatessen | maHall aTAHima mutanawiAHa | محل أطعمة متنوعة |
| department store | maHall tijaaree | محل تجاري |
| drugstore | Saydaleeya | صيدلية |
| fish store [fishmonger] | maHall samak | محل سمك |
| florist | maHall zuhoor | محل زهور |
| gift store | mahall hadaayaa | محل هدايا |
| greengrocer | maHall khuDaar | محل خضار |
| health food store | maHall aTAHima SiHHeeya | محل أطعمة صحية |
| jeweler | maHall mujauharaat | محل مجوهرات |

| | | |
|---|---|---|
| market | sooq | سوق |
| newsstand | kushk jaraa'id | كشك جرائد |
| pastry store | maHall Halawiyaat | محل حلويات |
| pharmacy [chemist] | ajzakhaana/Saydaleeya | أجزخانة/صيدلية |
| produce store | baqaala | بقالة |
| record/music store | maHall kaaseetaat | محل كاسيتات |
| shoe store | maHall aHzeeya | محل أحذية |
| shopping mall [centre] | markaz tijaaree | مركز تجاري |
| souvenir store | maHall hadaayaa tizkaareeya | محل هدايا تذكارية |
| sporting goods store | maHall adawaat riyaaDeeya | محل أدوات رياضية |
| supermarket | soobarmaarkit | سوبرماركت |
| toy store | maHall luAHb | محل لعب |

## Services خدمات

| | | |
|---|---|---|
| dentist | Tabeeb asnaan | طبيب أسنان |
| doctor | duktoor/Tabeeb | دكتور/طبيب |
| dry cleaner | maHall tanZeef malaabis | محل تنظيف ملابس |
| hairdresser (ladies'/men's) | Saaloon Hilaaqa (lin-nisaa/lir-rijaal) | صالون حلاقة (للنساء/للرجال) |
| hospital | mustashfaa | مستشفى |
| laundromat | maghsala (khidma zaateeya) | مغسلة (خدمة ذاتية) |
| optician | naZaaraatee | نظاراتي |
| police station | qism boolees | قسم بوليس |
| post office | maktab al-bareed | مكتب البريد |
| travel agency | maktab safar | مكتب سفر |

# Opening hours أوقات العمل

Opening hours for stores and banks vary from country to country. Often stores will close in the middle of the day and re-open in the afternoon. Times also vary seasonally and during Ramadan (➤ 34).

Friday is usually the official closing day, but in some areas this can extend to Saturday as well.

Stores and offices will be closed on Sundays in predominantly Christian areas.

| | | |
|---|---|---|
| When does the … open/shut? | *matta yaftaH/yaqfil* | ؟... متى يفتح/يقفل |
| Are you open in the evening? | *hal taftaH feel masaa* | هل تفتح في المساء؟ |
| Do you close for lunch? | *hal tuqfil li-fitrat al-ghadaa* | هل تقفل لفترة الغداء؟ |
| Where is the …? | *ayn …?* | أين ...؟ |
| cashier [cash desk] | *al-khazeena* | الخزينة |
| escalator | *as-silim al-kahrabaa'ee* | السلم الكهربائي |
| elevator [lift] | *al-maSAHd* | المصعد |
| store guide | *daleel al-maHall* | دليل المحل |
| first [ground (Brit.)] floor | *aT-Taabiq al-arDee* | الطابق الأرضي |
| second [first (Brit.)] floor | *aT-Taabiq al-awwal* | الطابق الأول |
| Where's the … department? | *ayn qism al …?* | أين قسم الـ ...؟ |

| | |
|---|---|
| مواعيد العمل الرسمية | business hours |
| مغلق لفترة الغداء | closed for lunch |
| مفتوح طوال اليوم | open all day |
| المدخل | entrance |
| سلم كهربائي | escalator |
| المخرج | exit |
| طوارئ/مخرج طوارئ | emergency/fire exit |
| مصعد | elevator [lift] |
| سلم | stairs |

132

# Service خدمة

| | |
|---|---|
| Can you help me? | *mumkin tusaAHidnee*<br>ممكن تساعدني؟ |
| I'm looking for … | *ana abHas AHn*<br>أنا أبحث عن … |
| I'm just browsing. | *ana atfarraj faqaT*<br>أنا أتفرج فقط. |
| It's my turn. | *dooree*<br>دوري. |
| Do you have any …? | *hal AHndak ayy*<br>هل عندك أي …؟ |
| I'd like to buy … | *ureed shiraa …*<br>أريد شراء … |
| Could you show me …? | *mumkin tureenee*<br>ممكن تريني …؟ |
| How much is this/that? | *bikam haaza/zaalik*<br>بكم هذا/ذلك؟ |
| That's all, thanks. | *hazaa kulluh, shukran*<br>هذا كله، شكرا. |

---

| | |
|---|---|
| صباح الخير/نهارك سعيد، سيدي/سيدتي. | Good morning/afternoon, madam/sir. |
| هل خدمك أحد؟ | Are you being served? |
| ماذا تحب؟ | What would you like? |
| هل هذا كل شيء؟ | Is that everything? |
| أي شيء آخر؟ | Anything else? |

---

– *mumkin usaAHidak?*
– *laa, shukran. ana atfarraj faqaT.*
– *hasanan …*
– *lau samaHt.*
– *nAHm, mumkin usaAHidak?*
– *bikam haaza?*
– *dAHnee at'akkad … haaza bi-AHishreen junayh.*

---

| | |
|---|---|
| خدمة الزبائن | customer service |
| خدمة ذاتية | self-service |
| عرض خاص | clearance |

133

## المفاضلة Preference

| | | |
|---|---|---|
| I want something … | *ureed shay* … | … أريد شيئا |
| It must be … | *yajib an yakoon* … | … يجب أن يكون |
| big/small | *kabeer/Sagheer* | كبير/صغير |
| cheap/expensive | *rakheeS/ghaalee* | رخيص/غال |
| dark/light | *ghaamiq/faatiH* | غامق/فاتح |
| genuine/imitation | *aSlee/taqleed* | أصلي/تقليد |
| light/heavy | *khafeef/thaqeel* | خفيف/ثقيل |
| oval/round/square | *bayDaawee/mustadeer/murabbAH* | بيضاوي/مستدير/مربع |
| I don't want anything too expensive. | *laa ureed ashyaa ghaalya jiddan* | لا أريد أشياء غالية جدا. |
| In the region of … pounds. | *fee Hudood … junayh* | في حدود … جنيه. |

| | |
|---|---|
| أي … تحب؟ | What … would you like? |
| لون/شكل | color/shape |
| نوع/كمية | quality/quantity |
| ما هو الصنف الذي تحبه؟ | What sort would you like? |
| ما المبلغ التقريبي الذي تفكر به؟ | What price range are you thinking of? |

| | | |
|---|---|---|
| Do you have anything …? | *hal AHndak ayy shay* …? | هل عندك أي شيء …؟ |
| larger/smaller | *akbar/aSghar* | أكبر/أصغر |
| better quality/cheaper | *afDal/arkhaS* | أفضل/أرخص |
| Can you show me …? | *mumkin tureenee* | ممكن تريني …؟ |
| that/this one | *zaalik/haaza* | ذلك/هذا |
| these/those ones | *haazihi/tilka* | هذه/تلك |
| the one in the window/ display case | *allazee feesh-shibbaak/ feeS-Sundooq al-AHrD* | الذي في الشباك/صندوق العرض |
| some others | *bAHD al-ashyaa al-ukhraa* | بعض الأشياء الأخرى |

## Conditions of purchase شروط الشراء

Is there a guarantee? *hal hunaak Damaan*
هل هناك ضمان؟

Are there any instructions with it? *hal mAHuh daleel*
هل معه دليل؟

## Out of stock نفاذ البضاعة

| | |
|---|---|
| أنا آسف، ليس موجودا عندنا. | I'm sorry, we haven't any. |
| البضاعة نفذت. | We're out of stock. |
| هل أستطيع أن أريك شيء آخر/ صنف مختلف؟ | Can I show you something else/ a different type? |
| هل تريدنا أن نطلبه لك؟ | Shall we order it for you? |

Can you order it for me? *mumkin taTlubuh lee*
ممكن تطلبه لي؟

How long will it take? *kam sa-tastaghriq*
كم ستستغرق؟

Where else can I get ...? *wa ayn aHSul AHlaa*
وأين أحصل على...؟

## Decision القرار

That's not quite what I want. *haaza laysa maa ureed biD-DabT*
هذا ليس ما أريد بالضبط.

No, I don't like it. *laa, laa yuAHjibnee*
لا، لا يعجبني.

That's too expensive. *haaza ghaalee jiddan* هذا غال جدا.

I'd like to think about it. *ureed at-tafkeer feel amr*
أريد التفكير في الأمر.

I'll take it. *sa-aakhuduh.* سآخذه.

---

– SabaaH al-khayr. ureed sweet sheert.
– bit-ta'keed. ayy laun?
– laun burtuqaalee, lau samaHt. wa ureed qiyaas kabeer.
– tafaDDal. at-taman khamseen junayh.
– haaza laysa maa ureeduh biD-DabT. shukran.

## الدفع Paying

| | | |
|---|---|---|
| Where do I pay? | ayn adfAH | أين أدفع؟ |
| How much is that? | bikam haaza | بكم هذا؟ |
| Could you write it down, please? | hal mumkin taktubuh, lau samaHt | هل ممكن تكتبه، لو سمحت؟ |

Do you accept traveler's checks [cheques]?
hal taqbal sheekaat siyaaHeeya
هل تقبل شيكات سياحية؟

I'll pay ...
sa-adfAH ...
سأدفع ...

by cash
naqdan
نقدا

by credit card
bi-biTaaqat itimaan
ببطاقة ائتمان

I don't have any smaller change.
laysa mAHaya Sarf aSghar
ليس معي صرف أصغر.

Sorry, I don't have enough money.
aasif. laa yoojad mAHaya nuqood kifaaya
آسف، لا يوجد معي نقود كفاية.

---

| كيف ستدفع؟ | How are you paying? |
|---|---|
| هذه الحوالة المصرفية رفضت. | This transaction has not been approved/accepted. |
| هذا الكرت غير ساري المفعول. | This card is not valid. |
| هل معك إثبات آخر لشخصيتك؟ | May I have further identification? |
| هل عندك صرف أصغر؟ | Do you have any smaller change? |

---

Could I have a receipt, please?
mumkin aakhud al-waSl, lau samaHt
ممكن آخذ الوصل، لو سمحت؟

I think you've given me the wrong change.
AHtaqid an hunaak khaTa feel-baaqee
أعتقد أن هناك خطأ في الباقي.

---

| الرجاء الدفع هنا | please pay here |
|---|---|
| سارق المعروضات سيقدم إلى المحاكمة | shoplifters will be prosecuted |

## Complaints شكاوى

| | |
|---|---|
| This doesn't work. | haaza laa yAHmal<br>هذا لا يعمل. |
| Can you exchange this, please? | mumkin tughayyir haaza,<br>lau samaHt<br>ممكن تغير هذا، لو سمحت؟ |
| I'd like a refund. | ureed istirjaAH nuqoodee<br>أريد استرجاع نقودي. |
| Here's the receipt. | haaza huwa al-eeSaal<br>هذا هو الإيصال. |
| I don't have the receipt. | al-eeSaal laysa mAHaya<br>الإيصال ليس معي. |
| I'd like to see the manager. | ureed an uqaabil al-mudeer<br>أريد أن أقابل المدير. |

## Repairs/Cleaning تصليح/تنظيف

Many towns in Egypt have ironing shops (**maqwagee**). For a modest price you can get your clothes expertly ironed. Some combine this with a cleaning service which works out at a fraction of what you would pay in an international hotel.

| | |
|---|---|
| This is broken. Can you repair it? | haaza maksoor. hal mumkin taSleeHuh<br>هذا مكسور. هل ممكن تصليحه؟ |
| Do you have … for this? | hal AHndak … li-haaza؟ هل عندك … لهذا؟ |
| a battery | baTaareeya بطارية |
| replacement parts | qiTAH ghiyaar قطع غيار |
| There's something wrong with … | hunaak khalal fee … هناك خلل في … |
| Can you … this? | hal mumkin … haaza؟ هل ممكن … هذا؟ |
| clean | tunaZZif تنظف |
| press | takwee تكوي |
| patch | turaqqiAH ترقّع |
| alter | tuAHddil تعدّل |
| When will it be ready? | matta sa-takoon jaahza<br>متى ستكون جاهزة؟ |
| This isn't mine. | haazihi laysat milkee<br>هذه ليست ملكي. |
| There's … missing. | hunaak … mafqood. هناك … مفقود. |

TIME ➤ 220; DATES ➤ 218

# Bank/Currency exchange office

## البنك/مكتب الصرافة

Most of the larger banks in Saudi Arabia and throughout the Gulf
have ATMs [cash machines], but they are not common in the rest of
the region, although some are starting to appear in big cities and international hotels. However, you can usually find a bank or a currency exchange
office that will allow you to withdraw money on an international credit card.

Traveler's checks [cheques] from well-known companies are also usually
accepted. If you carry a combination of cash and cards/checks you will be
able to keep your options open.

*Note:* It is better to avoid any black market in currency exchange as it can be
risky, and the difference in rates is often not significant.

| | |
|---|---|
| Where's the nearest …? | *ayn aqrab …?* أين أقرب …؟ |
| bank | *bank* بنك |
| currency exchange office [bureau de change] | *maktab taHweel al-AHumlaat* مكتب تحويل العملات |

| | |
|---|---|
| جميع المعاملات | all transactions |
| مكتب الصرف | currency exchange office |
| مفتوح/مغلق | open/closed |
| صرافون | cashiers |

## Changing money تبديل عملات

| | |
|---|---|
| Can I exchange foreign currency here? | *hal mumkin ughayyir AHumlaat ajnabeeya huna* هل ممكن أغيّر عملات أجنبية هنا؟ |
| I'd like to change some dollars/ sterling into riyal. | *ureed taghyeer doolaaraat/ junayhaat istarleeneeya ilaa riyaal* أريد تغيير دولارات/جنيهات إسترلينية إلى ريال. |
| I want to cash some traveler's checks [cheques]. | *ureed Sarf sheekaat siyaaHaeeya* أريد صرف شيكات سياحية. |
| What's the exchange rate? | *maa huwa siAHr aS-Sarf* ما هو سعر الصرف؟ |
| How much commission do you charge? | *kam takhud ka-AHmoola* كم تأخذ كعمولة؟ |
| I've lost my traveler's checks. These are the numbers. | *faqadt sheekaatee as-siyaaHeeya. haazihi hiya arqaamhaa* فقدت شيكاتي السياحية. هذه هي أرقامها. |

# Security أمن

| | |
|---|---|
| ممكن أرى ...؟ | Could I see ...? |
| جواز سفرك | your passport |
| بعض الإثباتات الشخصية | some identification |
| كرت البنك | your bank card |
| ما هو عنوانك؟ | What's your address? |
| أين تقيم؟ | Where are you staying? |
| إملاء هذه الاستمارة، لو سمحت. | Fill in this form, please. |
| وقع هنا، لو سمحت. | Please sign here. |

## ATMs [Cash machines] آلة سحب نقود من الحساب

| | |
|---|---|
| Can I withdraw money on my credit card here? | *hal astaTeeAH saHb nuqood bi-biTaaqat i'timaan huna* هل أستطيع سحب نقود ببطاقة ائتمان هنا؟ |
| Where are the ATMs [cash machines]? | *ayn aalaat saHb an-nuqood* أين آلات سحب النقود؟ |
| Can I use my ... card in the cash machine? | *hal astaTeeAH istiAHmaal biTaaqat ... fee aalat saHb an-nuqood haazihi* هل أستطيع استعمال بطاقة ... في آلة سحب النقود هذه؟ |
| The cash machine has eaten my card. | *aalat saHb an-nuqood akalat baTaaqtee* آلة سحب النقود أكلت بطاقتي. |

| | |
|---|---|
| automated teller [cash machine] | آلة سحب النقود |

| Currency | Countries using currency |
|---|---|
| **dinar** | Algeria, Bahrain, Iraq, Jordan, Kuwait, Libya, Tunisia |
| **pound (junayh)** | Egypt, Sudan |
| **pound (leera)** | Lebanon, Syria |
| **dirham** | Morocco, United Arab Emirates |
| **riyal** | Oman, Qatar, Saudi Arabia, Yemen |

*(Note: although the currency in different countries may have the same name, the value will vary enormously.)*

# الصيدلية Pharmacy

Pharmacies increasingly offer a wide range of imported toiletries and medicines, although the local alternatives will still be much cheaper.

You may find you can obtain drugs over the counter that would be prescription only back home, e.g., antibiotics or strong sedatives. The pharmacist will be able to advise you and even sometimes administer. If in doubt, get a second opinion before deciding what to take.

| | |
|---|---|
| Where's the nearest (all-night) pharmacy? | *ayn aqrab Saydaleeya munaawaba (Tawaal al-layl)*<br>أين أقرب صيدلية مناوبة (طوال الليل)؟ |
| What time does the pharmacy open/close? | *ayy SaAHa taftaH/tughliq aS-Saydaleeya*<br>أي ساعة تفتح/تغلق الصيدلية؟ |
| Can you make up this prescription for me? | *hal yumkinak tarkeeb haazihil waSfa aT-Tibbeeya lee*<br>هل يمكنك تركيب هذه الوصفة الطبية لي؟ |
| Shall I wait? | *hal antaZir*؟ هل أنتظر؟ |
| I'll come back for it. | *sa-AHood li-akhd-haa*<br>سأعود لأخذها. |

## Dosage instructions تعليمات الجرعة

| | |
|---|---|
| How much should I take? | *kam yajib an aakhud*<br>كم يجب أن آخذ؟ |
| How often should I take it? | *kam marra yajib an aakhud-haa*<br>كم مرة يجب أن آخذها؟ |

| | |
|---|---|
| خذ ... أقراص/... ملاعق صغيرة | Take ... tablets/... teaspoons |
| قبل/بعد الوجبات | before/after meals |
| مع ماء | with water |
| كاملة | whole |
| في الصباح/في المساء | in the morning/at night |
| لمدة ... أيام | for ... days |

## Asking advice طلب نصيحة

| What would you recommend for ...? | *bi-maazaa tinSaHnaa min ajl*<br>بماذا تنصحنا من أجل ... |
| a cold/a cough | *bard/suAHaal* برد/سعال |
| diarrhea | *ishaal* إسهال |
| hay fever | *Huma al-qash* حمى القش |
| insect bites | *ladgh al-Hasharaat* لدغ الحشرات |
| a sore throat | *alam feel Hanjara* ألم في الحنجرة |
| sunburn | *Harqat ash-shams* حرقة الشمس |
| motion [travel] sickness | *dawwaar as-safar* دوار السفر |
| an upset stomach | *alam feel baTn* ألم في البطن |
| Can I get it without a prescription? | *mumkin ashtareehaa bidoon waSfa Tibbeeya?* ممكن أشتريها بدون وصفة طبية؟ |
| Is it suitable for children? | *hal huwa munaasib lil-aTfaal*<br>هل هو مناسب للأطفال؟ |

## Over-the-counter treatment
## علاج دون إرشادات الطبيب

| Can I have ...? | *mumkin aakhud* ممكن آخذ...؟ |
| antihistamine | *muDaad lil-Hassaaseeya* مضاد للحساسية |
| antiseptic cream | *kreem muTTahir* كريم مطهر |
| aspirin | *asbareen* أسبرين |
| condoms | *ghishaa Tibbee* غشاء طبي |
| cotton [cotton wool] | *qutn Tibbee* قطن طبي |
| eye drops | *nuqaT li-tanZeef al-AHuyoon*<br>نقط لتنظيف العيون |
| gauze [bandages] | *Damaad* ضماد |
| insect repellent | *Taarid lil-Hasharaat* طارد للحشرات |
| pain killers | *musakkin al-alam* مسكن الألم |
| vitamin tablets | *aqraaS feetaameen* أقراص فيتامين |

## مستحضرات تجميل Toiletries

| | | |
|---|---|---|
| | I'd like … | *ureed* … أريد |
| | after shave | *AHiTr bAHd al-Hilaaqa*<br>عطر بعد الحلاقة |
| | after-sun lotion | *loosiyoon li-bAHd ash-shams*<br>لوسيون لبعد الشمس |
| deodorant | | *muzeel li-raa'iHat al-AHraq*<br>مزيل لرائحة العرق |
| razor blades | | *shafrat al-Hilaaqa* شفرة الحلاقة |
| sanitary napkins [towels] | | *fuwaT SiHHeeya (lis-sayyidaat)*<br>فوط صحية (للسيدات) |
| soap | | *Saaboon* صابون |
| suntan cream | | *kreem ash-shams* كريم الشمس |
| factor … | | *darajat quwa* … درجة قوة |
| tampons | | *Samaamaat quTneeya lis-sayyiddaat*<br>صمامات قطنية للسيدات |
| tissues | | *manaadeel waraq* مناديل ورق |
| toilet paper | | *waraq twaaleet* ورق تواليت |
| toothpaste | | *mAHjoon asnaan* معجون أسنان |

## Haircare العناية بالشعر

| | |
|---|---|
| brush/comb | *fursha/mishT* فرشاة/مشط |
| conditioner | *mukayyif ash-shAHr* مكيّف الشعر |
| hair mousse/gel | *muthabbit ash-shAHr/jal* مثبت الشعر/جل |
| hair spray | *isbraay lish-shAHr* اسبراي للشعر |
| shampoo | *shamboo* شامبو |

## For the baby للرضيع

| | |
|---|---|
| baby food | *TAHaam al-aTfaal* طعام الأطفال |
| baby wipes | *massaaHaat al-aTfaal* مساحات الأطفال |
| diapers [nappies] | *HafaaDaat* حفاضات |
| sterilizing solution | *saa'il maAHqqim* سائل معقم |

# Clothing ملابس

The markets are a good place to buy traditional items such as robes and headscarfs. Many countries also have a good range of locallymade western-style clothes. Alternatively, you could buy the material and have your clothes made-to-measure or copied from another item by one of the many tailors in the region.

## General بشكل عام

| | | |
|---|---|---|
| I'd like … | *ureed* | أريد …|
| Do you have any …? | *hal AHndak ayy* | هل عندك أي …؟ |

| | |
|---|---|
| ملابس نسائية | ladieswear |
| ملابس رجالية | menswear |
| ملابس للأطفال | childrenswear |

## Color لون

| | | |
|---|---|---|
| I'm looking for something in … | *abHas AHn shay bil-laun al* | أبحث عن شيء باللون الـ… |
| beige | *bayj* | بيج |
| black/white | *aswad/abyaD* | أسود/أبيض |
| blue/green | *azraq/akhDar* | أزرق/أخضر |
| brown | *bunnee* | بني |
| gray | *ramaadee* | رمادي |
| orange | *burtuqaalee* | برتقالي |
| purple | *banafsijee* | بنفسجي |
| red/pink | *aHmar/wardee* | أحمر/وردي |
| yellow | *aSfar* | أصفر |
| light (blue) | *(azraq) faatiH* | (أزرق) فاتح |
| dark (blue) | *(azraq) ghaamiq* | (أزرق) غامق |
| I want a darker/lighter shade. | *ureed nafs al-laun laakin bi-daraja aghmaq/afatH* | أريد نفس اللون لكن بدرجة أغمق/أفتح. |
| Do you have the same in …? | *AHndak nafs ash-shay bil-laun al …* | عندك نفس الشيء باللون الـ…؟ |

143

# Clothes and accessories ملابس و كماليات

| | | |
|---|---|---|
| belt | *Hizaam* | حزام |
| bikini | *bikeenee* | بكيني |
| blouse | *bilooza* | بلوزة |
| bra | *Hammaalat Sidr* | حمالة صدر |
| briefs | *sirwaal taHtaanee* | سروال تحتاني |
| cap | *kaab* | كاب |
| coat | *miAHTaf* | معطف |
| dress | *fustaan* | فستان |
| hat | *qubaAHa* | قبعة |
| jacket | *jaakeet* | جاكيت |
| jeans | *jeenz* | جينز |
| pants (U.S.) | *banTaloon* | بنطلون |
| panty hose [tights] | *shuraab Hareemee Taweel* | شراب حريمي طويل |
| raincoat | *miAHTaf lil-maTar* | معطف للمطر |
| scarf | *lifaaH* | لفاح |
| shirt | *qameeS* | قميص |
| shorts | *shoort* | شورت |
| skirt | *tannoora* | تنورة |
| socks | *shuraab* | شراب |
| stockings | *jawaarib Hareemee* | جوارب حريمي |
| suit | *badla* | بدلة |
| sweater | *kanza* | كنزة |
| sweatshirt | *sweet sheert* | سويت شيرت |
| swimming trunks | *maayoo rijaalee* | مايوه رجالي |
| swimsuit | *maayoo nisaa'ee* | مايوه نسائي |
| T-shirt | *tee-sheert* | تي-شيرت |
| tie | *krafatta* | كرفتة |
| trousers | *banTaloon* | بنطلون |
| underpants | *libaas daakhilee* | لباس داخلي |
| with long/short sleeves | *bi-akmaam Taweela/qaSeera* | بأكمام طويلة/قصيرة |
| with a V-/round neck | *bi-yaaqa sabAHa/mustadeera* | بياقة سبعة/مستديرة |

144

## Shoes أحذية

| | |
|---|---|
| boots | *boot* بوت |
| flip-flops | *shibshib Hammaam* شبشب حمام |
| running shoes [trainers] | *Hizaa riyaaDa* حذاء رياضة |
| sandals | *Sandal* صندل |
| shoes | *Hizaa* حذاء |
| slippers | *shibshib* شبشب |

## Walking/Hiking gear أمتعة السير/التنزه مشيا

| | |
|---|---|
| knapsack | *Haqeebat aZ-Zahr* حقيبة الظهر |
| hiking boots | *boot lil-mashy* بوت للمشي |
| waterproof jacket | *jaakeet waaqeeya min al-maa'* جاكيت واقية من الماء |

## Fabric قماش

| | |
|---|---|
| I want something in … | *ureed shay min* أريد شيئا من … |
| cotton | *al-quTn* القطن |
| denim | *al-jeenz* الجينز |
| leather | *al-jild* الجلد |
| linen | *al-kittaan* الكتان |
| wool | *aS-Soof* الصوف |
| Is this …? | *hal haaza* هل هذا … ؟ |
| pure cotton | *quTn khaaliS* قطن خالص |
| synthetic | *iSTinaAHee* اصطناعي |
| Is it hand/machine washable? | *hal huwa qaabil lil-ghaseel al-yadawee/bil-ghasaala* هل هو قابل للغسيل اليدوي/بالغسالة؟ |

| | |
|---|---|
| dry clean only | للتنظيف الجاف فقط |
| handwash only | غسيل يدوي فقط |
| do not iron | لا يكوى |

## هل تلائمك؟ Does it fit?

| | |
|---|---|
| Can I try this on? | *hal astaTeeAH an ujarrib haaza*<br>هل أستطيع أن أجرّب هذا؟ |
| Where's the fitting room? | *ayn ghurfat al-qiyaas*<br>أين غرفة القياس؟ |
| It fits well. I'll take it. | *innuh yulaa'imnee jiddan. sa-aakhuduh*<br>إنه يلائمني جدا. سآخذه. |
| It doesn't fit. | *laa yulaa'imnee*<br>لا يلائمني. |
| It's too … | *innuh … kateer*<br>إنه … كثيرا. |
| short/long | *qaSeer/Taweel*<br>قصير/طويل |
| tight/loose | *Dayyiq/waasiAH*<br>ضيق/واسع |
| Do you have this in size …? | *AHndak hazaa qiyaas …*<br>عندك هذا قياس …؟ |
| What size is this? | *maa huwa qiyaas haaza*<br>ما هو قياس هذا؟ |
| Could you measure me, please? | *mumkin takhud qiyaasee, lau samaHt*<br>ممكن تأخذ قياسي، لو سمحت؟ |

## قياس Size

The Middle East generally uses continental sizes and metric measures.

| | Dresses/Suits | | | | | | Women's shoes | | | |
|---|---|---|---|---|---|---|---|---|---|---|
| American | 8 | 10 | 12 | 14 | 16 | 18 | 6 | 7 | 8 | 9 |
| British | 10 | 12 | 14 | 16 | 18 | 20 | $4^{1/2}$ | $5^{1/2}$ | $6^{1/2}$ | $7^{1/2}$ |
| Continental | 36 | 38 | 40 | 42 | 44 | 46 | 37 | 38 | 40 | 41 |

| | Shirts | | | | Men's shoes | | | | | | | |
|---|---|---|---|---|---|---|---|---|---|---|---|---|
| American )<br>British ) | 15 | 16 | 17 | 18 | 5 | 6 | 7 | 8 | $8^{1/2}$ 9 | $9^{1/2}$ | 10 | 11 |
| Continental | 38 | 41 | 43 | 45 | 38 | 39 | 41 | 42 | 43 | 43 | 44 | 44 45 |

| | |
|---|---|
| كبير جدا extra large (XL) | |
| كبير large (L) | |
| وسط medium (M) | |
| صغير small (S) | |

| | |
|---|---|
| 1 centimeter (cm.) = 0.39 in. | 1 inch = 2.54 cm. |
| 1 meter (m.) = 39.37 in. | 1 foot = 30.5 cm. |
| 10 meters = 32.81 ft. | 1 yard = 0.91 m. |

# Health and beauty الصحة و الجمال

| | |
|---|---|
| I'd like a … | *ureed …* أريد … |
| facial | *tanZeef lil-wajh* تنظيف للوجه |
| manicure | *tajmeel al-aZaafir* تجميل الأظافر |
| massage | *tadleek* تدليك |
| waxing | *izaalat ash-shAHr bish-shamAH* إزالة الشعر بالشمع |

## Hairdresser/Hairstylist (الحلاق) المزين

It is usual to tip approximately 10% if you are happy with the service.

| | |
|---|---|
| I'd like to make an appointment for … | *ureed AHmal mawAHid li* أريد عمل موعد لـ … |
| Can you make it a bit earlier/later? | *mumkin tAHmil al-mauAHid abkar/mutakhkhar?* ممكن تعمل الموعد أبكر/متأخر؟ |
| I'd like a … | *ureed* …أريد |
| cut and blow-dry | *qaSS wa tansheef* قص وتنشيف |
| shampoo and set | *shamboo wa taSfeef* شامبو وتصفيف |
| trim | *taqleem* تقليم |
| I'd like my hair … | *ureed shAHree* … أريد شعري |
| highlighted | *mumayyash* مميش |
| permed | *mumawwaj* موج |
| Don't cut it too short. | *laa taqaSSuh aktar mimaa yanbaghee* لا تقصه أكثر مما ينبغي. |
| A little more off the … | *aktar qaleel min* … أكثر قليلا من |
| back/front | *al-khalf/al-amaam* الخلف/الأمام |
| neck/sides | *ar-raqaba/al-jawaanib* الرقبة/الجوانب |
| top | *al-qimma* القمة |
| That's fine, thanks. | *haaza mumtaaz, shukran* هذا ممتاز، شكرا! |

# Household articles أدوات منزلية

| | | |
|---|---|---|
| I'd like a/an ... | ureed | أريد ... |
| adapter | muHawwil | محول |
| alumin(i)um foil | raqaa'iq aluminyoom | رقائق ألمنيوم |
| bottle-opener | fattaaHat zujaajaat | فتاحة زجاجات |
| can [tin] opener | fattaaHat muAHlabaat | فتاحة معلبات |
| clothes pins [pegs] | milqaT malaabis | ملقط ملابس |
| corkscrew | fattaaHat nabeet | فتاحة نبيذ |
| light bulb | lamba | لمبة |
| matches | kibreet | كبريت |
| paper napkins | manaadeel waraq | مناديل ورق |
| plug | saddaada | سدادة |
| scissors | miqaSS | مقص |
| screwdriver | mifakk | مفك |

## Cleaning items مواد تنظيف

| | | |
|---|---|---|
| bleach | bleetsh | بليتش |
| dish cloth | minshafat SuHoon | منشفة صحون |
| dishwashing [washing-up] liquid | saa'il li-ghaseel aS-SuHoon | سائل لغسيل الصحون |
| garbage [refuse] bags | akyaas qimmaama | أكياس قمامة |
| detergent [washing powder] | mas-Hooq ghaseel al-malaabis | مسحوق غسيل الملابس |
| sponge | isfinj | إسفنج |

## Crockery/Cutlery الأواني/ملاعق، سكاكين، شوك

| | | |
|---|---|---|
| cups/glasses | fanaajeen/akwaab | فناجين/أكواب |
| knives/forks | sakaakeen/shuwak | سكاكين/شوك |
| spoons | malaAHiq | ملاعق |
| mugs | akwaaz | أكواز |
| plates | SuHoon | صحون |
| bowls | sulTaaneeyaat | سلطانيات |

# Jeweler جواهرجي

Could I see ...?     *mumkin araa*
ممكن أرى ...؟

| | |
|---|---|
| this/that | *haaza/zaalik.* هذا/ذلك. |
| It's in the window/ display cabinet. | *innaha feesh-shibbaak/ fee-khazaanat al-AHrD* إنها في شباك/خزانة العرض. |
| alarm clock | *munabbih* منبه |
| battery | *baTaareeya* بطارية |
| bracelet | *sawaar* سوار |
| brooch | *broosh* بروش |
| chain | *silsila* سلسلة |
| clock | *saAHat Haa'iT* ساعة حائط |
| earrings | *Halaq* حلق |
| necklace | *AHuqd* عقد |
| ring | *khaatim* خاتم |
| watch | *saAHa* ساعة |

## Materials مواد

| | |
|---|---|
| Is this real silver/real gold? | *hal haazihi faDDa Haqeeqeeya/ dahab Haqeeqee* هل هذه فضة حقيقية/ذهب حقيقي؟ |
| Is there a certificate for it? | *hal mAHahu shahaada?* هل معه شهادة؟ |
| Do you have anything in ...? | *hal AHndak ayy shay min* هل عندك أي شيء من ...؟ |
| copper | *an-naHHaas* النحاس |
| crystal | *al-baloor* البلور |
| diamond | *al-maas* الماس |
| gold | *ad-dahab* الذهب |
| gold plate | *qishrat dahab* قشرة ذهب |
| pearl | *al-lu'lu'* اللؤلؤ |
| pewter | *al-qaSdeer* القصدير |
| platinum | *al-balaateen* البلاتين |
| silver | *al-faDDa* الفضة |
| silver plate | *qishrat faDDa* قشرة فضة |
| wood | *al-khashab* الخشب |

## Newsstand [Newsagent]/
## Tobacconist. بائع الجرائد/الدخان

Larger newsstands usually carry English-language newspapers and magazines, although they may be expensive and a few days old. You may also be able to find local English-language papers which will give you news and details about events.

| | | |
|---|---|---|
| Do you sell English-language books/newspapers? | *hal tabeeAH kutub/jaraa'id bi-lugha al-injileezeeya* | هل تبيع كتب/جرائد باللغة الإنجليزية؟ |
| I'd like a/an/some ... | *ureed ...* | أريد ... |
| book | *kitaab* | كتاب |
| candy [sweets] | *sakaakir* | سكاكر |
| chewing gum | *libaan* | لبان |
| chocolate bar | *lauH shookalaata* | لوح شوكلاتة |
| (packet of) cigarettes | *(AHulbat) sajaa'ir* | (علبة) سجائر |
| cigars | *siijaar* | سيجار |
| dictionary | *qaamoos* | قاموس |
| Arabic–English | *AHrabee-injileezee* | عربي–إنجليزي |
| envelopes | *aZruf* | أظرف |
| guidebook of ... | *daleel siyaaHee AHn ...* | دليل سياحي عن ... |
| lighter | *walaAHa* | ولاعة |
| magazine | *majalla* | مجلة |
| map | *khareeTa* | خريطة |
| map of the town | *khareeTat al-madeena* | خريطة المدينة |
| road map of ... | *khareeTat ash-shawaariAH fee ...* | خريطة الشوارع في ... |
| matches | *kibreet* | كبريت |
| newspaper | *jareeda* | جريدة |
| American/English | *amreekeeya/injileezeeya* | أمريكية/إنجليزية |
| paper | *waraq* | ورق |
| pen | *qalam* | قلم |
| stamps | *TawaabiAH* | طوابع |
| tobacco | *tabgh* | تبغ |

# Photography تصوير

I'm looking for a ... camera.
abHas AHn kaameeraa
أبحث عن كاميرا ...

automatic
ootoomaateek أوتوماتيك

compact
muSaghghara مصغرة

disposable
tustAHmal marra waaHda
تستعمل مرة واحدة

I'd like a/an ...
ureed ... أريد ...

battery
baTaareeya بطارية

camera case
AHulba lil-kaameeraa علبة للكاميرا

flash (electronic)
flaash (iliktroonee) (إلكتروني) فلاش

filter
filtir فلتر

lens
AHdasa عدسة

lens cap
ghiTaa' lil-AHdasa غطاء للعدسة

## Film/Processing فيلم/تحميض

I'd like a ... film for this camera.
ureed feelm ... li-haazihil kaameeraa
أريد فيلم ... لهذه الكاميرا.

black and white
aswad wa abyaD أسود وأبيض

color
alwaan ألوان

24/36 exposures
arbAHa wa AHishreen/sitta wa
talaateen Soora صورة ٣٦/٢٤

I'd like this film developed,
please.
ureed taHmeeD hazaal feelm, lau samaHt
أريد تحميض هذا الفيلم، لو سمحت.

Would you enlarge this, please?
mumkin takbeer haazihi, lau samaHt
ممكن تكبير هذه، لو سمحت؟

How much do ... exposures
cost?
kam hiya ujrat taHmeeD ... Soora
كم هي أجرة تحميض ... صورة؟

When will the photos be ready?
matta sa-takoon aS-Suwar jaahza
متى ستكون الصور جاهزة؟

I'd like to collect my photos.
ureed an aakhud Suwaree
أريد أن آخذ صوري.

Here's the receipt.
haazaa huwa al-waSl
هذا هو الوصل.

# Police شرطة

You will need to report crimes, thefts or accidents to the police. Emergency numbers vary from country to country, but if you need to make an emergency call you can ask someone for the **an-najda** ("help") telephone number.

Where's the nearest police
station?

*ayn aqrab markaz shurTa*
أين أقرب مركز شرطة؟

Does anyone here speak
English?

*hunaak aHad yatkallam al-injileezeeya
huna*
هناك أحد يتكلم الإنجليزية هنا؟

I want to report a(n) …

*ureed an uballigh AHn*
أريد أن أبلغ عن...

accident/attack

*Haadis/iAHtidaa*
حادث/اعتداء

mugging/rape

*salb/ightiSaab*
سلب/اغتصاب

My child is missing.

*Tiflee mafqood.*
طفلي مفقود.

Here's his photo/her photo.

*haazihi Sooratuh/Soorathaa*
هذه صورته/صورتها.

Someone's following me.

*shakhS ma yatbAHnee.*
شخص ما يتبعني.

I need an English-speaking
lawyer.

*ureed muHamee yatkallam
al-injileezeeya.*
أريد محام يتكلم الإنجليزية.

I need to make a phone call.

*aHtaaj an atkallam AHlaal tilifoon*
أحتاج أن أتكلم على التلفون.

I need to contact the …
Consulate.

*aHtaaj ilaal ittiSaal bil-qunSuleeya …*
أحتاج إلى الاتصال بالقنصلية ... ...

American/British

*al-amreekeeya/al-bireeTaaneeya*
الأمريكية/البريطانية

---

| | |
|---|---|
| هل يمكنك وصفه/وصفها؟ | Can you describe him/her? |
| ذكر/أنثى | male/female |
| شعر أشقر/بني غامق/أحمر | blond/brunette/red-headed |
| شيب (أبيض) | gray-haired |
| بشعر طويل/قصير/بدون شعر (أصلع) | long/short hair/balding |
| الطول تقريبا ... | approximate height … |
| السن تقريبا ... | aged approximately … |
| كان/كانت يرتدي/ترتدي ... | He/She was wearing … |

# المفقودات/السرقة Lost property/Theft

| | |
|---|---|
| I want to report a theft/break-in. | ureed at-tableegh AHn saraqa/iqtiHaam<br>أريد التبليغ عن سرقة/اقتحام. |
| My car has been broken into. | HaSal iqtiHaam li-sayyaartee<br>حصل اقتحام لسيارتي. |
| I've been robbed/mugged. | laqad suriqt/sulibt. لقد سرقت/سلبت. |
| I've lost a ... | faqadt ... فقدت |
| A/an ... has been stolen from me. | laqad suriqat minnee<br>لقد سرقت مني ... |
| bicycle | darraaja دراجة |
| camera | kaameeraa كاميرا |
| (rental) car | sayyaara (mu'ajjara) سيارة (مؤجرة) |
| credit cards | baTaaqaat aD-Damaan<br>بطاقات الضمان |
| handbag | Haqeebat yad حقيبة يد |
| money | naqood نقود |
| passport | jawaaz as-safar جواز السفر |
| purse [wallet] | maHfaZa محفظة |
| ticket | tazkara تذكرة |
| watch | saAHa ساعة |
| What shall I do? | mazaa afAHl ماذا أفعل |
| I need a police report for my insurance claim. | ureed shihaadat ash-shurTa li-uqaddimhaa li-sharikat at-ta'meen<br>أريد شهادة الشرطة لأقدمها لشركة التأمين. |

| | |
|---|---|
| ما الذي ضاع؟ | What's missing? |
| ما الذي أُخذ؟ | What's been taken? |
| متى سرقت؟ | When was it stolen? |
| متى حصل الحادث؟ | When did it happen? |
| أين تقيم؟ | Where are you staying? |
| من أين أخذت؟ | Where was it taken from? |
| أين كنت وقتها؟ | Where were you at the time? |
| سنحضر لك مترجم. | We're getting an interpreter for you. |
| سننظر في الأمر. | We'll look into the matter. |
| الرجاء تعبئة هذه الاستمارة. | Please fill out this form. |

153

# Post office مكتب البريد

Mailboxes vary in color and shape from country to country. However, it is best to mail material at a post office. Sometimes hotels have their own mailboxes for postcards and letters, and these are also usually reliable.

## General queries أسئلة عامة

| | |
|---|---|
| Where is the nearest (main) post office? | *ayn aqrab maktab bareed (ra'eesee)* <br> أين أقرب مكتب بريد (رئيسي)؟ |
| What time does the post office open/close? | *matta yaftaH/yughliq maktab al-bareed* <br> متى يفتح/يغلق مكتب البريد ؟ |
| Does it close for lunch? | *hal yughliq waqt al-ghadaa* <br> هل يغلق وقت الغداء؟ |
| Where's the mailbox [postbox]? | *ayn Sundooq al-bareed* <br> أين صندوق البريد؟ |
| Is there any mail for me? | *hal hunaak rasaa'il lee* <br> هل هناك رسائل لي؟ |

## Buying stamps شراء طوابع

| | |
|---|---|
| A stamp for this postcard, please. | *TaabiAH li-haazal kaart, lau samaHt* <br> طابع لهذا الكارت، لو سمحت. |
| What's the postage for a letter to … | *maa hiya ujrat al-bareed li-risaala ilaa* <br> ما هي أجرة البريد لرسالة إلى …؟ |
| Is there a stamp machine here? | *hal hunaak aalat TawaabiAH huna* <br> هل هناك آلة طوابع هنا؟ |

---

| | |
|---|---|
| الطرود | parcels |
| موعد جمع البريد … | next collection … |
| صندوق البريد | general delivery [poste restante] |
| الطوابع | stamps |

---

– *ureed irsall haazihil kuroot ilaa amreekaa.*
– *kam kart?*
– *tisAHa, lau samaHt.*
– *al-majmooAH arbAHa dinaar.*

## Sending parcels إرسال طرود بريدية

| | |
|---|---|
| I want to send this package by ... | *ureed irsaal haazaT Tard bi* أريد إرسال هذا الطرد بـ ... |
| airmail | *al-bareed al-jauee* البريد الجوي |
| special delivery [express] | *al-bareed as-sareeAH* البريد السريع |
| registered mail | *bareed musajjal* بريد مسجل |
| It contains ... | *yaHtawee AHlaa ...* يحتوي على ... |

| | |
|---|---|
| إملاء شهادة الجمارك، لو سمحت. | Please fill in the customs declaration. |
| ما هي القيمة؟ | What's the value? |
| ماذا في الداخل؟ | What's inside? |

## الاتصالات السلكية و اللاسلكية Telecommunications

The major towns of the Arab world are rapidly becoming part of the international telephone network (▶ 127). In addition, hotels and office service bureaus in major cities often offer photocopying, word-processing and fax services, sometimes with translation facilities.

E-mail and Internet access in the Middle East is sporadic and ISPs (Internet Service Providers) may be limited to one or two approved companies.

| | |
|---|---|
| Do you have a photocopier? | *hal AHndak aalat naskh* هل عندك آلة نسخ؟ |
| I'd like to send a message ... | *ureed an abAHs risaala* أريد أن أبعث رسالة ... |
| by e-mail/fax | *bi-waasiTat al-eemayl/al-faaks* بواسطة الإي–ميل/الفاكس |
| What's your e-mail address? | *maa huwa AHunwaanak feel eemayl?* ما هو عنوانك في الإي–ميل؟ |
| Can I access the Internet here? | *hal mumkin istiAHmaal al-intarnat huna* هل ممكن استعمال الإنترنت هنا؟ |
| What are the charges per hour? | *maa huwal Hisaab fees saAHa* ما هو الحساب في الساعة؟ |
| How do I log on? | *kayf abda'* كيف أبدأ؟ |

# تذكارات Souvenirs

Here are some suggestions for souvenirs to take home. Many of these items can be found at the local markets (**sooq**), which offer a huge range of interesting articles. You will need to bargain, but try to find out price ranges before you go so you have some idea of what you should be paying.

| | | |
|---|---|---|
| How much is this? | *bikam haaza* | بكم هذا؟ |
| That's too much. I'll pay … | *haaza kateer. sa-adfAH* … | هذا كثير. سأدفع … |
| That's my last offer. | *haaza aakhir kalaam.* | هذا آخر كلام. |
| | | |
| long Egyptian robe | *gallaabeya* | جلابية |
| carpets | *sijaad* | سجاد |
| pottery | *awaanee fukhaareeya* | أواني فخارية |
| water pipe | *sheesha (naarjeela)* | شيشة (نارجيلة) |
| jewelry | *mujauharaat* | مجوهرات |
| backgammon board | *Taawlat zahr* | طاولة زهر |
| woodwork | *maSnooAHaat khashabeeya* | مصنوعات خشبية |
| leather goods | *maSnooAHaat jildeeya* | مصنوعات جلدية |
| sandals | *Sandal* | صندل |
| electrical goods | *baDaa'iAH kahrabaa'eeya* | بضائع كهربائية |

## هدايا Gifts

| | | |
|---|---|---|
| box of chocolates | *AHulbat shookaalaata* | علبة شوكولاتة |
| calendar | *raznaama* | رزنامة |
| key ring | *silsilat mafaateeH* | سلسلة مفاتيح |
| postcard | *kart boostaal* | كرت بوستال |
| tea towel | *fooTat maTbakh* | فوطة مطبخ |
| T-shirt | *tee-sheert* | تي—شيرت |

## Music موسيقى

| | |
|---|---|
| I'd like a... | *ureed* ... أريد |
| cassette | *shareeT kaaseet*<br>شريط كاسيت |
| compact disc | *usTuwaana koombaakt*<br>أسطوانة كومباكت |
| record | *usTuwaana*<br>أسطوانة |
| videocassette | *shareeT feedyoo* شريط فيديو |
| Who are the popular local singers/bands? | *man hum ash-har al-mughaneeyeen/<br>al-firaq al-maHalleeya*<br>من هم أشهر المغنين/الفرق المحلية؟ |

## Toys and games لعب وألعاب

| | |
|---|---|
| I'd like a toy/game ... | *ureed lAHba* ... أريد لعبة |
| for a boy | *li-walad* لولد |
| for a 5-year-old girl | *li-bint AHumrahaa khamas sanawaat*<br>لبنت عمرها خمس سنوات |
| ball | *kura* كرة |
| pail and shovel<br>[bucket and spade] | *dilw wa jaaroof* دلو وجاروف |
| chess set | *shaTranj* شطرنج |
| doll | *dumya* دمية |
| electronic game | *lAHba ileektrooneeya* لعبة إليكترونية |
| teddy bear | *dumya bi-shakl dubb* دمية بشكل دب |

## Antiques أنتيكات

| | |
|---|---|
| How old is this? | *kam AHumr haaza* كم عمر هذا؟ |
| Do you have anything from the ... era? | *AHndak ayy shay min AHhd*<br>عندك أي شيء من عهد ...؟ |
| Can you send it to me? | *hal tastaTeeAH irsaaluh lee*<br>هل تستطيع إرساله لي؟ |
| Will I have problems with customs? | *hal sa-takoon AHndee mushkila<br>mAHal jamaarik*<br>هل ستكون عندي مشكلة مع الجمارك؟ |
| Is there a certificate of authenticity? | *hal hunaak shihaada annahaa aSleeya*<br>هل هناك شهادة أنها أصلية؟ |

# Supermarket/Minimart
## سوبرماركت/بقالة

In Saudi Arabia and throughout the Gulf you will find huge hypermarkets, some local and some branches of international chains such as **Safeway** and **Spinnies**. In other parts of the region there are supermarkets, but generally on a smaller scale.

Most supermarkets offer a mix of imported/Western-style goods and locally produced goods.

## At the supermarket. في السوبرماركت.

| | |
|---|---|
| Excuse me. Where can I find a ...? | *lau samaHt. ayn ajid*<br>لو سمحت. أين أجد ...؟ |
| Do I pay for this here or at the checkout? | *hal adfAH huna am AHndal mughaadra*<br>هل أدفع هنا أم عند المغادرة؟ |
| Where are the carts [trolleys]/baskets? | *ayn al-AHrabaat/as-silaal*<br>أين العربات/السلال؟ |
| Is there a pharmacy here? | *hal hunaak Saydaleeya huna*<br>هل هناك صيدلية هنا؟ |

| | |
|---|---|
| نقدا فقط | cash only |
| مواد تنظيف | cleaning products |
| ألبان | dairy products |
| سمك طازج | fresh fish |
| لحم طازج | fresh meat |
| خضروات طازج | fresh produce |
| طعام مجمد | frozen foods |
| بضائع منزلية | household goods |
| دواجن | poultry |
| فواكه/خضار | fruit/vegetables |
| خبز وكيك | bread and cakes |

## Weights and measures
- **1 kilogram** or **kilo (kg.)** = **1000 grams (g.)**; **100 g.** = 3.5 oz.; **1 kg.** = 2.2 lb 1 oz. = **28.35 g.**; 1 lb. = **453.60 g.**
- **1 liter (l.)** = 0.88 imp. quart or 1.06 U.S. quart; 1 imp. quart = **1.14 l.**; 1 U.S. quart = **0.951 l.**; 1 imp. gallon = **4.55 l.**; 1 U.S. gallon = **3.8 l.**

# Food hygiene نظافة الطعام

| | |
|---|---|
| يؤكل خلال ... أيام من فتحه | eat within ... days of opening |
| يحفظ بالثلاجة | keep refrigerated |
| يمكن طبخه في الميكرويف | microwavable |
| سخنه قبل الأكل | reheat before eating |
| مناسب للنباتيين | suitable for vegetarians |
| يستخدم قبل ... | use by ... |

## At the minimart عند محل البقالة

| | |
|---|---|
| I'd like some of that/those. | ureed bAHD min haaza/haazihi أريد بعضا من هذا/هذه. |
| This one/those. | haaza/haazihi هذا/هذه. |
| To the left/right. | ilaal yasaar/yameen. إلى اليسار/اليمين. |
| Over there/Here. | hunaak/huna. هناك/هنا. |
| Which one(s)? | ayy minhaa أي منها؟ |
| That's all thanks. | hazaa kulluh, shukran. هذا كله، شكرا. |
| I'd like a ... | ureed ... أريد ... |
| kilo of apples | keeloo tufaaH كيلو تفاح |
| half-kilo of tomatoes | niSf keeloo TamaaTim نصف كيلو طماطم |
| 100 grams of cheese | meet graam jibna ١٠٠ غرام جبنة |
| liter of milk | leetr Haleeb ليتر حليب |
| half-dozen eggs | nuSf dastat bayD نصف دستة بيض |
| piece of cake | qiTAHt kayk قطعة كيك |
| carton of juice | kartoonat AHSeer كرتونة عصير |
| carton of milk | kartoonat Haleeb كرتونة حليب |
| jar of jam | barTumaan murabba برطمان مربى |
| bag of potato chips [crisps] | baakeet shibs (baTaaTis maqleeya) باكيت شبس (بطاطس مقلية) |
| can of cola | AHulbat koolaa علبة كولا |

## Provisions/Picnic مئونة/نزهة

| | | |
|---|---|---|
| butter | zibda | زبدة |
| cheese | jibna | جبنة |
| cookies [biscuits] | baskaweet | بسكويت |
| eggs | bayD | بيض |
| grapes | AHinab | عنب |
| ice cream | aayis kreem | آيس كريم |
| loaf of bread | ragheef khubz | رغيف خبز |
| milk | Haleeb | حليب |
| rolls | khubz mudawwar | خبز مدور |
| sausages | sujuq | سجق |
| soft drinks | kaazooza | كازوزة |
| tea bags | akyaas shay | أكياس شاي |

Bread (**khubz**) is very important to the Arabs and is eaten with every meal. It is often called **AHysh**, which literally means "life." It is considered disrespectful to throw away bread or drop it on the floor.

خبز (عيش شامي) **khubz (AHysh shaamee)**: Traditional Arabic bread is round, flat, and only slightly leavened.

عيش بلدي **AHysh baladee**: A wholemeal version of khubz.

خبز محمّص **khubz muHammas**: Bread crisped in the oven.

خبز مبسّس **khubz mubassis**: Tunisian semolina bread.

سميط **semiT**: Egyptian bread rings covered in sesame seeds.

# Health

Before you leave, make sure your health insurance policy covers illness and accidents while away from home. There is only a very basic system of state health care in most Arab countries, and you will be expected to pay doctors and dentists on the spot.

Almost all doctors in the region will have a good level of English – or at least know the medical terms. However, there may be occasions when you need to explain your problem in Arabic or use the tables on pages 164–165.

## Doctor/General دكتور/عام

| | |
|---|---|
| Where can I find a doctor/dentist? | ayn ajid duktoor/duktoor asnaan |
| | أين أجد دكتور/دكتور أسنان؟ |
| Where's there a doctor/dentist who speaks English? | ayn ajid duktoor/duktoor asnaan yatkallam al-injileezeeya |
| | أين أجد دكتور/دكتور أسنان يتكلم الإنجليزية؟ |
| What are the office [surgery] hours? | maa hiya mawaaAHeed al-AHiyaada |
| | ما هي مواعيد العيادة؟ |
| Could the doctor come to see me here? | hal yumkin lid-duktoor an yuzoornee huna |
| | هل يمكن للدكتور أن يزورني هنا؟ |
| Can I make an appointment ...? | mumkin aakhud mauAHid |
| | ممكن آخذ موعدا ...؟ |
| for today/tomorrow | lil-yaum/ghadan |
| | لليوم/غدا |
| as soon as possible | li-aqrab furSa mumkina |
| | لأقرب فرصة ممكنة |
| It's urgent! | innahaa Haala mustAHjila |
| | إنها حالة مستعجلة! |
| I've got an appointment with Doctor ... | AHndee mauAHid mAHa duktoor |
| | عندي موعد مع دكتور... |

– mumkin aakhud mauAHid li-aqrab
furSa mumkina?
– naHnu maHjoozeen tammaaman al-yaum.
hal al-Haala mustAHjila?
– nAHm.
– mumkin nAHmil lak Hajz as-sAHa AHshara wa
rubAH mAHa ad-duktoor shareef.
– as-sAHa AHshara wa rubAH. shukran jazeelan.

## Accident and injury حادث وإصابة

| | |
|---|---|
| ... is injured. | ... uSeeb/uSeebat. أصيب/أصيبت ... |
| my husband/wife | zaujee/zaujatee زوجي/زوجتي |
| my son/daughter | ibnee/bintee ابني/بنتي |
| my friend | Sadeeqee صديقي |
| my baby | raDeeAHee رضيعي |
| He/She is ... | huwa/hiya ... هو/هي |
| unconscious | faaqid al-wAHee فاقد الوعي |
| injured (seriously) | uSeeb (khaTeera) أصيب (خطيرة) |
| He/She is bleeding. | huwa/hiya yanzif/tanzif هو/هي ينزف/تنزف. |
| I have a/an ... | AHndee ... عندي |
| blister | kees maa' كيس ماء |
| boil | khuraaj خراج |
| bruise | kadma كدمة |
| burn | Harq حرق |
| cut | qaTAH قطع |
| graze | salkh سلخ |
| insect bite | ladghat Hashara لدغة حشرة |
| lump | waram ورم |
| rash | TafH jildee طفح جلدي |
| sting | Harqaan حرقان |
| strained muscle | tamazzuq AHDalee تمزق عضلي |
| swelling | waram ورم |
| wound | jurH جرح |
| My ... hurts. | ... yu'limnee. يؤلمني ... |

## Symptoms الأعراض

| | |
|---|---|
| I've been feeling ill for … days. | *ashAHur bil-maraD munzu … ayyaam*<br>أشعر بالمرض منذ … أيام. |
| I feel faint. | *ashAHur bi-ighmaa'* أشعر بإغماء. |
| I feel feverish. | *ashAHur bi-Humaa* أشعر بحمى |
| I've been vomiting. | *kunt atqayya'* كنت أتقيء. |
| I've got diarrhea. | *AHndee ishaal* عندي إسهال. |
| It hurts here. | *innahu yu'lim huna* إنه يؤلم هنا. |
| I have a/an … | *AHndee …* عندي … |
| backache | *alam feeZ-Zahr* ألم في الظهر |
| cold | *bard* برد |
| cramps | *taqalluSaat* تقلصات |
| earache | *alam feel uzun* ألم في الأذن |
| headache | *SudaAH* صداع |
| sore throat | *alam feel Halq* ألم في الحلق |
| stiff neck | *alam feel AHunuq* ألم في العنق |
| stomachache | *alam feel baTn* ألم في البطن |
| sunstroke | *Darbat shams* ضربة شمس |

## Health conditions الأوضاع الصحية

| | |
|---|---|
| I have arthritis. | *AHndee iltihaab bil-mafaaSil*<br>عندي التهاب بالمفاصل. |
| I have asthma. | *AHndee rabw* عندي ربو. |
| I am … | *ana …* أنا … |
| deaf | *aSamm* أصم |
| diabetic | *muSaab bis-sukaree* مصاب بالسكري |
| epileptic | *muSaab biS-SarAH* مصاب بالصرع |
| handicapped | *muAHaq* معاق |
| (… months) pregnant | *Haamil (bish-shahr al …)* حامل (بالشهر الـ …) |
| I have a heart condition. | *ana mareeD bil-qalb* أنا مريض بالقلب. |
| I have high blood pressure. | *AHndee irtifaAH bi-DaghT ad-dam*<br>عندي ارتفاع بضغط الدم. |
| I had a heart attack … years ago. | *kaan AHndee azma qalbeeya min … sineen.* كان عندي أزمة قلبية من … سنين. |

163

## Doctor's inquiries أسئلة الدكتور

| | |
|---|---|
| How long have you been feeling like this? | منذ متى تشعر هكذا؟ |
| Is this the first time you've had this? | هل هذه أول مرة تصاب بهذا؟ |
| Are you taking any other medication? | هل تأخذ أي أدوية أخرى؟ |
| Are you allergic to anything? | عندك حساسية من أي شيء؟ |
| Have you been vaccinated against tetanus? | هل أنت ملقح ضد التيتانوس؟ |
| Have you lost your appetite? | هل فقدت الشهية للطعام؟ |

## Examination الفحوص

| | |
|---|---|
| I'll take your temperature/ blood pressure. | سأقيس لك الحرارة/ضغط الدم. |
| Roll up your sleeve, please. | ارفع كمك، لو سمحت. |
| Please undress to the waist. | اخلع ملابسك العليا لو سمحت. |
| Please lie down. | استلق، لو سمحت. |
| Open your mouth. | افتح فمك. |
| Breathe deeply. | تنفس بعمق. |
| Cough, please. | أسعل، لو سمحت. |
| Where does it hurt? | أين تؤلمك؟ |
| Does it hurt here? | هل يوجد ألم هنا؟ |

## Diagnosis التشخيص

| | |
|---|---|
| I want you to have an X-ray. | أريدك أن تأخذ صورة بالأشعة. |
| I want a specimen of your blood/stools/urine. | أريد عينة من دمك/برازك/بولك. |
| I want you to see a specialist. | أريدك أن ترى أخصائي. |
| I want you to go to hospital. | أريدك أن تذهب إلى المستشفى. |
| It's broken/sprained. | إنها مكسورة/ملتوية. |
| It's dislocated/torn. | إنها مخلوعة/ممزقة. |

164

| | |
|---|---|
| عندك ... | You've got ... |
| التهاب الزائدة الدودية | appendicitis |
| التهاب المثانة | cystitis |
| انفلونزا | flu |
| تسمم غذاء | food poisoning |
| كسر | a fracture |
| حموضة في المعدة | gastritis |
| البواسير | hemorrhoids |
| فتاق | a hernia |
| التهاب في ... | an inflammation of ... |
| حصبة | measles |
| التهاب رئوي | pneumonia |
| عرق النسا | sciatica |
| التهاب اللوزتين | tonsilitis |
| ورم | a tumor |
| مرض تناسلي | venereal disease |
| إنه ملوث. | It's infected. |
| إنه معد. | It's contagious. |

## Treatment علاج

| | |
|---|---|
| سأعطيك ... | I'll give you ... |
| مطهر | an antiseptic |
| مسكن | a painkiller |
| سأصف لك ... | I'm going to prescribe ... |
| مضادات حيوية | a course of antibiotics |
| بعض التحاميل/اللبوس | some suppositories |
| هل عندك حساسية من أي دواء؟ | Are you allergic to any medicine? |
| خذ حبة واحدة ... | Take one pill ... |
| كل ... ساعات | every ... hours |
| ... مرات في اليوم | ... times a day |
| قبل/بعد كل وجبة | before/after each meal |
| عندما تتألم | in case of pain |
| لمدة ... أيام | for ... days |
| استشر طبيبا عندما تعود. | Consult a doctor when you get home. |

# Parts of the body أعضاء من الجسم

| | | |
|---|---|---|
| appendix | az-zaa'ida ad-doodeeya | الزائدة الدودية |
| arm | ziraaAH | ذراع |
| back | Zahr | ظهر |
| bladder | mathaana | مثانة |
| bone | AHuZma | عظمة |
| breast | thady | ثدي |
| chest | Sidr | صدر |
| ear | uzun | أذن |
| eye | AHyn | عين |
| finger | iSbAH | إصبع |
| foot | qadam | قدم |
| hand | yad | يد |
| head | ra's | رأس |
| heart | qalb | قلب |
| jaw | fakk | فك |
| joint | mifSal | مفصل |
| kidney | kilya | كلية |
| knee | rukba | ركبة |
| leg | saaq | ساق |
| liver | kibd | كبد |
| mouth | fam | فم |
| muscle | AHDala | عضلة |
| neck | raqaba | رقبة |
| nose | anf | أنف |
| rib | DilAH | ضلع |
| shoulder | kitif | كتف |
| skin | jild | جلد |
| stomach | baTn | بطن |
| thigh | fakhd | فخذ |
| throat | Hanjara | حنجرة |
| toe | iSbAH al-qadam | إصبع القدم |
| tongue | lisaan | لسان |
| tonsils | luwaz | لوز |
| vein | wareed | وريد |

# Gynecologist الطبيب النسائي

| | |
|---|---|
| I have ... | AHndee ... عندي |
| abdominal pains | amraaD jaufeeya<br>آلام جوفية |
| period pains | alam al-AHaada ash-shahreeya<br>ألم العادة الشهرية |
| a vaginal infection | talawwuth feel mahbal<br>تلوث في المهبل |
| I haven't had my period for ... months. | al-AHaada ash-shahreeya inqatAHat...<br>min ... shuhoor<br>العادة الشهرية انقطعت من ... شهور. |
| I'm on the Pill. | aakhud Huboob manAH al-Haml<br>آخذ حبوب منع الحمل. |

# Hospital المستشفى

| | |
|---|---|
| Please notify my family. | AHlim AHa'iltee, lau samaHt<br>أعلم عائلتي، لو سمحت. |
| I'm in pain. | ana AHndee alam. أنا عندي ألم. |
| I can't eat/sleep. | laa astaTeeAH al-akl/an-naum<br>لا أستطيع الأكل/النوم. |
| When will the doctor come? | matta sa-ya'tee ad-duktoor<br>متى سيأتي الدكتور؟ |
| Which ward is ... in? | fee ayy jinaaH ...؟ في أي جناح ...؟ |
| I'm visiting ... | ana azoor ... أنا أزور ... |

# Optician نظاراتي

| | |
|---|---|
| I'm short-sighted/<br>far- [long-] sighted. | ana qaSeer an-naZar/Taweel an-naZar<br>أنا قصير النظر/طويل النظر. |
| I've lost ... | faqadt ... فقدت ... |
| one of my contact lenses | iHda AHdsaatee al-laaSqa<br>إحدى عدساتي اللاصقة |
| my glasses/a lens | naZaartee/AHdsa نظاراتي/عدسة |
| Could you give me a replacement? | mumkin tAHTeenee badeel<br>ممكن تعطيني بديلاً؟ |

## طبيب أسنان Dentist

| I have toothache. | AHndee alam fee sinnee |
| | عندي ألم في سني. |
| This tooth hurts. | haazas sinn yu'allimnee |
| | هذا السن يؤلمني. |
| I've lost a filling/tooth. | faqadt Hashw/sinna. فقدت حشوا/سنة. |
| My gums are swollen. | AHndee iltihaab feel litha |
| | عندي التهاب في اللثة. |
| My gums are bleeding. | AHndee nazeef feel litha |
| | عندي نزيف في اللثة. |
| Can you repair this denture? | mumkin iSlaaH hazaaT Taqm |
| | ممكن إصلاح هذا الطقم؟ |
| I don't want it extracted. | laa ureed khalAHhaa |
| | لا أريد خلعها. |

| سأعطيك حقنة/مخدر موضعي. | I'm going to give you an injection/ a local anesthetic. |
| أنت تحتاج حشو/تاج الضرس | You need a filling/cap (crown). |
| يجب أن أخلعه. | I'll have to take it out. |
| أستطيع معالجته مؤقتا. | I can only fix it temporarily. |
| لا تأكل أي شيء لمدة ... ساعات. | Don't eat anything for ... hours. |

## الدفع والتأمين Payment and insurance

| How much do I owe you? | kam al-Hisaab؟ كم الحساب؟ |
| I have insurance. | AHndee ta'meen. عندي تأمين. |
| Can I have a receipt for my health insurance? | mumkin tAHTeenee eeSaal li-ta'meenee aS-SiHHee |
| | ممكن تعطيني إيصال لتأميني الصحي؟ |
| Would you fill in this health insurance form, please? | min faDlak, mumkin tamla istimaarat at-ta'meen aS-SiHHee |
| | من فضلك ممكن تملأ استمارة التأمين الصحي؟ |

# Dictionary
### English - Arabic

To enable correct usage, most terms in this dictionary are either followed by an expression or cross-referenced to pages where the word appears in a phrase. The notes below provide some basic grammar guidelines.

## Nouns

Nouns are either masculine or feminine. It is easy to tell them apart as almost all feminine nouns either refer to female people or end with **a**.

**al-** (the) is used for both genders. There is no equivalent of the English "a(n)".

| *masculine* | **al-walad** | the boy | *feminine* | **al-bint** | the girl |
| | **markib** | a boat | | **madeena** | a city |

Plurals are complicated and follow a number of different patterns. The plural can sound significantly different from the singular (➤ 216). The dictionary gives the plural for words you are most likely to encounter in this form.

## Adjectives

Adjectives come after the noun and agree in gender with the noun they are describing. Feminine adjectives, like nouns, usually end in **a**. If the noun has **al-**, then the adjective should also:

| **markib kabeer** | a big boat | **madeena kabeera** | a big city |
| **al-markib al-kabeer** | the big boat | **al-madeena al-kabeera** | a big city |

*Feminine* adjectives are used with all plurals except people:

| **maraakib kabeera** | big boats | **al-mudun al-kabeera** | the big cities |

## Verbs

Verbs are generally shown in the dictionary in present tense "he" form (*third person singular*). Different prefixes and endings are added to a present or past "stem". Although there are some variations, generally these prefixes and endings are as shown underlined below:

| | *present*<br>**yaktub** (write) | *past*<br>**katab** (wrote) |
|---|---|---|
| **ana** (I) | <u>a</u>ktub | katab<u>t(u)</u> |
| **anta** (you, m.) | <u>ta</u>ktub | katab<u>t(a)</u> |
| **anti** (you, f.) | <u>ta</u>ktub<u>ee(na)</u> | katab<u>ti</u> |
| **huwa** (he/it, m.) | <u>ya</u>ktub | katab |
| **hiya** (she/it, f.)* | <u>ta</u>ktub | katab<u>at</u> |
| **naHnu** (we) | <u>na</u>ktub | katab<u>naa</u> |
| **antum** (you, pl.) | <u>ta</u>ktub<u>oo(na)</u> | katab<u>tum</u> |
| **hum** (they) | <u>ya</u>ktub<u>oo(na)</u> | katab<u>oo</u> |

*All non-human plurals are grammatically *feminine singular* and so will also take this part of the verb:

| **al-rijaal wasal<u>oo</u>** | the men arrived | **al-maraakib wasal<u>at</u>** | the boats arrived |

**anything else?** أي شئ آخر؟
ayy shay aakhar

**apartment(s)** (شقق) شقة shaqqa (shuqaq)
28, 123

**appendix** *(part of body)* الزائدة الدودية
az-zaa'ida ad-doodeeya 166

**apples** تفاح tufaaH 49

**appointment** موعد mauAHid 147, 161

**approximately** تقريبا taqreeban 152

**apricots** مشمش mishmish 49

**Arabic** عربي AHrabee 11;
~ **language** اللغة العربية al-lugha
al-AHrabeeya 126; ~ **music**
موسيقى عربية mooseeqaa
AHrabeeya 111

**architect** مهندس معماري muhandis
mAHmaaree 103

**are there ...?** هل هناك ... ؟ hal hunaak 17

**area code** الرقم النداء الدولي raqm
an-nidaa' ad-daulee 127

**arm** ذراع ziraaAH 166

**around** *(time)* حوالي Hawaala 13

**arrive (in), to** يصل إلى yaSil
ilaa 68, 70, 75

**art gallery** معرض الفنون mAHraD
al-funoon 99

**arthritis** التهاب المفاصل iltihaab
al-mafaaSil 163

**artificial sweetener** سكر صناعي
sukkar SinaAH-ee 38

**artist** فنان fanaan 103

**ashtray** منفضة سجاير manfaDat
sajaayir 39

**ask: I asked for** طلبت Talabt 41

**aspirin** أسبرين asbireen 141

**asthma** ربو rabw 163

**at** *(place)* عند AHnda 12;
*(time)* الساعة as-sAHa 13

**at last!** أخيرا! akheeran 19

**athletics** ألعاب القوى alAHaab
al-quwa 114

**ATM** آلة سحب النقود
aalat saHb
an-nuqood 139

**attack** اعتداء iAHtidaa 152

**attractive** جذاب jazaab 157

**aubergine** باذنجان
baazinjaan 47

**aunt** خالة khaala *(maternal)* 120;
عمة AHmma *(paternal)* 120

**Australia** استراليا ostraalyaa 119

**authenticity** أصلية aSleeya 157

**automatic** *(car)* أوتوماتيك
otomateek 86

**automobile(s)**
(سيارات) سيارة
sayyarra(at)

**autumn** الخريف
al-khareef

**awful** مرعب murAHib 101;
شنيع shaneeAH 122

**B** **baby** (رضيع) طفل Tifl
(radeeAH) 39, 113, 162;
~ **food** طعام الأطفال TAHaam
al-aTfaal 142; ~ **wipes**
مساحات الأطفال masaaHaat
al-aTfaal 142

**babysitter** حاضنة HaaDina 113

**back** *(part of body)* ظهر Zahr 166;
*(rear)* الخلف al-khalf 147

**backache** ألم في الظهر alam
feeZ-Zahr 163

**backpacking**
السفر بحقيبة ظهر
as-safar bi-Haqeebat Zahr

**bad** سيء sayyi' 14

**badminton** تنس الريشة tanis
ar-reesha 114

**bag** *(luggage)* حقيبة Haqeeba 67;
*(packet)* باكيت baakeet 159

**baggage** حقائب / أمتعة amtiAHa/ Haqaa'ib 32, 69, 71; ~ **check** مكتب الأمانات maktab al-amaanaat 72; ~ **reclaim** استرداد الحقائب istirdaad al-Haqaa'ib 71

**Bahrain** البحرين al-baHrayn

**Bahraini** بحريني baHraynee

**bakery** مخبز makhbaz 129

**balcony** شرفة shurfa 29

**ball(s)** كرة (كرات) kura(at) 157

**ballet** باليه baalayh 108, 111

**bananas** موز mauz 49

**band(s)** (musical) فرقة (فرق) firqa (firaq) 111, 157

**bandage** ضماد Damaad 141

**bank(s)** بنك (بنوك) bank (bunook) 129, 138

**bar** بار baar 112

**barber** حلاق Hallaaq

**baseball** البايسبول al-baayisbool 114

**basement** دور أرضي door arDee

**basket(s)** سلة (سلال) salla (silaal) 158

**basketball** كرة السلة kurat as-salla 114

**bath** بانيو baanyo 21; ~ **towel** منشفة minshafa 27;

**bathroom** حمام Hammaam 26, 29

**battery(ies)** بطارية (بطاريات) baTaareeya(at) 88, 91, 137, 149, 151

**battle site** موقع المعركة mawqiAH al-mAHraka 99

**beach** شاطئ shaaTi' 117

**beans: brown (fava) beans** فول fool 48

**beard** لحية liHya

**beautiful** جميل jameel 14, 101

**because** لأن li'ann 14; ~ **of** بسبب bisabab 14

**bed** سرير sareer 21; ~ **and breakfast** السرير والفطور as-sareer wal-futoor

**bedding** أغطية السرير aghTiyyat as-sareer 29

**bedroom** غرفة نوم ghurfat naum 29

**beef** لحم بقري laHm baqaree 46

**beer** بيرة beera 49

**before** قبل qabl 13,165, 221

**begin, to** يبدأ yabda'

**beige** بيج bayj 143

**bell** جرس jaras 82

**belong: this belongs to me** هذا ملكي haaza milkee

**belt** حزام Hizaam 144

**berth** (sleeper) سرير sareer 73, 77

**best** الأفضل al-afDal

**better** أفضل afDal 14, 134

**between** بين bayn 221

**bib** صدرية الطفل Sidreeyat aT-Tifl

**bicycle(s)** دراجة (دراجات) daraaja(at) 74, 83, 153

**big** كبير kabeer 14, 134

**bigger** أكبر akbar 24

**bikini** بكيني bikeenee 144

**bill** (check) حساب Hisaab 32, 42

**bird(s)** طير (طيور) Tayr (Tuyoor) 106

**birthday** عيد ميلاد AHeed meelaad 219

**bite** (insect) لدغة ladgha

**bitten: I've been bitten by a dog** عضني كلب AHddanee kalb

**bitter** مر murr 41

**black** أسود aswad 143

**bladder** مثانة mathaana 166

**blanket** بطانية baTaaniya 27

**bleach** بليتش bleetsh 148

**bleed, to** ينزف yanzif 162

**blind** (window) شيش sheesh 25

**blister** كيس ماء (طب) kees maa' 162

**blocked** مسدود masdood 25

**blood** دم dam 164; **~ group**
فصيلة الدم faSeelat ad-damm;
**~ pressure** ضغط الدم DaghT
ad-dam 164

**blouse** بلوزة bilooza 144

**blow-dry** تنشيف tansheef 147

**blue** أزرق azraq 143

**boarding card** بطاقة الصعود baTaaqat
aS-SuAHood 70

**boat** مركب markib 81; **~ trip**
رحلة بالمركب riHla bil-markib 81, 97

**body** جسم jism 166

**boil** (medical) خراج khuraaj 162

**boiler** سخان sakh-khaan 29

**bone** عظمة AHaZma 166

**bonnet** (of car) غطاء المحرك ghaTaa
al-muHarrik 90

**book(s)** كتاب (كتب) kitaab (kutub)
11, 150

**booklet of tickets**
كتيب من التذاكر
kutayyeb min at-tazaakir 79

**bookshop** مكتبة maktaba 129

**boot** (of car) صندوق السيارة Sundooq
as-sayyaara 90

**booted: my car has been booted**
سيارتي ربطت بملزم sayyaaratee
rubiTat bi-mulzim 87

**boots** بوت boot 145

**boring** ممل mumill 101

**born: I was born in …** ولدت في …
wulidt fee

**botanical garden** حديقة النبات
Hadeeqat an-nabaat 99

**bottle(s)** زجاجة (زجاجات) zujaaja(at) 37;
**~-opener** فتاحة زجاجات fattaaHat
zujaajaat 148

**bowel** أمعاء amAHaa

**bowl(s)** سلطانية (سلطانيات)
sulTaaneeya(at) 148

**boxing** (sport) الملاكمة
al-mulaakma 114

**boy(s)** ولد (أولاد) walad
(awlaad) 120, 157

**boyfriend** صاحب
SaaHib 120

**bra** حمالة صدر Hamaalat Sidr 144

**bracelet** سوار sawaar 149

**brake pad** تيل الفرامل teel
al-faraamil 82

**brakes** فرامل faraamil 91

**bread** خبز khubz 38, 43

**break, to** يكسر yaksar 28; **~ down, to**
يعطل yAHTal 28; **~down truck**
ونش AHTl 88; **~down truck**
winsh 88; **~-in** اقتحام iqtiHaam 153

**breast** (part of body) ثدي thady 166

**breathe, to** يتنفس yatnaffas 92, 164

**bridge** جسر jisr 96, 107

**Britain** بريطانيا bireeTaanya 119

**British** بريطانية bireeTaanee 152

**broken** مكسور maksoor 25, 137, 164

**bronchitis** التهاب شعبي iltihaab
shuAHbee

**brooch** بروش broosh 149

**brother** أخ akh 120

**brown** بني bunnee 143

**browse, to** يتفرج yatfarraj 133

**bruise** كدمة kadma 162

**brush** فرشاة fursha 142

**bucket** دلو dilw 157

**building** مبنى mabnaa

**built: was built** بُني buniya 103

**bulletin board**
لوحة البيانات
lauHat al-bayaanaat 26

**bureau de change**
مكتب تغيير عملات maktab
taghyeer AHumlaat 138

**burn** حرق Harq 162

**bus(es)** (أوتوبيسات) أوتوبيس
ootoobees(aat) 70;
**~ route** مسلك الأوتوبيس
maslak al-ootoobees 96;
**~ station** محطة الأوتوبيس
maHaTTit al-ootoobees
77, 78; **~ stop** موقف الأوتوبيس
mawqaf al-ootoobees 65, 69;
**by ~** بالأوتوبيس
bil-ootoobees 123;
**long-distance ~** أوتوبيس (رحلات)
ootoobees (riHlaat) 77

**business: on business** في رحلة عمل
fee riHlit AHmal 66

**business class** درجة رجال الأعمال
rijaal al-AHmaal 68

**busy** (occupied) مشغول mashghool 125

**butane gas** غاز البيوتان ghaaz
al-biyootaan 31

**butcher** جزار jazzaar 129

**butter** زبدة zibda 38, 43, 160

**button(s)** زر (أزرار) zurr (azraar)

**buy, to** يشتري yashtaree 125

**by** (+ means of transportation) بـ bi- 17;
**by car** بالسيارة bis-sayyaara 94;
**by** (near) بقرب bi-qurb 36;
**by** (time) خلال khilaal 13;
**by credit card** ببطاقة الائتمان
bi-biTaaqat al-i'timaan 17

**bye!** وداعا! wadaAHan

**cabbage** كرنب/ملفوف kurunb/
malfoof 47

**cabin** كابينة kaabeena 81

**cable TV** تلفزيون كوابل tilifizyoon
kawaabil 22

**café** مقهى maqhaa 35

**calendar** رزنامة raznaama 156

**call, to** (telephone) يتصل بـ
yattaSil bi 127

**call the police!** اتصل بالشرطة!
ittaSil bish-shurTa 92

**camera** كاميرا kaameeraa
151, 153; **~ case** علبة للكاميرا
AHulba lil-kaameeraa 151; **~ store**
محل كاميرات maHall kaameeraat 129; **automatic ~**
كاميرا أوتوماتيك kaameeraa
ootoomaateek 151; **compact ~**
كاميرا مصغرة kaameeraa
muSaghghara 151

**camp (to)** يخيم yukhayyim 31

**campbed** سرير سفر sareer safar 31

**camping** تخييم takhyeem 31

**campsite** مخيم mukhayyam 30, 123

**can** (tin) علبة AHulba 159;
**~ opener** فتاحة معلبات
fattaaHat muAHlabaat 148

**can I?** ممكن؟ mumkin 18

**Canada** كندا Kanadaa 119

**cancel, to** يلغي yulghee 68

**cancer** (disease) مرض السرطان
maraD as-saraTaan

**candy** سكاكر sakaakir 150

**cap** كاب kaab 144

**car(s)** سيارة (سيارات) sayyaara(at) 81,
85, 86, 88, 90–91, 153; **~ ferry**
معدية السيارات mAHdeeyat
as-sayyaaraat 81; **~ hire**
سيارة للاستئجار sayyaara lil-isti'jaar
70; **~ park** ركن/كراج سيارات
rakn/garaaj sayyaaraat 26, 87, 96;
**~ rental** تأجير سيارة ta'jeer sayyaara
86; **2-door ~** سيارة ببابين sayyaara
bi-baabayn 86; **4-door ~**
سيارة بأربع أبواب sayyaara bi-arbAH
abwaab 86; **by ~** بالسيارة
bis-sayyaara 95, 123

**car** (train compartment) مقطورة
maqToora 74

**carafe** إبريق ibreeq 37

cinema سينما seenamaa 96, 110

claim check بطاقة الاسترداد biTaaqat al-istirdaad 71

clean (adj) نظيف naZeef 14, 41, 39

clean, to ينظف yunaZZif 137

cliff منحدر munHadar 107

cloakroom حجرة المعاطف Hujrat al-mHaaTif 109

clock ساعة حائط sAHat Haa'iT 149

close (near) قريب qareeb 95

close, to يغلق yughliq 100, 140

clothes ملابس malaabis 144;
~ pins [pegs] ملابس ملقط milqaT malaabis 148;
~ shop محل ملابس maHall malaabis 129

clothing store محل ملابس maHall malaabis 129

cloudy غائم ghaa'im 122

clubs (golf) مضارب (جولف) maDaarib (golf) 116

coach (long-distance bus) أوتوبيس (رحلات) ootoobees (riHlaat) 77;
~ station محطة الأوتوبيس maHaTTit al-ootoobees 77

coach (train compartment) مقطورة maqToora 74

coast ساحل saaHil

coat معطف miAHTaf 144; ~ check حجرة المعاطف Hujrat al-mHaaTif 109;
~hanger(s) (علاقات) ملابس AHilaaqa(at) malaabis

cockroach(es) (صراصير) صرصار SirSaar (SaraaSeer)

coffee قهوة qahwa 51

cold (adj) بارد baarid 14, 41, 122

cold (sickness) برد bard 141, 163

collect, to يأخذ ya'khud 151

color(s) (ألوان) لون laun (alwaan) 134, 143

comb مشط mishT 142

come back, to يرجع yarjAH 36

commission عمولة AHmoola 138

compact disc أسطوانة كومباكت usTuwaana koombaakt 157

company (business) شركة sharika

complain, to يشكو yashkoo 137

complaint(s) (شكاوى) شكوى shakwa (shakaawee) 41

composer (music) مؤلّف mu'allif 111

computer كمبيوتر kumbiyootar

concert حفلة موسيقية Hafla mooseeqeeya 108

concession تصريح خاص taSreeH khaaSS

condoms غشاء طبي ghishaa Tibbee 141

conductor قائد الفرقة qaa'id al-firqa 111

confirm, to يؤكّد yu'akkid 22, 68

congratulations! مبروك! mabrook

connection (transportation) مواصلة muwaaSla 76

constipation إمساك imsaak

consulate قنصلية qunSuleeya 152

consult, to (doctor) يستشير yastasheer 165

contact, to يتصل yattaSil 28

contact lenses عدسات لاصقة AHdsaat laaSqa 167

contain, to يحتوي على yaHtawee AHlaa 69, 155

contraceptive مانع الحمل maaniAH al-Haml

cook (chef) طباخ Tabbaakh

cook, to يطبخ yaTbukh

cooker فرن furn 29

cookies بسكويت baskaweet 160

cooking (cuisine) الطبخ aT-Tabkh

**coolbox** علبة تبريد AHulbat tabreed

**copper** نحاس naHaas 149

**corkscrew** فتاحة نبيذ fattaaHat nabeet 148

**corn** ذرة dura 47

**corner** زاوية zaaweeya 95

**correct** صحيح SaHeeH

**cosmetics** مستحضرات تجميل mustHDaraat tajmeel

**cot** سرير للطفل sareer lil-Tifl 22

**cottage** شاليه shaalay 28

**cotton** قطن quTn 145; [cotton wool] قطن طبي quTn Tibbee 141

**cough** (noun) سعال suAHaal 141

**cough, to** يسعل yasAHl 164

**could I have?** ممكن آخذ؟ mumkin aakhud 18

**country (countries)** دولة (دول) dawla (duwal)

**courgette** كوسة koosa 47

**courier** (guide) مرشد murshid

**course** (of meal) طبق Tabaq; (of medicine) دورة علاج daurat AHilaaj

**crab** كبوريا kaaboorya 44

**cracked wheat** برغل burghul 48

**cramps** تقلصات taqalluSaat 163

**crèche** دار الحضانة daar al-HaDaana

**credit card** بطاقة الائتمان baTaaqat al-itimaan 42, 136

**crib** سرير للطفل sareer lil-Tifl 22

**crockery** أواني awaanee 29, 148

**crossroad** تقاطع taqaaTiAH 95

**crowded** مزدحم muzdaHim 31

**crown** (dental) تاج (أسنان) taaj (asnaan) 168

**cruise** (noun) رحلة بحرية riHla baHreeya

**crutches** عكازات AHkkaazaan

**crystal** بلور balloor 149

**cucumber** خيار khiyaar 47

**cup(s)** فنجان (فناجين) finjaan (fanaajeen) 39, 148

**cupboard** خزانة khazaana

**curlers** مشابك لف الشعر mushaabik laff ash-shAHr

**currency** عملات AHumlaat 67; ~ **exchange office** مكتب تغيير عملات maktab taghyeer AHumlaat 138

**curtains** ستائر sataa'ir

**customer service** خدمة الزبائن khidmat az-zabaa'in 133

**customs** (airport) جمارك jamaarik 67, 157; ~ **declaration** شهادة الجمرك shihaadat al-jumruk 155

**D** **damaged** تالف taalif 28

**damn!** لعين! lAHeen 19

**damp** (n/adj) رطوبة / رطب rutooba/raTib

**dance** (n) رقص raqS 111

**dance, to** يرقص yurqus 124

**dangerous** خطر khaTir

**dark** (without light) مظلم muZlim 24; (color) غامق ghaamiq 14, 134, 143

**darker** (color) أغمق aghmaq 143

**dates** (fruit) بلح balaH 49

**daughter** بنت bint 120, 162

**dawn** فجر fajr 221

**day(s)** يوم (أيام) yaum (ayyaam) 97, 122; ~ **ticket** تذكرة لطول اليوم tazkara li-Tool al-yaum; ~ **trip** رحلة لطول اليوم riHla li-Tool al-yaum

**dead** (battery) فارغة faargha 88

**deaf** أصم aSamm 163

**deck chair** كرسي الشاطئ kursee ash-shaaTi' 117

**A-Z**

deep عميق AHmeeq
degrees (temperature)
درجات الحرارة
darajaat al-Haraara
delay تأخير ta'kheer 70
delicious لذيذ lazeez 14
denim جينز jeenz 145
dental floss
شريط لتنظيف الأسنان
shareeT li-tanZeef al-asnaan
dentist طبيب أسنان Tabeeb asnaan 131,
161, 168
dentures (أسنان) طقم Taqm
(asnaan) 168
deodorant مزيل لرائحة العرق muzeel
li-raa'iHat al-AHraq 142
department قسم qism 132;
~ store محل تجاري maHall
tijaaree 129
departure lounge قاعة الرحيل
qaaAHa ar-raHeel 69
deposit عربون AHraboon 24, 83
describe, to يصف yaSif 152
desert صحراء SaHraa' 106, 107;
~ track(s) طريق (طرق) صحراوي
Tareeq (Turuq) SaHraawee 106
destination وجهة wijha
details تفاصيل tafaaSeel
detergent منظف munaZZif
detour تحويل taHweel 96
developing (photos) تحميض
taHmeeD 151
diabetes مرض السكري marD
as-sukkaree
diabetic مصاب بالسكري muSaab
bis-sukkaree 39, 163
diagnosis تشخيص
tashkheeS 164
dialling code رقم النداء الدولي
raqm an-nidaa
ad-daulee 127
diamond الماس al-maas 149

diapers حفاضات HafaaDaat 142
diarrhea إسهال ishaal 141, 163;
I have ~ عندي إسهال AHndee ishaal
dice زهر اللعب zahr al-lAHb
dictionary قاموس qaamoos 150
diesel ديزل deezil 87
diet: I'm on a diet
أنا أتبع نظام غذائي
ana atbAH naZaam ghizaa'ee
difficult صعب SAHb 14
dining car عربة الطعام AHrabit
aT-TAHaam 77
dining room حجرة الطعام Hujrat
aT-TAHaam 26
dinner jacket سترة العشاء
sutrat al-AHashaa'
dinner: to have dinner يتعشى
yatAHashshaa 124
direct مباشر mubaashir 74
direction(s) (اتجاهات) اتجاه ittijaah(aat) 94;
in the ~ of باتجاه bittijaah 95
director (of company) مدير mudeer
dirty وسخ wisikh 14, 28
disabled معاق muAHaaq 22
discotheque ديسكو deeskoo 112
discount(s) (تخفيضات) تخفيض
takhfeeD(aat) 24, 74, 100
disgusting مقرف muqrif
dish cloth منشفة صحون minshafat
SuHoon 148
dishwashing detergent سائل لغسيل الصحون
saa'il li-ghaseel aS-SuHoon 148
dislocated مخلوع makhlooAH 164
display cabinet خزانة العرض
khazaanat al-AHrD 149
display case صندوق العرض Sundooq
al-AHrD 134
distilled water مقطرة
مياه miyaah muqaTTara
dive, to يغطس yaghTas 117
diversion تحويل taHweel 96
divorced مطلق muTallaq 120

**dizzy: I feel dizzy** أشعر بدوار
ashAHur bi-dawaar

**doctor** دكتور doktoor 92, 131, 161, 167

**doctor's office [surgery]** عيادة
AHiyaada 161

**doll** دمية dumya 157

**dollar(s)** دولار(ات) dolaar(aat) 67, 138

**door(s)** باب (أبواب) baab (abwaab) 25, 29

**double** (cabin) لشخصين li-shakhSayn 81;
**~ bed** سرير مزدوج sareer muzdawij 21;
**~ room** غرفة لشخصين ghurfa
li-shakhSayn 21

**downstairs** تحت taHt 12

**downtown area** وسط المدينة wasT
al-madeena 99

**draught** (wind) تيار الهواء tayyaar
al-hawaa

**dress** فستان fustaan 144

**drink(s)** مشروب (مشروبات) mashroob(aat)
37, 70, 125, 126

**drink, to** يشرب yishrab 37

**drinking water** ماء الشرب maa'
ash-shurb 30

**drive, to** يسوق yasooq 93

**driver** سائق saa'iq

**driver's license** شهادة السواقة
shahaadat as-sawaaqa 93

**drowning: someone is drowning!**
هناك شخص يغرق! hunaak shakhS yaghriq

**drugstore** صيدلية Saydaleeya 129

**dry cleaner** محل تنظيف ملابس maHall
tanZeef malaabis 131

**dubbed** (movie) مدبلج mudablaj 110

**duck** بط baTT 46

**during** خلال khilaal

**dustbin** صندوق الزبالة Sundooq
iz-zibaala 30

**duvet** غطاء سميك للنوم ghaTaa'
sameek li-naum

**E** **e-mail** إي-ميل
eemayl 155;
**~ address**
عنوان في الإي-ميل
AHunwaan feel eemayl 155

**ear** أذن uzun 166; **~ drops**
نقط للأذن nuqaT lil-uzun; **~ache**
ألم في الأذن alam feel uzun 163

**earlier** أبكر abkar 147

**early** مبكر mubakkir 221

**earrings** حلق Halaq 149

**east** شرق sharq 95

**easy** سهل sahl 14

**eat, to** يأكل ya'kul 41, 139, 167

**economy class** الدرجة السياحية
ad-daraja as-siyaaHiyya 68

**eggs** بيض bayD 160; **boiled ~**
بيض مسلوق bayD maslooq 43;
**fried ~** بيض مقلي bayD maqlee 43;
**scambled ~** بيض ممزوج bayD
mamzooj 43

**eggplant** باذنجان baazinjaan 47

**Egypt** مصر muSr 119

**Egyptian** مصري muSree

**elastic** (adj) مطاطي maTaaTee

**electric outlet(s)** مواقع لأخذ الكهرباء
mauqiAH (mawaaqiAH) li-akhd
al-kahrabaa 30

**electric shaver** آلة حلاقة كهربائية aalat
Halaaqa kahrabaa'eeya

**electricity** كهرباء kahrabaa' 28
**~ meter** عداد الكهرباء AHddaad
al-kahrabaa 28

**electronic** إلكتروني iliktroonee;
**~ game** لعبة إلكترونية lAHba
iliktrooneeya 157

**elevator(s)** مصعد (مصاعد) maSAHd
(maSaaAHid) 26, 132

**A-Z**

**else: something else** شئ آخر shay aakhir

**embassy** سفارة sifaara

**emergency exit** مخرج طوارئ makhraj Tawaari' 132

**Emirates** الإمارات al-imaaraat;
**from the ~** إماراتي imaaraatee

**empty** فارغ faarigh 14

**end, to** ينتهي yantahee 108

**engaged** (to be married) خاطب khaaTib 120

**engine** محرك muHarrik 82, 91

**engineering** هندسة handasa 121

**England** إنجلترا injilteraa 119

**English** إنجليزي injileezee 67; (language) الإنجليزية al-injileezeeya 150, 152, 161;
**~speaking** يتكلم إنجليزي yatkallam injileezee 98, 152

**enjoy, to** يستمتع yastamtiAH 123

**enough** كفاية kifaaya 15, 42, 136

**ensuite bathroom** حمام تابع للغرفة Hamaam taabiAH lil-ghurfa

**entertainment guide** دليل لأماكن الترفيه daleel li-amaakin at-tarfeeh

**entry visa** تأشيرة الدخول ta'sheerat ad-dukhool

**envelope(s)** ظرف (أظرف) Zarf (aZruf) 150

**epileptic** مصاب بالصرع muSaab biS-SarAH 163

**equipment** معدات muAHidaat 116

**error** خطأ khaTa'

**escalator** سلم كهربائي sillim kahrabaa'ee 132

**essential** ضروري Darooree 89

**estate agent** وكيل عقاري wakeel AHqaaree

**evening** المساء al-masaa 221;
**in the ~** في المساء feel masaa 221;
**~ dress** ملابس السهرة malaabis as-sahra 112

**every day** كل يوم kull yaum

**every week** كل أسبوع kull usbooAH 13

**examination** (medical) فحص (طبي) faHS (Tibbee)

**example: for example** مثلا masalan

**except** ما عدا maa AHdaa

**excess baggage** أمتعة زيادة amtiAHa ziyaada 69

**exchange rate** سعر الصرف siAHr aS-Sarf 138

**exchange, to** يغيّر yughayyir 137, 138

**excluding** بدون bidoon 24

**excursion** جولة سياحية منظمة jaula siyyaaHeeya munaZZama 97

**excuse me** (apology) آسف aasif 10;
(attention) لو سمحت lau samaHt 10, 94

**exhausted** (very tired) منهك munhak 106

**exit** مخرج makhraj 70, 132

**expensive** غال ghaalee 14, 134

**expiration [expiry] date** تاريخ الانتهاء taareekh al'intihaa 109

**exposure** (photos) صورة Soora 151

**extension** (telephone) امتداد imtidaad 128

**extra** (adj) إضافي iDaafee 27

**eye** عين AHyn 166

**F** **fabric** قماش qumaash 145
**facial** تنظيف للوجه tanZeef lil-wajh 147

facilities تسهيلات tas-heelaat 22

faint: to feel faint يشعر بإغماء yashAHur bi-ighmaa' 163

fairground مدينة الملاهي madeenat al-malaahee 113

falconry صيد بالصقور SayD biS-Suqoor 115

fall (season) الخريف al-khareef 219

family (families) عائلة (عائلات) AH'ila(at) 74; my ~ عائلتي AH'iltee 66, 120, 167

famous شهير shaheer

fan (cooling) مروحة marwaHa 25, 91

far بعيد bAHeed 95; how ~ is it? كم تبعد؟ kam tabAHud 72

fare أجرة ujra 78

farm مزرعة mazrAHa 107

fast بسرعة bi-surAHa 93

fast food وجبات سريعة wajbaat sareeAHa 35, 40

fat دهن duHn 39

father أب ab 120

faucet حنفية Hanafeeya 25

favorite مفضل mufaDDal

fax فاكس faaks 155

feeding bottle زجاجة الرضيع zujaajat ar-raDeeAH

feel ill, to يشعر بالمرض yashAHur bil-maraD

ferry معدية mAHdeeya 81; by ~ بالمعدية bil-mAHdeeya 123

feverish, to feel يشعر بحمى yashAHur bi-Huma 163

few بعض bAHD 15

fiancé(e) خطيب/خطيبة khaaTeeb/khaaTeeba

field حقل Haql 107; ~ hockey الهوكي al-hookee 115

fifth خامس khaamis 217

fight (brawl) مشاجرة mushaajara

figs تين teen 49

fill in, to (a form) يملأ yamla 168

filling (dental) حشو (أسنان) Hashw (asnaan) 168

film (camera) فيلم (كاميرا) feelm (kaameeraa) 151; (movie) فيلم feelm 108, 110; black and white ~ فيلم أسود و أبيض feelm aswad wa abyaD 151; color ~ فيلم ألوان feelm alwaan 151

filter فلتر filtir 151

find, to يجد yajid 18

fine (going well) بخير bi-khayr 19; ~, thanks بخير، الحمد لله bi-khayr, al-Hamdu lilaah 118

fine (penalty) غرامة gharaama 93

finger إصبع iSbAH 166

fire حريق Hareeq; ~ alarm إنذار الحريق inzaar al-Hareeq; ~ department [brigade] المطافئ al-muTaafi' 92; ~ escape سلم الحريق sillim al-Hareeq; ~ extinguisher طفاية الحريق Tafaayat al-Hareeq

firewood حطب HaTab

first [أولى] awwil [fem: oolaa] 68, 75, 132, 217; ~ class الدرجة الأولى ad-daraja al-oolaa 68, 73

fish سمك samak; ~ restaurant مطعم سمك matAHm amak 35; ~ soup شوربة سمك shoorbit samak 43; ~ store محل سمك maHall samak 129

fishing rod سنارة sinaara

fishing, to go يذهب لصيد السمك yazhab li-Sayd as-samak

fit, to (clothes) يلائم yulaa'im 146

fitting room غرفة القياس ghurfat al-qiyaas 146

**fix, to** يصلح yuSalliH 168

**flannel** فوطة صغيرة fooTa Sagheera

**flash (electronic)** (فلاش (إليكتروني) flaash (ileektroonee) 151

**flashlight** بطارية جيب baTaareeyat jayb 31

**flat** (tire) ثقب thuqb 83, 88

**flea** برغوث barghooth

**flight** رحلة riHla 68, 70; ~ **number** ... الرحلة رقم ... ar-riHla raqm 68

**flip-flops** شبشب حمام shibshib Hammaam 145

**floor** (level) طابق Taabiq 132

**florist** محل زهور maHall zuhoor 129

**flour** طحين TaHeen 39

**flower(s)** (زهر) zahra (zahr) 106

**fly** (insect) ذبابة dubaaba

**follow, to** يتبع yitbAH 95, 152

**food** طعام TAHaam 39, 41; ~ **poisoning** تسمم tasammum 165

**foot** قدم qadam 166; ~ **path** ممر المشاة mamarr al-mushaa

**football** (soccer) كرة القدم kurat al-qadam 115

**for** (+ length of time) لمدة li-muddat 13, 23

**foreign currency** عملات أجنبية AHumlaat ajnabeeya 138

**forest** غابة ghaaba 107

**forget: I've forgotten** نسيت naseet 42

**fork(s)** (شوك) shauka (shuwak) 39, 41, 148

**form** استمارة istimaara 168

**fortnight** أسبوعان usbooAHayn

**fortunately** لحسن الحظ liHusn al-HaZZ 19

**fountain** نافورة naafoora 99

**four-wheel drive** الدفع الرباعي ad-dafAH ar-rubaaAHee 86

**fourth** رابع raabiAH 217

**foyer** (hotel/theater) بهو bahw

**fracture** كسر kasr 165

**frame** إطار iTaar 167

**free** (not busy) فاض faaDee 124

**freezer** فريزر fireezir 29

**French dressing** صلصة الخل SalSat al-khall 38

**French fries** بطاطس مقلية baTaaTis maqleeya 38

**frequent: how frequent ...?** كم عدد ...؟ kam AHdad 75

**frequently** مرارا miraaran

**fresh** (food) طازج Taazij 41

**Friday** (يوم) الجمعة (yaum) al-jumAHa 218

**fridge** ثلاجة tallaaja

**fried** مقلي maqlee

**friend(s)** (أصدقاء) Sadeeq (aSdiqaa') 162

**frightened, to be** يخاف yukhaaf

**from** من min 12, 119; **from ... to** من ... إلى min ... ilaa 13

**front** الأمام al-amaam 147; ~ **door** الباب الرئيسي al-baab ar-ra'eesee 26

**fruit** فواكه fawaakih 49; ~ **juice** عصير فواكه AHseer fawaakih 43

**frying pan** مقلاة maqlaa 29

**fuel** (gasoline) وقود wuqood 86

**full** مليان malyaan 14; ~ **board** إقامة كاملة iqaama kaamla 24

**fun: to have fun** يستمتع yastamtiAH

**furniture** أثاث athaath

**fuse(s)** (electric) صمام الكهرباء Samaam(aat) al-kahrabaa; ~ **box** علبة صمامات الكهرباء AHilbat Samaamaat al-kahrabaa 28

**G** game (match) ماتش
maatsh 114

garage كراج garaaj 88

garbage bag(s) قمامة (أكياس)
كيس kees (akyaas) qammaama 148

garden حديقة Hadeeqa

gas bottle(s) أنبوبة (أنابيب) الغاز anbooba
(anaabeeb) al-ghaaz 28

gas station محطة بنزين maHaTTat
banzeen 87

gasoline بنزين benzeen 88

gate (airport) بوابة bawwaaba 70

genuine أصلي aSlee 134

get off, to (bus) ينزل yanzil 79

get to, to يصل إلى yaSil ilaa 70, 77;
how do I get to ...? كيف أصل إلى ...؟
kayf aSil ilaa 72, 94

gift هدية hadeeya 67, 156; ~ shop
محل هدايا maHall hadaayaa 129

girl(s) بنت (بنات) bint (banaat) 120, 157

girlfriend صاحبة Saahba 120

give, to يعطي yuAHTee

glass(es) كوب (أكواب) koob (akwaab)
37, 39, 148

glasses (optical) نظارات naZaara 167

gloves قفاز qafaaz

go, to يذهب yaz-hab 18; let's go!
هيا بنا نذهب! hayyaa bina naz-hab;
~ back يرجع yirjAH 95
~ for a walk يتمشى yatmashshaa 124

goggles نظارات بحر naZaaraat baHr

gold ذهب dahab 149; ~ plate
قشرة ذهب qishrat dahab 149

golf الجولف al-goolf 115; ~ course
أرض الجولف farD al-gool 115

good جيد jayyid 14, 35;
~ afternoon مساء الخير
masaa al khayr 10;
~ evening مساء الخير
masaa al khayr 10;

~ morning صباح الخير sabaaH
al khayr 10; ~ night
تصبح على خير
tiSbaH AHla khayr 10;
Good God! يا إلهي!
yaa ilaahee 19

good-bye مع السلامة maAH
as-salaama 10

gram غرام ghraam 159

grandparents الجد والجدة
al-jadd wal-jadda

grapes عنب AHinab 49, 160

grass عشب AHushb

gratuity بقشيش baqsheesh

gray رمادي ramaadee 143

graze سلخ salkh 162

greasy (hair) دهني dihnee

green أخضر akhDar 143; ~ beans
فاصوليا خضراء faSoolya khaDra 47;
~ pepper فلفل أخضر filfil akhDar 47;
~grocer محل خضار maHall khuDaar 129

ground (noun) أرض arD 31;
(adj) أرضي arDee 132; ~cloth
حصيرة HaSeera 31; ~sheet
حصيرة HaSeera 31

group مجموعة majmooAH 66

guarantee ضمان Dammaan 135

guavas جوافة jawaafa 49

guide (tour) مرشد (سياحي) murshid
(siyyaaHee) 98

guidebook دليل سياحي daleel
siyaaHee 100

guitar جيتار geetaar

Gulf (Persian) الخليج al-khaleej 119

guy rope حبل الخيمة Habl
il-khayma 31

gynecologist طبيب نسائي Tabeeb
nisaa'ee 167

**H**

**hair** شعر shAHr 147; **~ spray** اسبراي للشعر isbraay lish-shAhr 142; **~cut** حلاقة الشعر Halaaqat ash-shAHr; **~dresser** صالون حلاقة Saaloon Hallaaqa 131, 147; **~stylist** مزين (للشعر) muzayyin (lish-shAHr) 147

**half** نصف nuSf 217; **~ an hour** نصف ساعة nuSf saAHa 217; **~ board** نصف إقامة nuSf iqaama 24; **~ past ...** ... ونصف ... wa nuSf 220

**hammer** مطرقة miTraqa 31

**hand** يد yad 166; **~ washable** يغسل باليد yughsal bil-yad 145

**handbag** حقيبة يد Haqeebat yad 153

**handicapped** معاق muAHaq 163

**handkerchief** منديل mindeel

**hanger** (clothes) علاقة AHlaaqa 27

**happen: what happened?** ماذا حدث؟ maazaa Hadas 93

**harbor** ميناء بحري meenaa baHree

**hat** قبعة qubAHa 144

**have: can I have?** ممكن آخذ؟ mumkin aakhud 18

**have to** (must) يجب أن yajib an 79

**hay fever** حمى القش Huma al-qash 141

**head** رأس ra's 166; **~ waiter** المتر al-mitr 41; **~ache** صداع SudaAH 163

**health** صحة SiHHa; **~ food store** محل أطعمة صحية maHall aTAHima SiHHeeya 129; **~ insurance** تأمين صحي ta'meen SiHHee 168

**hear, to** يسمع yasmAH

**hearing aid** سماعة (لثقيلي السمع) samaaAHa

**heart** قلب qalb 166; **~ attack** أزمة قلبية azma qalbeeya 163; **~ condition** مريض بالقلب mareeD bil-qalb 163

**heat** تدفئة tadfi'a 25

**heating** تدفئة tadfi'a 25

**heavy** ثقيل taqeel 14, 69, 134

**height** طول Tool 152

**hello** السلام عليكم as-salaam AHlaykum 10; مرحبا marHaban 118

**helmet** خوذة khooza 82

**help: can you help me?** ممكن تساعدني؟ mumkin tusaAHidnee 18, 92

**hemorrhoids** البواسير al-bawaaseer 165

**her** ها haa (on end of word) 16; **hers** لها lahaa 16

**here** هنا hunaa; **here it is** ها هو هنا haa huwa huna 17

**hi!** أهلا! ahlan 10

**high** مرتفع martafiAH 122; **~ blood pressure** (ارتفاع) ضغط الدم (irtifaAH) DaghT ad-dam 163

**highlighted** (hair) مميش mumayyish 147

**hill** تل tall 107

**his** ـه uh (on end of word) 16; لـ lahu 16

**hitchhiking** طلب توصيل Talb tauSeel 83

**hobby(-ies)** هواية (هوايات) hiwaaya(at) 121

**holiday** إجازة ijaaza 123; **~ resort** منتجع muntajAH; **on ~** في إجازة fee ijaaza 66

**home** بيت bayt; **we're going home** سنعود إلى بيتنا sa-nAHood ilaa baytnaa

**homosexual** (adj) شاذ جنسي shaazz jinseeyan

**honey** عسل AHsal 43; **~moon** شهر العسل shahr al-AHsa1;

**hood** (of car) غطاء المحرك ghaTaa al-muHarrik 90

**insist: I insist** أنا أصر على
ana aSirr AHLaa

**instead of** بدل
badal

**instructions** تعليمات
tAHleemaat 135

**instructor** معلم / مدرب muAHallim/
madarrib

**insulin** انسولين insooleen

**insurance** تأمين ta'meen 86, 89, 93, 168;
**~ card** شهادة التأمين shahaadat
at-ta'meen 93; **~ company**
شركة التأمين sharikat at-ta'meen 93, 153;
**full ~** تأمين شامل ta'meen shaamil 86

**interest(s)** (hobby) هواية (هوايات)
hiwaaya(at) 121

**interesting** مثير للاهتمام mutheer
lil-ihtimaam 101

**International Student Card**
بطاقة طالب عالمية baTaaqat Taalib
AHlameeyya 29

**Internet** الإنترنت al-intarnat 155

**interpreter** مترجم mutarjim 93, 153

**intersection** تقاطع taqaaTiAH 95

**introduce, to** يقدّم yuqaddim 118

**invitation** دعوة dAHwa 124

**invite, to** يدعو yadAHoo 124

**Iraq** العراق al-AHiraaq

**Iraqi** عراقي AHiraaqee

**Ireland** إرلندا irlandaa 119

**is it ...?** هل هو ... ؟ hal huwa 17

**is there ...?** هل هناك ... ؟ hal hunaak 17

**is this ...?** هل هذا ... ؟ hal haaza ... 145

**Italian** إيطالي eeTaalee 35

**items** مواد mawaad 69

**J**

**jacket** جاكيت jaakeet 144

**jam** مربى murabba 43

**jammed** مزنوق maznooq 25

**jar** برطمان barTumaan 159

**jaw** فك fakk 166

**jazz** الجاز al-jaaz 111

**jeans** جينز jeenz 144

**jellyfish** قنديل البحر qindeel al-baHr

**jet lag: I'm jet lagged**
أشعر بدوار السفر ashAHur bi-dawaar as-safar

**jetski** دراجة مائية darraaja
maa'eeya 117

**jeweler** جواهرجي jawaahirjee 149

**Jewish** (adj) يهودي yahoodee

**job: what's your job?** ما هي وظيفتك؟
maa hiya waZeeftak?

**joint** (body) مفصل mifSal 166

**joke** دعابة duAHaaba

**Jordan** الأردن al-urdunn

**Jordanian** أردني urdunnee

**journalist** صحافي SaHaafee

**judo** الجودو al-joodoo 115

**jug** إبريق ibreeq

**juice** عصير AHSeer 50

**jump leads** أسلاك تشغيل بطارية السيارة
aslaak tashgheel baTaareeyat
as-sayyaara

**junction** (intersection) تقاطع طريق
taqaaTuAH Tareeq

**K**

**keep: keep the change!**
احتفظ بالباقي iHtafiZ bil-baaqee

**ketchup** كتشب ketchup

**kettle** غلاية ghalaaya 29

**key(s)** مفتاح (مفاتيح) miftaaH (mafaateeH)
(mafaateeH) 27, 28, 88; **~ ring**
سلسلة مفاتيح silsilat mafaateeH 156

**kiddie pool** مسبح للأطفال masbaH
lil-aTfaal 113

**kidney** كلية kilya 166

**kilo(gram)** كيلو keeloo 159

**kilometer** كيلومتر keeloomatr

**kind** (*pleasant*) لطيف laTeef

**kind: what kind of ...** ما نوع هذا الـ ...
maa nooAH haazal ...

**kiosk** كشك kushk

**kitchen** مطبخ maTbakh 29

**knapsack** حقيبة الظهر Haqeebat
iZ-Zahr 31, 145

**knee** ركبة rukba 166

**knife (knives)** (سكاكين) سكين sikkeen
(sakaakeen) 39, 41, 148

**knight** (*chess*) حصان الشطرنج HuSaan
ash-shaTranj

**Kuwait** الكويت al-kuwayt

**Kuwaiti** كويتي kuwaytee

**L** **ladder** سلم sillim
**ladies' fingers** بمية bamya 47

**lake** بحيرة buhayra 107

**lamb** ضاني Daanee 46

**lamp** مصباح miSbaaH 25, 29

**language course** دورة لدراسة لغة daura
li-diraasat lugha

**large** كبير kabeer 40, 110

**larger** أكبر akbar 134

**last** أخير akheer 68, 75;
آخر aakhir 80

**last, to** يدوم yadoom

**later** متأخر mutakhkhar 147, 221

**laugh, to** يضحك yaDHak 126

**laundromat** (خدمة ذاتية) مغسلة maghsala
(khidma zaateeya) 131

**laundry** (*service*) مغسلة maghsala 22

**lawyer** محام muHaamee 152

**laxative** مسهل musahhil

**lead, to** يؤدي إلى yu'addee ilaa 94

**lead-free** (*gas/petrol*) دون رصاص
doon raSaaS 87

**learn, to** يتعلم
yatAHallam

**leather** جلد jild 145

**leave, to** (*depart*) يغادر
yughaadir 32, 70, 81;
(*deposit*) يترك yatruk 72;
**leave me alone!** اتركني وحدي
utruknee waHdee 126; **I've left
my bag** تركت حقيبتي tarakt Haqeebtee

**Lebanese** لبناني lubnaanee 35

**Lebanon** لبنان Lubnaan

**left** يسار yasaar 95; **on the ~**
على اليسار AHlal yasaar 95

**left-luggage office** مكتب الأمانات
maktab al-amaanaat 71

**leg** ساق saaq 166

**legal** قانوني qaanoonee

**lemon** ليمون laymoon 38

**lemonade** ليمونادة laymoonaada

**length** طول Tool

**lens** عدسة AHDasa 151, 167; **~ cap**
غطاء للعدسة ghiTaa' lil-AHDasa 151

**lentils** عدس AHds 48; **lentil soup**
شوربة عدس shoorbit AHds 43

**less** أقل aqall 15

**lesson(s)** (دروس) درس dars (duroos)

**letterbox** صندوق الخطابات
Sundooq al-khaTaabaat

**lettuce** خس khass 47

**level** (*even*) مستو mustawee 31

**library** مكتبة maktaba

**Libya** ليبيا leebeeyaa

**Libyan** ليبي leebee

**lifeguard** منقذ munqiz 117

**lift** (*elevator*) مصعد miSAHad 26

**light(s)** (أنوار) نور noor (anwaar) 82, 83;
**~ bulb** لمبة lamba 148

**light** (*adj. – color*) فاتح faatiH 14, 134, 143;
(*adj. – weight*) خفيف khafeef 14, 134

**lighter** (color) أفتح aftaH 143; (with more light) أكثر إنارة aktar inaara 24

**lighter** (cigarette) ولاعة walaAHa 150

**like** (similar to) مثل misl

**like, to** يحب yuHibb 111, 119, 121; **I like it** أحبه uHibbuh 101; **I don't like it** أنا لا أحبه laa uHibbuh 101; **I'd like** أريد ureed 18

**limousine** ليموزين leemoozeen

**linen** كتان kittaan 145

**lipstick** أحمر شفاة aHmar shifaa

**liter(s)** لتر(ات) litr(aat) 87, 159

**little** (small) صغير Sagheer

**live, to** يسكن yaskun 119

**liver** كبد kibd 166

**living room** غرفة جلوس ghurfat juloos 29

**loaf of bread** رغيف خبز ragheef khubz 150

**lobby** (theater/hotel) قاعة qaAHa

**lobster** استاكوزا istaakooza 44

**local** محلي maHallee 35, 37

**lock** قفل qifl 25, 82, 90

**long** طويل Taweel 144, 146

**look for, to** يبحث عن yabHas AHn 133, 143

**loose** واسع waasiAH 146

**lorry** شاحنة shaaHina

**lose, to** يفقد/يضيع yafqad/yuDeeAH **I've lost ...** فقدت ... faqadt 138, 153

**lost property office** مكتب المفقودات maktab al-mafqoodaat 72

**lost-and-found** مكتب المفقودات maktab al-mafqoodaat 72

**love: I love you** أنا أحبك ana uHibbak

**lovely** ممتاز mumtaaz 122

**low** منخفض munkhafiD 122

**low-fat** قليل الدهن qaleel ad-dihn

**luck: good luck** حظ سعيد HaZZ sAHeed 219

**luggage check** مكتب الأمانات maktab al-amaanaat 71

**luggage locker(s)** خزانة (خزائن) الحقائب khazaanat (khazaa'in) al-Haqaa'ib 71

**lump** ورم waram 162

**lunch** غداء ghadaa 98

**lung** رئة ri'a

**M** **madam** مدام madaam

**magazine** مجلة majalla 150

**magnificent** جميل جدا jameel jiddan 101

**maid** خادمة khaadima

**mail** بريد bareed 27; **by ~** بالبريد bil-bareed 22; **~box** صندوق البريد Sundooq al-bareed 154

**mail, to** يرسل بالبريد yarsil bil-bareed

**main** رئيسي ra'eesee 129, 154

**make-up** مكياج mikyaaj

**mallet** مطرقة خشبية miTraqa khashabeeya 31

**man (men)** رجل (رجال) rajul (rijaal)

**manager** مدير mudeer 25, 41, 137

**mango** منجا manga 40, 49

**manicure** تجميل الأظافر tajmeel al-aZaafir 147

**manual** (car) يدوي yadawee

**map** خريطة khareeTa 94, 106, 150

**mark** مارك maark 67

**market(s)** سوق (أسواق) sooq (aswaaq) 99, 131

**married** متزوج mutzawwij 120

**mascara** ماسكارا maskaaraa

**mask** (diving) قناع الغوص qinaaAH al-ghauS

**massage** تدليك tadleek 147

**matches** كبريت kibreet 31, 148, 150

**matter: it doesn't matter** لا يهم laa yuhimm; **what's the matter?** ماذا بك؟ mazaa bik

**mattress** مرتبة martaba 31

**may I?** ممكن؟ mumkin 18

**maybe** ربما rubbamaa

**me** أنا ana

**meal(s)** وجبة (وجبات) wajba(at) 38, 42, 125, 165

**mean, to** يقصد yaqSud; **what does this mean?** ما معنى هذا؟ maa maAHna haaza 23

**measles** حصبة HaSba 165

**measurement** قياس qiyaas

**meat** لحم laHm 41; **~ soup** شوربة لحم shoorbit laHm 43; **~balls** كفتة kufta 46

**medication** دواء dawaa 164, 165

**medium** متوسط mutawassiT 122

**meet, to** يلتقي yaltaqee 125; **pleased to meet you** تشرفنا tasharrafnaa 118; **meeting place** نقطة اللقاء nuqTit al-liqaa' 12

**member(s)** (of club) عضو (أعضاء) ADoo (AHDaa) 112, 116

**mention: don't mention it** عفوا AHfwan 10

**menu** قائمة الطعام qaa'imat aT-TAHaam

**message(s)** رسالة (رسائل) risaala (rasaa'il) 27

**metal** معدن mAHdan

**meter** (taxi) عداد AHdaad 84

**metro** مترو (أنفاق) metroo (anfaaq) 80; **~ station** محطة المترو maHaTTit al-metroo 80

**microwave (oven)** فرن الميكروويف furn al-meekroooweef

**midday** منتصف النهار muntaSaf an-nahaar

**midnight** منتصف الليل muntaSaf al-layl 220

**migraine** صداع شديد SudaaAH shadeed

**mileage** مسافة masaafa 86

**milk** حليب Haleeb 43, 160

**million** مليون milyoon 217

**mind: do you mind?** هل عندك مانع؟ hal AHndak maaniAH 76; **I don't mind** لا أمانع laa umaaniAH 19

**mine** لي lee 16; **it's mine!** هذا لي! hazaa mulkee

**mineral water** مياه معدنية miyaah mAHdaneeya

**mini-bar** البار الصغير al-baar aS-Sagheer 32

**mint tea** شاي بنعنع shaay bi-nAHnAH 51

**minute** دقيقة daqeeqa

**mirror** مرآة miraaya 82

**missing** مفقود mafqood 137, 152

**mistake** خطأ khaTa 35, 41, 42

**mobile home** بيت متنقل bayt mutanaqqil

**modern** حديث Hadees 14

**Modified American Plan (M. A. P.)** نصف إقامة nuSf iqaama 24

**moisturizer (cream)** كريم مرطب kreem muraTTib

**monastery** دير dayr 99

**Monday** (يوم) الاثنين (yaum) al-itnayn 218

**money** فلوس fuloos 42; نقود nuqood 136, 153; **~ order** حوالة نقدية Huwaala naqdeeya; **~-belt** حزام حفظ النقود Hizaam HafZ an-nuqood

**month(s)** شهر (أشهر) shahr (ashhur) 218

**monthly** شهري shahree 79

**moped** دراجة نارية صغيرة darraaja naareeya Sagheera 83

**more** أكثر aktar 15; **I'd like some more ...** أريد المزيد من ... ureed al-mazeed min 39

**morning** صباح SabaaH; **in the ~** صباحا SabaaHan 221

**Moroccan** مغربي maghribee

**Morocco** المغرب al-maghrib 119

**Moslem** مسلم muslim

**mosque** جامع jaamiAH 96, 99, 105

**mosquito bite** لدغة الباعوض ladghat al-baaAHooD

**mother** أم umm 120

**motorbike** دراجة نارية darraaja naareeya 83

**motorboat** زورق بخاري zauraq bukhaaree 117

**mountain** جبل jabal 107; **~ pass** ممر جبلي mamarr jabalee 107; **~ range** سلسلة جبلية silsila jabaaleeya 107

**mountaineering** تسلق الجبال tasalluq al-jibaal 115

**moustache** شوارب shawaarib

**mouth** فم fam 164, 166

**movie** (سينمائي) فيلم feelm (seenamaa'ee) 108, 110; **~ theater** سينما seenimaa 96, 110

**Mr.** السيد as-sayyid

**Mrs.** السيدة as-sayyida

**mugging** سلب salb 152

**muscle** عضلة AHDla 166

**museum** متحف matHaf 99

**music** موسيقى mooseeqaa 111, 121 **~ store** محل كاسيتات maHall kaaseetaat 131

**musician** عازف الموسيقى AHaazif al-mooseeqaa

**mussels** بلح البحر balaH al-baHr 44

**must: I must** لابد أن laa budd an

**mustard** مسطردة musTarda 38

**my** ي ee (on end of word) 16

**myself: I'll do it myself** سأفعل هذا بنفسي sa'afAHal haaza bi-nafsee

**N** **name** اسم ism 22, 36, 118, 120; **my name is ...** اسمي ismee ... 22, 118; **what's your name?** ما اسمك؟ maa ismak 118

**napkin** منديل المائدة mindeel al-maa'da 39

**nappies** حفاضات HafaaDaat 142

**narrow** ضيق Dayyiq 14

**national** وطني waTanee

**nationality** جنسية jinseeya

**near** قريب من qareeb min 12; **nearby** قريب qareeb 21; **nearest** أقرب aqrab 80, 88, 92, 129, 140, 154

**neck** رقبة raqaba 147, 166; **round ~** ياقة مستديرة yaaqa mustadeera 144; **V-~** ياقة سبعة yaaqa sabAHa 144

**necklace** عقد AHuqd 149

**need: I need to ...** ... أحتاج أن aHtaaj an ... 18

**nephew** ابن الأخ أو الأخت ibn al-akh aul ukht

**nerve** عصب AHSab; **nervous system** الجهاز العصبي al-jahaaz al-AHaSabee

**never** أبدا abadan 13; **~ mind** ولا يهمك walaa yuhimmak 10

**new** جديد jadeed 14; **New Year** رأس السنة ra's as-sana 219

**newspaper** جريدة jareeda 150

**newsstand [newsagent]** بائع جرائد baa'iAH jaraa'id 150

**next** قادم qaadim 68, 75, 77, 80;
~ **to** بجانب bijaanib 12, 95

**nice** لذيذ lazeez

**niece** ابنة الأخ أو الأخت ibnat al-akh au al-ukht

**night** ليلة layla; **at ~** بالليل bil-layl 221; **~club** نادي ليلي naadee laylee 112

**no** لا laa 10; **no way!** لا مجال! laa majaal 19

**no-one** لا أحد laa aHad 16

**noisy** مزعج muzAHij 14

**non-alcoholic** بدون كحول bidoon kuHool 50

**non-smoking** عدم التدخين AHdam at-tadkheen 36

**none** لا شيء laa shay 15, 16

**noon** ظهر Zuhr 220

**normal** عادي AHdee 67

**north** شمال shamaal 95

**nose** أنف anf 166

**not yet** ليس بعد laysa bAHd 13

**nothing** لا شيء آخر laa shay 15;
~ **else** لا لا شيء آخر laa laa shay aakhar 15

**notify, to** يعلم yuAHlim 167

**now** الآن al-aan 13,84

**number(s)** رقم (أرقام) raqm (arqaam) 138; **sorry, wrong number** آسف، النمرة غلط aasif, an-nimra ghalaT

**nurse** ممرضة mumarriDa

**nylon** نايلون naayloon

---

**o'clock: it's ... o'clock.**
... الساعة as-saAHa ... 220

**oasis** واحة waaHa 102, 107

**occasionally** من حين إلى آخر min Heen ilaa aakhar

**occupied** (busy) مشغول mashghool 14

---

**octopus** أخطبوط akhTabooT 44

**of course** طبعا TabAHan 19

**office** مكتب maktab

**often** كثيرا kateer 13

**oil** زيت zayt

**okay** حسنا Hasanan 10

**okra** بمية bamya 47

**old** (non-human) قديم qadeem 14;
(human) عجوز AHjooz 14;
**~-fashioned** قديم (زي) qadeem 14

**olive oil** زيت زيتون

**Oman** عمان AHumaan

**Omani** عماني Omanee

**omelette** عجة AHjja 43

**on** (+ day, date) في fee 13;
~ **foot** ماشيا maashiyan 17, 95;
~ **my own** وحدي waHdee 120; ~ **the left** على اليسار AHlal yasaar 12; ~ **the right** على اليمين AHlal yameen 12; ~ **the spot** فورا fauran 93; **on/off switch** مفتاح التشغيل miftaaH at-tashgheel

**once** مرة marra 217

**one** واحد waaHid; **one like that** واحد مثل ذلك waaHid misl zaalik 16

**one-day** (ticket) يومية yaumeeya 79

**one-way** (ticket) ذهاب zahaab 65, 68, 73;
~ **street** طريق باتجاه واحد Tareeq bittijaah waaHid 96

**onion** بصل baSal 47

**open** مفتوح mafTooH 14; **~-air** مكشوف makshoof 117

**open, to** يفتح yaftaH 76, 132, 140

**opening hours** المواعيد al-muwaaAHeed 100

---

opera أوبرا oobraa 108, 111; ~ house دار الأوبرا daar al-oobraa 99, 111

operation عملية AHamaleeya

opposite مقابل muqaabil 12

optician نظاراتي naZaaraatee 131, 167

or أو au

orange (color) برتقالي burtuqaalee 143

oranges برتقال burtuqaal 49

orchestra أوركسترا oorkistraa 111

order, to (request) يطلب yaTlub 32, 37, 41, 135

our نا naa (on end of word) 16

ours لنا linaa 16

outrageous جنوني junoonee 89

outside خارج khaarij 12; في الخارج feel khaarij 36

oval بيضاوي bayDaawee 134

oven فرن furn

over there هناك hunaak 36, 76

overcharge: I've been overcharged دفعت أكثر من اللازم dafAHt aktar min al-laazim

overdone (food) كثير السوا kateer as-siwaa 41

overheat تسخين أكثر من اللازم taskheen aktar min al-laazim

own: on my own وحدي waHdee 65

owner المالك al-maalik

oyster محار maHHaar 44

**P** p.m. بعد الظهر baAHd aZ-Zuhr

pack of cards علبة من ورق اللعب AHulba min waraq al-lAHb

package طرد Tard 155

packet of cigarettes علبة سجائر AHulbat sajaa'ir 150

paddling pool مسبح للأطفال masbaH lil-aTfaal 113

padlock قفل qifl

pail دلو dilw

pain ألم alam 167; ~killer مسكن (الألم) musakkin (al-alam) 141, 165

paint, to يرسم بالألوان yarsim bil-alwaan; painter رسام rassaam; painting لوحة lauHa

pajamas بيجاما beejaamaa

palace قصر qaSr 99

Palestine فلسطين filasTeen

Palestinian فلسطيني filasTeenee

palpitations ضربات القلب المتزايدة Darabaat al-qalb al-mutzaayida

pants (U.S.) بنطلون banTaloon 144

panty hose شراب حريمي طويل shuraab Hareemee Taweel 144

paper ورق waraq 150; ~ napkins مناديل ورق manaadeel waraq 148

paraffin بارافين baaraafeen 31

paralysis شلل shalal

parents: my parents والديّ waalidayya 120

park حديقة عامة Hadeeqa AHama 96, 99, 107

parking ركن rakn 87; ~ lot ركن السيارات rakn as-sayyaaraat 87, 96; ~ meter عداد الركن AHdaad ar-rakn 87

parliament building مبنى البرلمان mabna al-barlamaan 99

party (social) حفلة Hafla 124

passport جواز سفر jawaaz safar 66, 69; joint ~ جواز (سفر) مشترك jawaaz (safar) mushtarak 66

pasta مكرونة makaroona 48

**pastry store** محل حلويات maHall Halweeyaat 131

**patch, to** يرقع yuraqqiAH 137

**patient** (*sick person*) المريض al-mareeD

**pavement** رصيف raSeef; **on the ~** على الرصيف AHlar raSeef

**pay, to** يدفع yadfaAH 42, 67, 136;

**payment** سداد (مبلغ) saddaad (mablagh)

**pay phone** هاتف عام haatif AHaam

**peaches** خوخ khookh 49

**peak** قمة qimma 107

**pearl** اللؤلؤ al-lu'lu' 149

**peas** بسلة bisilla 47

**pebbly** (*beach*) صخري Sakhree 117

**pedal** (*bicycle/car*) دواسة dawaasa 82, 91

**pedestrian crossing** ممر للمشاة mamarr lil-mashaah 96

**pedestrian zone** منطقة المشاة manTiqat al-mashaah 96

**pedicure** تجميل أظافر القدمين tajmeel aZaafir al-qadamayn

**pen(s)** قلم (أقلام) qalam (aqlaam) 150

**penicillin** بنسلين binisileen 165

**penknife** مطواة miTwaa 31

**people** ناس naas 92, 119

**pepper** فلفل filfil 38

**per: ~ day** باليوم bil yaum 83, 86;
**~ hour** فى الساعة fees saAHa 155;
**~ night** لليلة li-layla 21; **~ week** بالأسبوع bil usbooAH 83, 86

**perhaps** ربما rubbamaa 19

**period** (*menstrual*) العادة الشهرية al-AHaada ash-shahreeya 167
**~ pains** ألم العادة الشهرية alam al-AHaada ash-shahreeya 167

**permed** (*hair*) موج mumawwaj 147

**petrol** بنزين banzeen 87, 88; **~ station** محطة بنزين maHaTTat banzeen 87

**pharmacy** أجزخانة/صيدلية ajzakhaana/Saydaleeya 131, 140, 158

**phone, to** يطلب بالهاتف yaTlub bil-haatif

**photo** صورة Soora 116; **to take a ~** يأخذ صورة ya'hkud Soora

**photocopier** آلة نسخ aalat naskh 155

**photograph(s)** صورة (صور) Soora (Suwar) 98

**photographer** مصور muSawwir

**photography** تصوير taSweer 151

**phrase** عبارة AHibaara 11

**pickup truck** شاحنة صغيرة shaaHina Sagheera

**piece** قطعة qiTAHa 69, 159

**pigeon** حمام Hamaam 46

**pill** حبة Habba 165; **the Pill** (*contraceptive*) حبوب منع الحمل Huboob manAH al-Haml 167

**pillow** وسادة wisaada 27;
**~ case** كيس الوسادة kees al-wisaada

**pineapples** أناناس anaanaas 49

**pink** وردي wardee 143

**pizzeria** محل بيتزا maHall beetza 35

**plain** (*not patterned*) سادة saada

**plane** طائرة Taa'ira 68; **by ~** بالطائرة biT-Taa'ira 123

**plant** (*noun*) نبات nabaat

**plastic bag(s)** كيس (أكياس) بلاستك kees (akyaas) balaastik

**plate(s)** صحن (صحون) SaHn (SuHoon) 39, 148

**platform(s)** رصيف (أرصفة) raSeef (arSifa) 72, 76

**platinum** بلاتين balaateen 149

**play** (*theater*) مسرحية masraHeeya 110;
**~wright** كاتب المسرحية kaatib al-masraHeeya 110

play, to يلعب yalAHb 121; (music) يعزف yAHzif 111; ~ group مجموعة لعب majmooAHat lAHb 113

playground ملعب malAHb 113

playing field أرض الملعب arD al-malAHab 96

pleasant مرض murDee 14

please من فضلك min faDlak 10

plug سدادة saddaada 148

plumber سباك sabbaak

plums برقوق barqooq 49

pneumonia التهاب رئوي iltihaab ri'awee 165

point to, to يشير إلى yusheer ilaa 11

poison سم samm; poisonous سام saamm

police شرطة shurTa 92, 152; ~ station مركز الشرطة markaz ash-shurTa 96, 152

pollen count نسبة غبار الطلع nisbat ghubaar aT-TalAH 122

pomegranates رمان rummaan 49

pond بركة birka 107

pop (music) البوب al-boob 111

popular مشهور mash-hoor 111

port (harbor) ميناء بحري meenaa' baHree

porter شيال shayyaal 71

portion مقدار miqdaar 39

possible: as soon as possible بأسرع ما يمكن bi-asrAH maa yumkin

post (mail) بريد bareed; ~ office مكتب البريد maktab al-bareed 96, 131, 154; ~box صندوق البريد Sundooq al-bareed 154; ~card كرت (بوستال) kart (boostaal) 154, 156; ~man ساعي البريد saaAHee al-bareed; postage أجرة البريد ujrat al-bareed 154

potatoes بطاطس baTaaTis 38, 47

pound(s) sterling جنيه (جنيهات) إسترليني junayh(aat) istarleenee 67, 138

power cut انقطاع التيار الكهربائي inqiTaAH at-tayyaar al-kahrabaa'ee

power point(s) مواقع لأخذ الكهرباء mauqiAH (mawaaqiAH) li-akhd al-kahrabaa 30

prawn جمبري/قريدس jambaree/ quraydis 44

pregnant حامل Haamil 163

premium (gas/petrol) ممتاز mumtaaz 87

prescribe, to يصف (الدواء) yaSif 165

prescription وصفة (طب) waSfa 140, 141

present (gift) هدية hideeya

press, to يكوي yakwee 137

pretty جميل jameel

price سعر sAHr 24

primus stove موقد البريموس mauqad il-bareemoos 31

prison سجن sijn

probably من المحتمل min al-muHtamal 19

produce store بقالة baqqaala 131

program برنامج barnaamij 109

pronounce, to ينطق yanTuq

pullover كنزة kanza

pump مضخة maDakhkha 82, 87

puncture ثقب thuqb 83, 88

pure (cotton) قطن (خالص) (quTn) khaalis 145

purple بنفسجي banafsijee 143

purse (Brit.) محفظة maHfaZa 153

put: where can I put ...? أين أضع الـ ...؟ ayn aDAH al ...

pyramid(s) هرم (أهرام) haram (ahraam) 102

**Q** Qatar قطر qaTar
Qatari قطري qaTaree
**quality** (type) نوع nauAH 134
**quantity** كمية kimmeeya 134
**quarter** ربع rubAH 217
**quarter past ...** والربع
... war-rubAH 220; **quarter to ...**
... إلا ربعاً ... ilaa rubAH 220
**question** سؤال su'aal
**queue, to** يصطف yaSTaff 112
**quick** سريع sareeAH 14
**quickest: what's the quickest way?**
ما هي أسرع طريقة؟ maa hiya
asrAH Tareeqa
**quickly** بسرعة bi-surAHa 17
**quiet** هادئ haadi' 14
**quieter** أهدأ ahda' 24, 126

**R** rabbit (meat) أرانب araanib 46
race سباق sibaaq;
racetrack [racecourse]
مضمار السباق miDmaar as-sibaaq 114
**racket** (sports) مضرب miDrab 116
**radiator** خزان الماء khazaan
al-maa' 91
**railroad [railway]** سكك حديدية
sikak Hadeedeeya
**rain, to** تمطر tumTir 122
**raincoat** معطف للمطر miAHTaf
lil-maTar 144
**rape** اغتصاب ightiSaab 152
**rare** (steak) قليل السواء qaleel
as-siwaa'; (unusual) نادر naadir
**rash** (skin) طفح جلدي TafH
jildee 162
**rate: special rate** أسعار خاصة
asAHaar khaaSSa 86

**razor** موس الحلاقة
moos al-Hilaaqa;
**~ blade** شفرة الحلاقة
shafrat al-Hilaaqa 142
**reading** قراءة qiraa'a 121
**ready** جاهز jaahiz 89, 137, 151
**real** (genuine) حقيقي Haqeeqee 149
**really?** بجد؟ bijadd 19
**receipt** وصل waSl 32, 89, 136, 151
**reception (desk)** مكتب الاستقبال
maktab al-istiqbaal
**receptionist** موظف الاستقبال muwaZZaf
al-istiqbaal
**recommend, to** ينصح yinSaH 21,
35, 141; **can you recommend ...?**
ممكن تنصحنا ... ؟ mumkin tinSaHnaa 108;
**what do you recommend?**
بماذا تنصحنا؟ bi-maaza tinSaHnaa 37
**record** (music) أسطوانة ustuwaana 157
**red** أحمر aHmar 143; **~ wine**
نبيذ أحمر nabeet aHmar 49
**reduction(s)** (in price) تخفيض (تخفيضات)
takhfeeD(aat) 68
**refrigerator** ثلاجة tallaaja 29
**refund** (نقود) استرجاع istirjaAH
(nuqood) 137
**refuse bag(s)** كيس (أكياس) قمامة kees
(akyaas) qimaama 148
**region** منطقة minTaqa 106
**registered mail** البريد المسجل al-bareed
al-musajjal
**registration number** رقم السيارة
raqm as-sayyaara 88
**regular** (gas/petrol) عادي AHdee 87;
(size) متوسط mutawassiT 110
**religion** ديانة diyyaana
**remember** يتذكر yatzakkar; **I don't**
**remember** أنا لا أتذكر ana laa atzakkar
**rent, to** يستأجر yasta'jir 29, 86, 116;
**I'd like to rent** أريد استئجار ureed
isti'jaar 83

**sales rep.** مندوب مبيعات
mandoob mabeeAHaat

**sales tax** ضريبة Dareeba 24

**salt** ملح malH 38, 39

**salty** مالح maaliH

**same: the same ...** نفس الـ...
nafs al-... 74; **same-day** بنفس اليوم
bi-nafs al-yaum 74

**sand** رمل raml; **~ dune** كثيب رملي
kuthayb ramlee 107; **sandy** (beach)
رملي ramlee 117

**sandals** صندل Sandal 145

**sandwich** سندويتش sandawitsh 40

**sanitary napkins [towels]**
فوطة صحية للسيدات fuwaT SiHHeeya
lis-sayyidaat 142

**satellite TV** تلفزيون فضائي tilifizyoon
faDaa'ee

**satin** (القماش) (الساتان) (qumaash)
as-saataan

**satisfied: I'm not satisfied with this**
أنا غير راض عن هذا ana ghayr
raadee AHn haaza

**Saturday** (يوم) السبت (yaum)
as-sabt 218

**sauce** صلصة SalSa 38

**saucepan** إناء صغير inaa' Sagheer 29

**Saudi** سعودي sAHoodee

**Saudi Arabia** السعودية as-sAHoodeeya

**sauna** السونا as-sauna 26

**sausages** سجق sujuq 46, 160

**say** يقول yaqool; **how do you say ...?**
كيف تقول ...؟ kayf taqool ...

**scarf** لفاح lifaaH 144

**scheduled flight**
رحلة طيران مجدولة
riHlat Tayaraan mujadwala

**school** مدرسة madrasa 96

**scissors** مقص miqaSS 148

**Scotland** اسكوتلندا iskootlandaa 119

**screwdriver** مفك mifakk 148

**sea** بحر baHr 107;
**~front** على البحر
AHlal baHr;
**~sick: I feel seasick**
أشعر بدوار البحر
ashAHur bi-dawaar al-baHr

**season ticket** تذكرة موسمية
tazkara mausimeeya

**seat(s)** (مقاعد) مقعد maqAHd
(maqaa'id) 73, 76, 108, 109; **~ belt**
حزام الأمان Hazaam al-amaan 90;
**aisle ~** مقعد بقرب الممر maqAHd
bi-qurb al-mamarr 69; **window ~**
مقعد بجانب الشباك maqAHd bi-jaanib
ish-shibaak 69

**second** ثاني taanee 217; **~ class**
درجة ثانية daraja tanya 73;
**~-hand** مستعمل mustAHmal

**secretary** سكرتيرة sakriteera

**sedative** مهدئ mahaddi'

**see, to** يرى yara 18; (witness) يشاهد
yashaahid 93; **see you soon!**
إلى اللقاء! ilaal liqaa 126

**self-employed** صاحب مهنة حرة
SaaHib mihna Hurrah 121

**self-service** خدمة ذاتية khidma
zaateeya 87, 133

**sell, to** يبيع yabeeAH 133

**send, to** يرسل yursil 155

**senior citizen(s)** (مسنين) مسن
musinn(een) 74

**separated** (in marriage) منفصل
munfaSil 120

**separately** منفصلين munfasileen 42

**serious** جاد jaadd

**service(s)** خدمات khidma(at) 131;
**is service included?**
هل الخدمة ضمن الحساب؟
hal il-khidma Dimn
il-Hisaab 42

**serviette** منديل المائدة mindeel al-maa'da 39

**set menu** طبق اليوم Tabaq al-yaum 37

**shady** مظلل muZallal 31

**shallow** ضحل DaHil

**shampoo** شامبو shamboo 142

**shape(s)** شكل (أشكال) shakl (ashkaal) 134

**share, to** يشارك yushaarik

**sharp** حاد Haadd 69

**shaving brush** فرشاة الحلاقة furshat al-Hilaaqa

**shaving cream** كريم الحلاقة kreem al-Hilaaqa

**she** هي hiya

**sheath** (contraceptive) غشاء طبي ghishaa' Tibbee

**sheet(s)** (bedding) ملاءة (ملاءات) milaaya(at) 28

**shirt** قميص qameeS 144

**shock** (electric) صدمة كهربائية Sadma kahrabaa'ee

**shoes** حذاء Hizaa 145; **shoe laces** رباط الحذاء ribaaT al-Hizaa; **shoe polish** ورنيش أحذية warneesh aHzeeya; **shoe repair** تصليح أحذية taSleeH aHzeeya; **shoe store** [**shop**] محل أحذية maHall aHzeeya 131

**shop(s)** محل (محلات) maHall(aat); **~ assistant** بائع في محل baa'iAH fee maHall

**shopping: go ~** يتسوق yatsawwaq 124; **~ basket** سلة المشتريات sillat al-mushtarayaat; **~ mall** [**centre**] مركز تجاري markaz tijaaree 129, 131

**shore** (sea/lake) شاطئ shaaTi'

**short** قصير qaSeer 14, 144, 146, 147

**shorts** شورت shoort 144

**shoulder** كتف kitif 166

**shovel** جاروف jaaroof 157

**show, to** يري yuree 133; **can you show me?** ممكن تريني؟ mumkin tureenee 94, 106

**shower** دش dush 21, 26, 30

**shrimp** جمبري/قريدس jambaree/ quraydis 44

**shut** (closed) مغلق mughlaq 14

**shut, to** يقفل yuqfil 132

**side(s)** جانب (جوانب) jaanib (jawaanib) 147; **~ order** طلب جانبي Talab jaanibee 38

**sight: far- [long-] sighted** طويل النظر Taweel an-naZar 167; **near- [short-] sighted** قصير النظر qaSeer an-naZar 167

**sights** معالم mAHaalim

**sightseeing tour** جولة لزيارة المعالم jaula li-ziyaarat al-mAHaalim 97

**sign** (road) لافتة laafta 93

**signpost** لافتة laafta

**silk** حرير Hareer

**silver** فضة faDDa 149; **~ plate** قشرة فضة qishrat faDDa 149

**singer(s)** مغن (مغنيون) mughanee(yeen) 157

**single** (cabin) لشخص li-shakhS 81; (not married) عازب AHaazib 120; (ticket) ذهاب (فقط) zahaab (faqaT) 65, 68, 73; **~ room** غرفة لشخص ghurfa li-shakhS 21

**sink** مغسل maghsal 25

**sister** أخت ukht 120

**sit, to** يجلس yajlis 36, 76, 126

**sit down, please** اجلس، من فضلك ijlis, min faDlak

**size** قياس qiyaas 116, 146

skiing التزحلق على الجليد at-tazaHluq AHlaal jaleed 115

skin جلد jild 166

skirt تنورة tannoorra 144

sleep, to ينام yanaam 167

sleeper car عربة نوم AHrabit naum 73

sleeping bag حقيبة للنوم Haqeeba lil-naum 31

sleeping pill منوم munawwim

sleeve(s) كم (أكمام) kumm (akmaam) 144

slippers شبشب shibshib 145

slow بطيء baTee' 14; **slow down!** هدئ السرعة! hadi' as-surAHa; **slowly** ببطء bi-buT' 11, 17, 94

small صغير Sagheer 14, 24, 40, 110, 134; **smaller** أصغر aShgar 136

smoke, to يدخن yudakhkhin 126

smoking تدخين tadkheen 36

snacks وجبات خفيفة wajbaat khafeefa

snack bar مطعم سناك maTAHm snaak 72

sneakers حذاء رياضة Hizaa riyaaDa

snorkel أنبوبة التنفس anboobat at-tanaffus

soap صابون Saaboon 27, 142; **~ powder** مسحوق الغسيل masHooq al-ghaseel

soccer كرة القدم kurat al-qadam 115

socket فيش كهرباء feesh kahrabaa'

socks شراب shuraab 144

soft drink كازوزة kaazooza 110, 160

solarium شرفة حمام شمسي shurfat Hammaam shamsee 22

sole (shoes) نعل nAHl

some بعض bAHD

someone أحد ما aHad maa 16

something شيء ما shay maa 16

sometimes أحيانا aHyaanan 13

somewhere أي مكان ayy makaan 108

son ابن ibn 120, 162

soon قريبا qareeban 13; **as soon as possible** أقرب فرصة ممكنة aqrab furSa mumkina 161

sore ملتهب multahib; **~ throat** ألم في الحلق alam feel Halq 141, 163

sorry آسف aasif 10

sort(s) صنف (أصناف) Sanf (aSnaaf) 134

soup شوربة shoorba 43

sour حازق Haaziq 41

south جنوب janoob 95

South Africa جنوب أفريقيا janoob afreeqyaa

South African جنوب أفريقي janoob afreeqee

souvenir تذكار tizkaar 98, 156 **~ store** محل هدايا تذكارية maHall hadaayaa tizkaareeya 131

space (e.g. in campsite) مكان makaan 30

spade جاروف jaaroof 157

spare (extra) إضافي iDaafee

speak, to يتكلم yatkallam 11, 18, 41, 67, 128; **~ to s.o.** يتكلم مع yatkallam mAHa 128; **do you speak English?** تتكلم إنجليزي؟ tatkallam injileezee 11

specialist أخصائي akhSaa'ee 164

spectacles نظارات naZaaraat

spicy كثير البهار kateer al-buhaar

sponge إسفنج isfinj 148

spoon(s) ملعقة (ملاعق) milAHaqa (malaAHiq) 39, 41, 148

**sport** رياضة
riyaaDa 114, 121;
**sports club** نادٍ رياضي
naadee riyaaDee
115; **sports ground**
أرض الملعب arD al-malAHab 96;
**sporting goods store** محل أدوات رياضية
maHall adawaat riyaaDeeya 131

**sprained** ملتوٍ multawee 164

**spring** (season) الربيع ar-rabeeAH 219

**square** مربع murabbAH 134

**squash** الإسكواش al-iskwaash 115

**squid** سبيط subbayT 44

**stadium** مدرج mudarraj 96

**stain** بقعة buqAHa

**stairs** سلم sillim 132

**stamp(s)** طابع (طوابع) TaabiAH
(TawaabiAH) 150, 154

**stand in line, to** يصطف yaSTaff 112

**start, to** يبدأ yabda' 98, 108

**station** محطة maHaTTa 96

**statue** تمثال timthaal 99

**stay** (noun) إقامة iqaama 32

**stay, to** (remain) يبقى yibqaa 65;
(reside) يقيم yuqeem 23, 123

**steak house** مطعم لحم ستيك maTAHm
laHm steek 35

**steering wheel**
عجلة القيادة
AHjalat al-qiyaada 90

**sterilizing solution**
سائل معقم
saa'il muAHqqim 142

**still: I'm still waiting**
أنا لا أزال منتظرا
ana la azaal muntaZiran

**sting** حرقان Haraqaan 162

**stockings** جوارب حريمي jawaarib
Hareemee 144

**stolen: ... has been stolen**
سُرق ... suriqa ... 71

**stomach** بطن baTn 166; ~ache
ألم في البطن alam feel baTn 163

**stop** (bus/metro) محطة maHaTTa 79, 80;
**next stop!**
المحطة القادمة! al-maHaTTa al-qaadima 79;
**which stop?** أي محطة؟ ayy
maHaTTa 80

**stop, to** يتوقف yatwaqqaf 77;
يقف عند yaqif 98; **stop at**
يقف عند yaqif AHnd 75, 77

**stopcock** محبس maHbas 28

**store(s)** محل (محلات) maHall(aat) 129;
**~ guide** دليل المحل daleel
al-maHall 132

**stove** فرن furn 28, 29

**straight ahead** على طول AHla Tool 95

**strained muscle**
تمزق عضلي
tamazzuq AHDalee 162

**strange** غريب ghareeb 101

**straw** (drinking) ماصة maaSSa

**strawberries** فراولة faraawla 49

**stream** جدول jadwal 107

**street** شارع shaariAH; **main [high] ~**
الشارع الرئيسي ash-shaariAH
ar-ra'eesee 96; **side ~**
طريق جانبي Tareeq jaanibee 95

**strong** (potent) قوي المفعول qawee
al-mafAHool

**student(s)** طالب (طلاب) Taalib
(Tulaab) 74, 100, 121

**study, to** يدرس yadrus 121

**stunning** مذهل muzhil 101

**subtitled** (movie) مترجم mutarjam 110

**subway** (metro) مترو (أنفاق) metro
(anfaaq) 80; **~ station**
محطة المترو maHaTTit metro 80

**Sudan** السودان as-soodaan

**Sudanese** سوداني soodaanee

**sugar** سكر sukkar 38, 39

**suggest, to** يقترح yaqtariH 123

**suit** بدلة badla 144

**suitable (for)** مناسب (لـ) munaasib (li)

**A-Z**

summer الصيف aS-Sayf 219

sun شمس shams; **~bathe, to**
يأخذ حمام شمس ya'khud Hamaam
shams; **~burn** حرقة الشمس
Harqat ash-shams 141; **~glasses**
نظارات شمس naZaarat shams;
**~stroke** ضربة شمس Darbat
shams 163; **~tan cream**
كريم الشمس kreem ash-shams 142;

**sunny** مشمس mushmis 31

Sunday (يوم) الأحد (yaum) al-aHad 218

superb ممتاز mumtaaz 101

supermarket سوبرماركت
soobarmaarkat 131, 158

supervision إشراف ishraaf 113

supplement(s) إضافة (إضافات)
iDaafa(at) 68

suppositories تحاميل/لبوس
taHaameel/luboos 165

sure: are you sure?
هل أنت متأكد؟ hal anta mutakkid

surfboard لوح ركوب الموج
rukoob al-mauj 117

surname اسم العائلة ism al-AHaaila

sweater كنزة kanza 144

sweatshirt سويت شيرت sweet
sheert 144

sweet (taste) حلو Hilw

sweets سكاكر sakaakir 150

swelling ورم waram 162

swim, to يسبح yasbaH 117

swimming السباحة as-sibaaHa 115;
**~ pool** حمام سباحة
HamMaam
sibaaHa 117; **~ trunks** مايوه رجالي
maayoo rijaalee 144

swimsuit مايوه نسائي maayoo
nisaa'ee 144

switch (light) مفتاح النور miftaaH an-noor 25

swollen, to be متورم mutwarrIm

symptoms أعراض AHraaD 163

synthetic
اصطناعي
iSTinaAHee 145

Syria سوريا sooreeyaa

Syrian سوري sooree

**T** T-shirt تي-شيرت tee-sheert 144, 156
**table** مائدة maa'da 36, 112;

table tennis تنس الطاولة tanis
aT-Taawla 115

tablet(s) قرص qurS (aqraaS) 140

take, to يأخذ yakhud; **~ medicine**
يأخذ دواء yakhud dawaa 140;
**I'll take it** سآخذه sa-aakhuduh 135;
**taken** (reserved) محجوز maHjooz 76

talcum powder بودرة تلك boodrat talk

talk, to يتكلم yatkallam

tall طويل Taweel 14

tampons صمامات قطنية للسيدات
Samaamaat qutneeya lis-sayyidaat 142

tan سمرة الشمس sumrat ash-shams

tap حنفية Hanafeeya 25

taxi(s) تاكسي (تاكسيات) taaksee(yaat)
70, 71, 84; **shared ~** سرفيس
sarfees 78; **~ stand [rank]**
موقف تاكسي mawqif taaksee 96

tea شاي shaay 51; **~ bags**
أكياس شاي
akyaas shaay 160; **~ towel**
فوطة مطبخ fooTat maTbakh 156; **~spoon**
ملعقة صغيرة milAHaqa Sagheera 140

teacher مدرس mudarris

team(s) فريق (فرق) fareeq
(firaq) 115

teddy bear دمية بشكل دب dumya
bi-shakl dubb 157

telephone تلفون tilifoon 22, 92, 127;
**~ number** رقم التلفون raqm
at-tilifoon 127

**tell: can you tell me?** ممكن تقول لي؟
mumkin taqool lee?
18, 79

**temperature** (body)
حرارة (الجسم) Harraara 164

**temple** معبد mAHbad 99

**temporarily** مؤقتا mu'aqqatan 89, 168

**tennis** التنس at-tanis 115; ~ **court(s)**
ملعب (ملاعب) التنس malAHab
(malaaAHib) at-tanis 115

**tent(s)** خيمة (خيام) khayma (khiyaam)
30, 31; ~ **peg(s)** وتد (أوتاد) الخيمة
awatad (autaad) il-khayma 31;
~ **pole** عامود الخيمة AHamood
il-khayma 31

**terrible** سيء جدا sayyi' jiddan 19;
فظيع faZeeAH 101

**thank you** شكرا shukran 10

**that one** ذلك zaalik 16, 134

**that's all** هذا كله haaza kulluh 133

**theater** مسرح masraH 96, 110

**theft** سرقة saraqa 153

**their** هم hum (on end of word) 16

**theirs** لهم lahum 16

**then** (time) في هذا الوقت fee haazal
waqt 13

**there** هناك hunaak 12
**there is/are** هناك hunaak 17;
**there it is** ها هو هناك haa huwa
hunaak 17

**thermometer** مقياس الحرارة miqyaas
al-Harraara

**thermos flask** ترموس tirmoos

**these ones** هذه haazihi 134

**they** هم hum

**thick** سميك sameek

**thief** لص liSS

**thigh** فخذ fakhd 166

**thin** رفيع rafeeAH

**think: I think** أظن aZunn 76;
أعتقد AHtaqid 42; **think about**
يفكر في yufakkir fee; **what do you think of ...**
ما رأيك في ...؟ maa ra'yak fee 119

**third** (adj.) ثالث taalit 217;
~ **party insurance** تأمين الطرف الثالث
ta'meen aT'Taraf at-taalit

**third** (noun) ثلث tult 217

**thirsty** عطشان AHTshaan

**this one** هذا haaza 16, 134

**those ones** تلك tilka 134

**thousand** ألف alf 217

**throat** حنجرة Hanjara 166

**through** من خلال min khilaal

**thundery** راعد raAHid 122

**Thursday** (يوم) الخميس (yaum)
al-khamees 218

**ticket(s)** تذكرة (تذاكر) tazkhara (tazaakir)
65, 69, 73, 74, 100, 114, 153;
~ **office** شباك التذاكر shabbaak
at-tazaakir 72

**tie** كرفتة krafatta 144

**tight** ضيق Dayyiq 146

**tights** شراب حريمي طويل shuraab
Hareemee Taweel 144

**till receipt** إيصال الدفع eeSaal
ad-dafAH

**time** وقت waqt; **free** ~ وقت حر
hurr 98; **on** ~ في موعده fee
mauAHiduh 75; **what time ...?**
أي ساعة ...؟ ayy saaAHa 68;
**what's the time?** كم الساعة؟
kam as-saAHa 220

**timetable** جدول المواعيد
jadwal al-mawaaAHeed 75

**tin opener** فتاحة معلبات
fattaaHat muAHlabaat 148

**tire(s) [tyre(s)]** إطار (إطارات)
iTaar(at) 90

**tired** متعب mutAHb

**tissues** مناديل ورق manaadeel
waraq 142

**to** *(place)* إلى ilaa 12

**toast** خبز محمص khubz
muHammaS 43

**tobacco** تبغ tabgh 150

**today** اليوم al-yaum 124, 161, 218

**toe** إصبع القدم iSbAH al-qadam 166

**toilet** مرحاض marHaaD 29; **~ paper**
ورق الحمام waraq al-Hammam 25, 29

**tomatoes** طماطم TamaaTim 47

**tomato soup** شوربة طماطم shoorbit
TamaaTim 43

**tomorrow** غدا ghadan 84, 161, 218

**tongue** لسان lisaan 166

**tonight** الليلة al-layla 110, 124;
**for tonight** لهذه الليلة li-haazihil
layla 109

**tonsilitis** التهاب اللوزتين iltihaab
al-lauzatayn 165

**tonsils** لوز luwaz 166

**too** جداً jiddan 93, 135; كثيرا kateer 146;
**~ much** كثير جدا kateer jiddan 15

**tooth (teeth)** سنة (أسنان) sinna
(asnaan) 168; **~brush**
فرشاة الأسنان furshat al-asnaan;
**~ache** ألم الأسنان
alam al-asnaan; **~paste** معجون أسنان
mAHjoon asnaan 142

**top** قمة qimma 147

**torch** بطارية جيب baTaareeyat
jayb 31

**torn** مقطوع maqTooAH; **~ muscle**
تمزق tamazzuq

**tough** *(food)* عسير المضغ
AHseer al-maDgh 41

**tour** جولة jaula 97;
**~ representative**
مندوب سياحي
mandoob siyaaHee 27

**tourist(s)** سائح (سائحون)
saa'iH (saa'iHeen);

~ **office**
مكتب السياحة
maktab
as-siyyaaHa 97

**tow truck** ونش winsh 88

**tower** برج burj 99

**town** مدينة madeena 70, 94;
**~ hall** دار البلدية daar al-baladeeya 99;
**old ~** مدينة قديمة madeena
qadeema 96, 99

**toy** لعبة lAHba 157; **~ store**
محل لعب maHall luAHb 131

**traditional** تقليدي taqleedee 35

**traffic** حركة المرور Harakat al-muroor;
**~ jam** احتقان المرور iHtiqaan
al-muroor; **~ violation [offence]**
مخالفة مرور mukhaalfat muroor

**trailer** بيت متنقل bayt mutanaqqil 30, 81

**train** قطار qiTaar 72, 75, 76;
**~ station** محطة القطار maHaTTat
al-qiTaar 72; **by ~** بالقطار
bil-qiTaar 123

**trainers** حذاء رياضة Hizaa riyaaDa 145

**tram** ترام traam

**transfer** تحويل taHweel

**transit, in** ترانزيت traanzeet

**translate, to** يترجم yutarjim 11

**translation** ترجمة tarjama

**translator** مترجم mutarjim

**trash** زبالة zibaala 28;
**~can** صندوق الزبالة Sundooq
iz-zibaala 30

**travel** سفر safar; **~ agency**
مكتب سفر maktab safar 131;
**~ sickness** دوار السفر dawwaar
as-safar 141

**traveler's check(s) [cheque(s)]**
شيك (شيكات) سياحي (سياحية)
sheek(aat) siyaaHee(ya) 136, 138

**tray** صينية Seeneeya

tree(s) شجرة (شجر) shajara (shajar) 106

trim (hair) تقليم taqleem 147

trip (journey) رحلة riHla 75, 77, 97, 123

trolley(-ies) عربة (عربات) AHraba(at) 158

trousers بنطلون banTaloon 144

truck شاحنة shaaHina

true: that's true هذه الحقيقة hazihil Haqeeqa 19; that's not true هذا غير صحيح haazaa ghayr SaHeeH

trunk (of car) صندوق السيارة Sundooq as-sayyaara 90

try on, to يجرب yajarrib 146

Tuesday (يوم) الثلاثاء (yaum) at-talaat 218

tumor ورم waram 165

Tunisia تونس toonis

Tunisian تونسي toonisee

tunnel نفق nafaq

turkey ديك رومي deek roomee 46

turning منعطف munAHTaf 95

TV تلفزيون tilifizyoon 22

tweezers ملقاط milqaaT

twice مرتان marratayn 217

twin bed بسريرين bi-sareerayn 21

type نوع nauAH 109

typical تقليدي taqleedee 37

U.S. أمريكا amreeka 119

ugly قبيح qabeeH 14, 101

U.K. المملكة المتحدة al-mamlaka al-mutaHida

ulcer قرحة qurHa

uncle عم/خال AHmm (paternal) / khaal (maternal) 120

unconscious فاقد الوعي faaqid al-wAHee 92, 162

under تحت taHt

underdone (food) قليل السوا qaleel as-siwaa 41

underpants لباس داخلي libaas daakhilee 144

underpass نفق nafaq 96

understand, to يفهم yafham 11; do you understand? هل تفهم؟ hal tafham 11; I don't understand لا أفهم laa afham 11

uneven (ground) غير مستوٍ ghayr mustawee

unfortunately للأسف lil-asaf 19, 126

United States الولايات المتحدة al-wilaayaat al-mutaHida

unleaded petrol بنزين خالي الرصاص banzeen khaalee ar-raSaaS

unlimited mileage دون تحديد المسافة doon taHdeed al-masaafa

unlock, to يفتح (القفل) yaftaH (al-qifl)

unpleasant غير مرض ghayr murDee 14

unscrew, to يفك (بمفك) yafakk (bi-mifakk)

until لغاية li-ghaayat 221

up to حتى Hatta 12

upset stomach ألم في البطن alam feel baTn 141

upstairs فوق fouq 12

urgent مستعجل mustAHjil 161

use, to يستعمل yastAHmil 139

vacant فارغ faarigh 14

vacate, to يخلى yukhlee 32

vacation إجازة ijaaza 123; on ~ في إجازة fee ijaaza 66

**vaccinated against** ملقح ضد mullaqaH Didd 164

**validate, to** يوثق yuwassiq

**valley** وادٍ waadee 107

**value** قيمة qeema 155

**valve** محبس maHbas 28

**vanilla** فانيلا faneela 40

**VAT** ضريبة Dareeba 24

**veal** بتلو bitilloo 46

**vegetables** خضار khuDaar 38;
   **vegetable soup** شوربة خضار shoorbit khuDaar 43

**vegetarian** نباتي nabaatee 35, 39

**vehicle registration document**
   أوراق السيارة awraaq as-sayyaara 93

**vein** وريد wareed 166

**ventilator** فتحة تهوية fatHat tahweeya

**very** جداً jiddan 17; **very good**
   ممتاز mumtaaz 42

**video game** ألعاب الفيديو
   alAHaab al-feedyoo

**video recorder** مسجل الفيديو
   mussajil al-feedyoo

**viewpoint** مكان مرتفع للمشاهدة
   makaan murtifiAH lil-mushaahda 99

**village** قرية qarya 107

**vinaigrette** صلصة الخل
   SalSat al-khall 38

**visa** تأشيرة ta'sheera

**visit** (noun) زيارة ziyaara 119, 123

**visit, to** يزور yazoor 167; **places to ~**
   أماكن للزيارة amaakin liz-ziyaara 123;
   **visiting hours** مواعيد الزيارة
   mawaaAHeed az-ziyaara

**vitamin tablets** أقراص فيتامين
   aqraS feetaameen 141

**volleyball** الكرة الطائرة
   al-kura aT-Taa'ira 115

**voltage** فولت foolt

**vomit, to** يتقيء
   yatqayya' 163

**waiting room** صالة الانتظار Saalit il-intiZaar 72

**Waiter!** يا جرسون! yaa garsoon 37

**Waitress!** يا آنسة! yaa aanisa 37

**wake someone, to** يصحّي
   yuSaHHee

**wake-up call** مكالمة الإيقاظ
   mukaalmat al-eeqaaZ

**Wales** ويلز waylz 119

**walk home, to** يمشي للبيت
   yimshee lil-bayt 65

**walking boots** بوت للمشي boot lil-mashy

**wallet** محفظة maHfaZa 42, 153

**want, to** يريد yureed 18

**ward** (hospital) جناح jinaaH 167

**warm** ساخن saakhin 14

**washbasin** حوض الغسيل
   HauD al-ghaseel

**washing machine** غسالة الملابس
   ghasaalat al-malaabis 29

**washing powder** مسحوق غسيل الملابس
   mas-Huq ghaseel al-malaabis 148

**washing-up liquid** سائل لغسيل الصحون
   saa'il li-ghaseel aS-SuHoon 148

**wasp** دبور dabboor

**watch** ساعة saAHa 149, 153

**water** ماء maa' 87; **~ bottle**
   زجاجة مياه zujaajat miyaah
   **~ heater** سخان الماء sakh-khaan al-maa' 28; **~ pipe** شيشة sheesha 51;
   **~ skis** لوح التزحلق على الماء lauH at-tazaHluq AHlaal maa' 117;
   **mineral ~** مياه معدنية miyaah mAHdaneeya 50

water melons بطيخ baTTeekh 49

waterfall شلال shallaal 107

waterproof مقاوم للماء muqaawim lil-maa'; ~ jacket جاكيت واقية من الماء jaakeet waaqeeya min al-maa' 145

wave(s) موجة mauja (mauj)

waxing إزالة الشعر بالشمع izaalat ash-shAHr bish-shamAH 147

way: I've lost my way أنا تهت ana tuht 94

we نحن naHnu

wear, to يرتدي yartadee 152

weather طقس Taqs 122; ~ forecast تنبؤات الجو tanabu'aat al-jau 122

wedding (زواج) فرح faraH (zawaaj); ~ ring خاتم الزواج khaatim az-zawaaj

Wednesday (يوم) الاربعاء (yaum) al-arbAHa 218

week(s) (أسابيع) أسبوع usbooAH (asaabeeAH) 97, 218

weekend نهاية الأسبوع nihaayat al-usbooAH 218

weekly (ticket) أسبوعي usbooAHee 79

weight وزن wazn

welcome مرحبا marHaban

well I never! مش معقول! mish maAHqool 19

well-done (steak) كثير السواء kateer as-siwaa'

Welsh (adj.) ويلزي waylzee

west غرب gharb 95

wetsuit بذلة غوص badlat ghauS

what? ما/ماذا؟ maa/maaza; what's your name? ما اسمك؟ maa ismak; what do you do? (job) بماذا تعمل؟ bi-maaza tAHmil 121; what kind of? من أي نوع؟ min ayy nauAH 106

wheel (عجلة) دولاب doolaab (AHjala)

wheelchair كرسي متحرك kursee mutHarrik

when? متى؟ matta 13

where? أين؟ ayn 12; where are you from? من أين أنت؟ min ayn anta 119

which? أي؟ ayy 16

white أبيض abyaD 143; ~ wine نبيذ أبيض nabeet abyaD 49

who? مَن؟ man 16

whole: the whole day طول النهار Tool an-nahaar

whose? لمن؟ liman 16

why? لماذا؟ limaaza 14

wide واسع waasiAH 14

wife زوجة zauja 120, 162

wildlife الحياة البرية al-Hayaat al-barreeya

window(s) (شبابيك) شباك shibbaak (shabaabeek) 25, 76, 90, 149; ~ seat مقعد بجانب الشباك maqAHad bijaanib ash-shibbaak

windshield [windscreen] الزجاج الأمامي az-zujaaj al-amaamee 90

windy مذرو بالرياح mazroo bir-riyaaH 122

winter الشتاء ash-shitaa 219

with مع maAH 17

withdraw, to (money) يسحب yasHab 139

within (time) خلال khilaal 13

without بدون bidoon 17

witness(es) (شهود) شاهد shaahid (shuhood)

wood خشب khashab 149

wood (forest) غابة ghaaba 107

wool صوف Soof 145

work, to يعمل yAHmil 83; this doesn't work هذا لا يعمل haaza laa yAHmal 137; ~ for يعمل لحساب yAHmal li-Hisaab 121

**worse** أسوأ aswa' 14

**worst** الأسوأ al-aswa'

**wound** (*cut*) جرح jurH 162

**write down, to** يكتب yaktub 136

**wrong** (*incorrect*) خطأ khaTaa 88, 136;

~ **number** رقم غلط raqm ghalaT 128

**x-ray** صورة بالأشعة Soora
bil-ashiAHa 164

**yacht** يخت yakht

**year** سنة sana 218

**yellow** أصفر aSfar 143

**Yemen** اليمن al-yaman

**Yemeni** يمني yamanee

**yes** نعم naAHm 10

**yesterday** أمس ams 218

**yoghurt** لبن زبادي laban zabaadee

**you** (*masc./fem./plural*) أنت/أنتِ/أنتم
anta/anti/antum

**young** صغير السن Sagheer as-sinn 14

**your** ك ak (*fem:* ik) (*on end of word*) 16

**yours** لك lak (*fem:* lik) 16

**youth hostel** بيت الشباب
bayt ash-shabaab 29

**zero** صفر Sifr 216

**zipper** سوستة soosta

**zuchini** كوسة koosa 47

# Glossary
*Arabic - English*

This Arabic-English glossary covers all the areas where you may need to decode written Arabic: hotels, public buildings, restaurants, stores, ticket offices, airports, and stations. The Arabic is written in large type to help you identify the word(s) from the signs you see around you.

## General عام

| يسار | yasaar | LEFT |
|---|---|---|
| يمين | yameen | RIGHT |
| دخول | dukhool | ENTRANCE |
| خروج | khurooj | EXIT |
| دورة المياه | daurat al-miyaah | TOILETS |
| رجال | rijaal | MEN (TOILETS) |
| سيّدات | sayyidaat | WOMEN (TOILETS) |
| ممنوع التدخين | mamnooAH at-tadkheen | NO SMOKING |
| خطر | khaTar | DANGER |
| ممنوع الدخول | mamnooAH ad-dukhool | NO ENTRY |

| | | |
|---|---|---|
| اجذب/ادفع | ijzib/idfAH | PULL/PUSH |
| المفقودات | al-mafqoodaat | LOST PROPERTY |
| ممنوع السباحة | mamnooAH as-sibaaHa | NO SWIMMING |
| ماء للشرب | maa' lish-shurb | DRINKING WATER |
| خاصّ | khaaSS | PRIVATE |
| انذار الحريق | inzaar al-Hareeq | FIRE ALARM |
| ممنوع السير على الحشائش | mamnooAH as-sayr AHlal Hashaa'ish | KEEP OFF THE GRASS |
| احترس من البوية | iHtaris min al-booya | WET PAINT |
| درجة أولى | daraja oolaa | FIRST CLASS |
| درجة ثانية | daraja taanya | SECOND CLASS |
| سقف منخفض | saqf munkhafiD | LOW CEILING |

## علامات الطريق Road Signs

| | | |
|---|---|---|
| قف | qif | STOP |
| الزم اليمين | ilzam al-yameen | KEEP RIGHT |
| الزم اليسار | ilazam al-yasaar | KEEP LEFT |
| اتجاه واحد | ittijaah waaHid | ONE WAY |
| لا تتخطى | laa tatkhaTa | NO PASSING |
| ممنوع الوقوف | mamnooAH al-wuqoof | NO PARKING |
| طريق سريع | Tareeq sareeAH | HIGHWAY [MOTORWAY] |
| بوابة رسوم | bawaabat rusoom | TOLL |
| اشارات مرور | ishaaraat muroor | TRAFFIC LIGHTS |
| تقاطع | taqaaTuAH | JUNCTION |
| هدى السرعة | Hidee as-surAHa | SLOW |

| | | |
|---|---|---|
| معلومات | mAHloomaat | INFORMATION |
| رصيف ١ | raSeef waaHid | PLATFORM 1 |
| بوابة ١ | bawaaba waaHid | GATE 1 |
| الجمارك | al-jamaarik | CUSTOMS |
| الجوازات | al-jawaazaat | IMMIGRATION |
| وصول | wuSool | ARRIVALS |
| مغادرة | mughaadara | DEPARTURES |
| خزائن الأمتعة | khazaa'in al-amtiAHa | LUGGAGE LOCKERS |
| استلام الحقائب | istilaam al-Haqaa'ib | LUGGAGE RECLAIM |
| باصات | baaSaat | BUSES |
| تأجير السيّارات | ta'jeer as-sayyaaraat | CAR RENTAL |
| القطارات | al-qiTaaraat | TRAINS |

# الفندق/المطعم Hotel/Restaurant

| معلومات | mAHloomaat | INFORMATION |
| الاستقبال | al-istiqbaal | RECEPTION |
| محجوز | maHjooz | RESERVED |
| مخرج الطوارئ | makhraj aT-tawaari' | EMERGENCY/ FIRE EXIT |
| ماء ساخن | maa' saakhin | HOT (WATER) |
| ماء بارد | maa' baarid | COLD (WATER) |
| للعاملين فقط | lil-AHaamileen faqaT | STAFF ONLY |
| قسم للعائلات | qism lil-AHaa'ilaat | FAMILY SECTION |
| الشرفة/ الحديقة | ash-shurfa/al-Hadeeqa | TERRACE/GARDEN |
| بار | baar | BAR |

# محلات Stores

| | | |
|---|---|---|
| مفتوح | maftooH | OPEN |
| مغلق | mughlaq | CLOSED |
| غداء | ghadaa | LUNCH |
| قسم الـ... | qism al ... | ... DEPARTMENT |
| دور | door | FLOOR |
| مصعد | maSAHd | ELEVATOR [LIFT] |
| سلّم كهربائي | sillim kahrabaa'ee | ESCALATOR |
| صرّاف | Sarraaf | CASHIER |
| تخفيضات | takhfeeDaat | SALE |

| | | |
|---|---|---|
| الدخول مجاناً | *ad-dukhool majaanan* | FREE ADMISSION |
| للكبار | *lil-kubaar* | ADULTS |
| للأطفال | *lil-aTfaal* | CHILDREN |
| للطلبة | *liT-Talaba* | STUDENTS |
| هدايا تذكارية | *hidaayaa tizkaareeya* | SOUVENIRS |
| مرطبات | *muraTTibaat* | REFRESHMENTS |
| ممنوع اللمس | *mamnooAH al-lams* | DO NOT TOUCH |
| ممنوع التصوير | *mamnooAH at-taSweer* | NO PHOTOGRAPHY |
| سكوت | *sukoot* | SILENCE |
| ممنوع الدخول | *mamnooAH ad-dukhool* | NO ACCESS |

# Public Buildings المباني العامة

| | | |
|---|---|---|
| مستشفى | *mustashfaa* | HOSPITAL |
| طبيب | *Tabeeb* | DOCTOR |
| طبيب أسنان | *Tabeeb asnaan* | DENTIST |
| شرطة | *shurTa* | POLICE |
| بنك | *bank* | BANK |
| مكتب البريد | *maktab al-bareed* | POST OFFICE |
| حمام السباحة | *Hamaam as-sibaaHa* | SWIMMING POOL |
| مبنى البلدية | *mabnaa al-baladeeya* | TOWN HALL |
| موقف تاكسي | *mauqaf taaksee* | TAXI STAND [RANK] |
| متحف | *matHaf* | MUSEUM |

# Reference

| Numbers | 216 | Public holidays | 219 |
|---|---|---|---|
| Days/ | | Time | 220 |
| Months/Dates | 218 | Maps | 222 |
| Greetings | 219 | Quick reference | 224 |

## Numbers

### GRAMMAR

1. Unlike the rest of the script, Arabic numbers are written from left to right (as in English). Arabic numbers vary from Western numerals (although they are related) as shown here:

   0 = ٠  1 = ١  2 = ٢  3 = ٣  4 = ٤  5 = ٥  6 = ٦  7 = ٧  8 = ٨  9 = ٩

2. When counting nouns, Arabic uses a special "dual" ending **-ayn** (or **-tayn** for words which end in the feminine **a**) rather than the number 2. So "a book" is **kitaab**, "2 books" is **kitaabayn**; "a city" is **madeena**, "2 cities" is **madeenatayn**.

3. Plurals are made by using a large number of different patterns. They can sound very different from the singular, e.g., **kitaab** (book)/**kutub** (books). They are shown for the most important words in the dictionary if you need them (➤ 169–207).

4. Numbers 3–10 are followed by the *plural*, but numbers above 10 are followed by the *singular*:

| a (1) book | **kitaab** | 10 books | **AHshara kutub** |
|---|---|---|---|
| 2 books | **kitaabayn** | 11 books | **Hadashar kitaab** |
| 3 books | **talaata kutub** | 100 books | **mi'a kitaab** |

| | | | |
|---|---|---|---|
| 0 | *Sifr* صفر | 6 | *sitta* ستة |
| 1 | *waaHid* واحد | 7 | *sabAHa* سبعة |
| 2 | *itnayn* اثنان | 8 | *tamaanya* ثمانية |
| 3 | *talaata* ثلاثة | 9 | *tisAHa* تسعة |
| 4 | *arbAHa* أربعة | 10 | *AHshara* عشرة |
| 5 | *khamsa* خمسة | 11 | *Hadashar* أحد عشر |

| | | | | |
|---|---|---|---|---|
| 12 | *itnashar* اثنا عشر | 70 | *sabAHeen* سبعون | |
| 13 | *talaatashar* ثلاثة عشر | 80 | *tamaaneen* ثمانون | |
| 14 | *arbAHatashar* أربعة عشر | 90 | *tisAHeen* تسعون | |
| 15 | *khamastashar* خمسة عشر | 100 | *mi'a* مئة | |
| 16 | *sittatashar* ستة عشر | 101 | *mi'a wa waaHid* مئة وواحد | |
| 17 | *sabHatashar* سبعة عشر | 201 | *mi'a wa itnayn* مئة وائنان | |
| 18 | *tamaantashar* ثمانية عشر | 200 | *mi'atayn* مائتان | |
| 19 | *tisAHtashar* تسعة عشر | 500 | *khamsa mi'a* خمسمائة | |
| 20 | *AHishreen* عشرون | 1,000 | *alf* ألف | |
| 21 | *waaHid wa AHishreen* واحد وعشرون | 10,000 | *AHsharat aalaaf* عشرة آلاف | |
| 22 | *itnayn wa AHishreen* اثنان وعشرون | 1,000,000 | *milyoon* مليون | |
| 23 | *talaata wa AHishreen* ثلاثة وعشرون | first | *awwal/oola* أول/أولى | |
| 24 | *arbAHa wa AHishreen* أربعة وعشرون | second | *taanee* ثاني | |
| 25 | *khamsa wa AHishreen* خمسة وعشرون | third | *taalit* ثالث | |
| 26 | *sitta wa AHishreen* ستة وعشرون | fourth | *raabiAH* رابع | |
| 27 | *sabAHa wa AHishreen* سبعة وعشرون | fifth | *khaamis* خامس | |
| 28 | *tamaanya wa AHishreen* ثمانية وعشرون | once | *marra* مرة | |
| 29 | *tisAHa wa AHishreen* تسعة وعشرون | twice | *marratayn* مرتان | |
| 30 | *talaateen* ثلاثون | three times | *talaat marraat* ثلاث مرات | |
| 31 | *waaHid wa talaateen* واحد وثلاثون | a half | *nuSf* نصف | |
| 32 | *itnayn wa talaateen* اثنان وثلاثون | half an hour | *nuSf saAHa* نصف ساعة | |
| 40 | *arbAHeen* أربعون | a quarter | *rubAH* ربع | |
| 50 | *khamseen* خمسون | a third | *tult* ثلث | |
| 60 | *sitteen* ستون | a pair of … | *zauj min …* زوج من … | |
| | | a dozen | *dazayna* دزينة | |
| | | 1999 | *alf wa tisAHa mi'a wa tisAHa wa tisAHeen* ألف وتسعمائة وتسعة وتسعون | |
| | | 2001 | *alfayn wa waaHid* ألفان وواحد | |
| | | the 1990s | *al-tisAHeenaat* التسعينات | |

# Days الأيام

| | | |
|---|---|---|
| Monday | *(yaum) al-itnayn* | (يوم) الاثنين |
| Tuesday | *(yaum) at-talaat* | (يوم) الثلاثاء |
| Wednesday | *(yaum) al-arbAHa* | (يوم) الأربعاء |
| Thursday | *(yaum) al-khamees* | (يوم) الخميس |
| Friday | *(yaum) al-jumAHa* | (يوم) الجمعة |
| Saturday | *(yaum) as-sabt* | (يوم) السبت |
| Sunday | *(yaum) al-aHad* | (يوم) الأحد |

# Months الشهور

Following are the Arabic names for the months of the Christian calendar (with alternatives used in some Arab countries, e.g., Syria). The Islamic lunar **hijra** calendar (➤ 219) also has 12 months, but is 10 to 11 days shorter.  A.D. 2000 is A.H. 1419/1420 in the **hijra** calendar.

| | | |
|---|---|---|
| January | *yanaayir (kaanoon at-taanee)* | يناير (كانون الثاني) |
| February | *fabraayir (shabbaT)* | فبراير (شباط) |
| March | *maaris (azaar)* | مارس (آذار) |
| April | *abreel (neesaan)* | إبريل (نيسان) |
| May | *maayoo (ayyaar)* | (مايو) أيار |
| June | *yoonyoo (Hazeeraan)* | يونيو (حزيران) |
| July | *yoolyoo (tamooz)* | يوليو (تموز) |
| August | *aghusTus (aab)* | أغسطس (آب) |
| September | *sibtambir (aylool)* | سبتمبر (أيلول) |
| October | *uktoobar (tishreen al-awwal)* | أكتوبر (تشرين الأول) |
| November | *noofambir (tishreen at-taanee)* | نوفمبر (تشرين الثاني) |
| December | *deesimbir (kaanoon al-awwal)* | ديسمبر (كانون الأول) |

# Dates تواريخ

| | | |
|---|---|---|
| It's … | *innahu …* | إنه … |
| July 10 | *AHshara yoolyoo (tamooz)* | ١٠ يوليو (تموز) |
| yesterday | *ams* | أمس |
| today | *al-yaum* | اليوم |
| tomorrow | *ghadan* | غدا |
| next week | *al-usbooAH al-qaadim* | الأسبوع القادم |
| on [at] the weekend | *fee AHTlat nihaayat al-usbooAH* | في عطلة نهاية الأسبوع |

## Seasons فصول السنة

| | |
|---|---|
| spring | الربيع *ar-rabeeAH* |
| summer | الصيف *aS-Sayf* |
| fall [autumn] | الخريف *al-khareef* |
| winter | الشتاء *ash-shitaa* |
| in spring | في الربيع *feel rabeeAH* |
| during the summer | خلال الصيف *khilaal aS-Sayf* |

## Greetings تحيات

A general greeting that you can use on someone's birthday and on most major festivals is **kull sana wa anta bi-khayr**, meaning "Every year and you are well."

| | |
|---|---|
| Happy birthday! | عيد ميلاد سعيد! *AHeed meelaad sAHeed!* |
| Happy New Year! | عام سعيد! *AHaam saAheed!* |
| Congratulations! | مبروك! *mabrook!* |
| Good luck! | حظ سعيد! *HaZZ sAHeed!* |

## Public holidays العطلات الرسمية

National holidays vary from country to country, but most observe both the Western and Islamic New Years and other major Islamic holidays. As the Islamic months are shorter, Muslim festivals will move in relation to the Gregorian calendar, but for the foreseeable future the Islamic year begins in spring. The Muslim months and major festivals are:

| *Islamic month* | *Major Islamic holidays* |
|---|---|
| **al-muharram** | 1st: Islamic New Year |
| | 10th: Ashura |
| **safar** | |
| **rabee al-awwal** | 12th: Prophet's birthday |
| **rabee at-taanee** | |
| **jumadee al-awwal** | |
| **jumadee al-aakhra** | |
| **rajab** | 27th: Laylat al-ma'raj |
| **shabaan** | |
| **ramadaan** | |
| **shawwaal** | 1st–4th: Eid al-Fitr |
| **zuu al-qa'da** | |
| **zuu al-Hijja** | 10th–16th Eid al-Adha |

# Time الساعة

| | |
|---|---|
| Excuse me, can you tell me the time? | *kam as-saAHa, lau samaHt* كم الساعة، لو سمحت؟ |
| It's … | *as-saAHa …* الساعة … |
| five past one | *waaHda wa khamsa* الواحدة وخمس |
| ten past two | *itnayn wa AHshara* الثانية وعشرة |
| a quarter past three | *talaata war-rubAH* الثالثة والربع |
| twenty past five | *khamsa wa tult* الخامسة وثلث |
| twenty-five past four | *arbAHa wa khamsa wa AHishreen daqeeqa* الرابعة وخمسة وعشرون دقيقة |
| half past six | *sitta wa nuSf* السادسة والنصف |
| twenty-five to seven | *sabAHa wa khamsa wa talaateen daqeeqa* السادسة وخمسة وثلاثون دقيقة |
| twenty to eight | *tamaanya ilaa tult* الثامنة إلا ثلث |
| a quarter to nine | *tisAHa ilaa rubAH* التاسعة إلا ربعا |
| ten to eleven | *Hadashar ilaa AHshara* الحادية عشرة إلا عشر |
| five to ten | *AHshara ilaa khamas daqaa'iq* العاشرة إلا خمس دقائق |
| twelve o'clock noon/midnight | *itnashar Zuhran/muntaSaf al-layl* الثانية عشرة ظهرا/منتصف الليل |

| at dawn | *fajran* فجرا |
|---|---|
| in the morning | *SabaaHan* صباحا |
| during the day | *khilaal an-nahaar* |
| | خلال النهّار |

| before lunch | *qabl al-ghadaa* قبل الغداء |
|---|---|
| after lunch | *bAHd al-ghadaa* بعد الغداء |
| in the afternoon | *bAHd aZ-Zuhr* بعد الظهر |
| in the evening | *feel masaa* في المساء |
| at night | *bil-layl* بالليل |

I'll be ready in five minutes.    *sa-akoon jaahiz bAHd khamas daqaa'iq*
سأكون جاهز بعد خمس دقائق.

He'll be back in a quarter of an hour.    *sa-yarjAH khilaal rubAH saAHa*
سيرجع خلال ربع ساعة.

She arrived half an hour ago.    *waSalat munzu nuSf saAHa*
وصلت منذ نصف ساعة.

The train leaves at 13:04.    *yughaadir al-qiTaar as-saAHa waaHda wa arbAH daqaa'iq*
يغادر القطار الساعة الواحدة وأربع دقائق.

10 minutes late/early    *mutakhkhar/mubakkir bi-AHshar daqaa'iq*
متأخر/مبكر بعشرة دقائق

from 9:00 to 5:00    *min as-saAHa tisAHa ilaa khamsa*
من الساعة ٩ إلى ٥.

between 8:00 and 2:00    *bayn as-saAHa tamaanya wa itnayn*
بين الساعة ٨ و٢.

Will you be back before …?    *hal sa-tirjAH qabl*
هل سترجع قبل …؟

We'll be here until …    *sa-nakoon huna li-ghaayat*
سنكون هنا لغاية …

# Quick reference مراجعة سريعة

| | | |
|---|---|---|
| Good morning. | SabaaH al-khayr | صباح الخير. |
| Good afternoon/ evening. | masaa al-khayr | مساء الخير. |
| Hello. | ahlan/salaam | أهلاً/سلام. |
| Good-bye. | mAHas salaama | مع السلامة. |
| Excuse me! (getting attention) | lau samaHt | لو سمحت! |
| Pardon? | AHfwan | عفواً؟ |
| Sorry! | aasif | آسف! |
| Please. | min faDlak | من فضلك. |
| Thank you. | shukran | شكراً. |
| Do you speak English? | hal tatkallam al-injileezeeya | هل تتكلم الإنجليزية؟ |
| I don't understand | laa afham. | لا أفهم. |
| Where is/are ...? | ayn | أين ...؟ |
| Where are the bathrooms [toilets]? | ayn al-Hammaamaat | أين الحمامات؟ |

# Emergency حالات طارئة

| | | |
|---|---|---|
| Help! | an-najda | النجدة! |
| Go away! | inSarif/imshee | انصرف/امشي! |
| Leave me alone! | utruknee waHdee | اتركني وحدي! |
| Call the police! | ittaSil bish-shurTa | اتصل بالشرطة! |
| Stop thief! | imsik Haraamee | امسك حرامي! |
| Get a doctor! | ittaSil bi-duktoor | اتصل بدكتور! |
| Fire! | Hareeq | حريق! |
| I'm ill. | ana mareeD | أنا مريض. |
| I'm lost. | ana tuht | أنا تهت. |
| Can you help me? | hal mumkin tusaAHidnee | هل ممكن تساعدني؟ |

224